**JACKIE MILBURN**

This book is dedicated to my mother. Without her, it could not have been written.

MAINSTREAM / SPORT

# JACKIE MILBURN

## A MAN OF TWO HALVES

## JACK MILBURN

MAINSTREAM
PUBLISHING
EDINBURGH AND LONDON

First published in Great Britain in 2003 by
MAINSTREAM PUBLISHING COMPANY
(EDINBURGH) LTD
7 Albany Street
Edinburgh EH1 3UG

ISBN 1 84018 893 6

A catalogue record for this book is available
from the British Library

Typeset in Cheltenham and Apollo
Printed and bound in Great Britain by
Cox & Wyman Ltd

# Acknowledgements

I wish to acknowledge the following people for their valuable help and inspiration:

Wendy Pilmer head of regional and local programmes at the BBC; Tony Parker at the BBC; Mike Neville at TTTV; Jeff Brown at the BBC (formerly TTTV); Ged Clarke and the two Pauls of North Star Television; Sir Bobby Charlton; Sir Bobby Robson; Sir Tom Finney; Big Jack Charlton; Charlie Crowe; Malcolm Macdonald; Alan Shearer; John Gibson; Ronnie and Joan Coulson; Rosemary Clark; Lindisfarne's Ray Laidlaw (still the best band on the planet!); Tony 'the keyboard' Davis at Cluny Studios; Stu Aitken; David Langdown at Bubbles; Ron, Cath and Vicky at Harleys in Rothbury (and their prize-winning carrot cake which kept my eyes sharp as I burned the midnight oil); all at Mainstream; and finally, my wife Yasmin, for her patience.

# Contents

# Prologue

My mother, my sister Betty and I sat in numbed silence around my mother's kitchen table, blankly staring at its top. During the early hours of that morning, 9 October 1988, my father had quietly passed away.

Realisation dawned and we struck up a heart-rending exchange as to what the funeral arrangements should be. We decided on a simple, quiet service for family and close friends only, but were faced with the problem that Dad had known so many people. For advice, and to make the necessary arrangements, we contacted Peter Grenfell, a local Ashington undertaker and family friend. Peter listened, but quickly disagreed with our intentions, reminding us that: 'Jackie also belonged to the people and many of them will no doubt want to pay their last respects too.'

The rest of the morning was spent telephoning relatives and friends to inform them and somehow the news broke in the media. Through streaming eyes we witnessed my father's death as it was broadcast on national TV and radio and I think we were all amazed at the widespread demonstration of such deep sympathy. One of the many who rang to offer condolences was former Newcastle United manager Arthur Cox who, mid-conversation, suddenly broke down, apologising profusely as he was forced to replace the receiver. Like us, everyone seemed stunned.

Peter Grenfell called round the next day to tell us he had now discussed the matter with several Newcastle city officials and those concerned at St Nicholas's Cathedral. Both parties were in agreement to holding a special service there. The ball of grief had begun to turn and we simply rolled with it.

By sheer coincidence, that Monday morning, Newcastle United sacked their current manager and former goalkeeper Willie McFaul, and I'll never forget his reply to reporters when asked how he felt about losing his job. 'Don't think about me. Think about the grief that Laura Milburn must be suffering.' What a selfless man.

That evening, Betty and I went to our separate homes, leaving an exhausted Mum to sleep, and it was then that the whole thing hit me personally. I spent the entire night crying my eyes out just sitting under a blanket in the hallway next to the telephone, praying that Dad would, one way or another, be able to ring. I am not wholly religious, but do hold my own beliefs, and all I wanted was some kind of an 'after life' sign that would show me he was OK. Strange as it may seem, that is just what I reckon happened only a couple of days later – to my mind anyway.

As Betty and I sat talking in Mum's kitchen, a red butterfly fluttered in through the narrow gap of the open-top window and then floated over our heads before circling the room to make its way back out. I know it's easy to be sceptical and dismiss the whole notion, but when you are grieving and call upon some manner of a sign . . . well, who knows?

I was the one who registered Dad's death at Ashington Registrar's Office and it certainly wasn't a pleasant experience. In one hand I held his birth certificate, dated 11 May 1924, and in the other his death certificate, dated 9 October 1988, and, for a split-second, it felt as if I was holding his entire 64 years in my hands, as though it had all passed in the blink of an eye. Anyone who has ever experienced that will know just what I mean.

On Thursday, 13 October, the funeral cortège, saluted by several of the fire-fighters of the station immediately opposite Mum's house in Bothal Terrace, drove at a snail's pace from the street and up towards Ashington's main street. None of us could believe the magnificent turnout. There appeared to be thousands of folk lining both sides of the street, young and old and many of them in tears just as we were, and incredibly, we viewed the same scene all the way to Newcastle city centre.

Even along the dual carriageway leading there, where there was no obvious place for anyone to stand, silent people with bowed heads waited on the bridges spanning its width. The marvellous police motorcycle escort controlled and sometimes stopped the other traffic for the entire 15-mile journey, and not once did the cortege have to raise or even drop its even speed.

After the Cathedral service, Dad was taken past his beloved St James' Park and then on to the crematorium at the city's West End, and it was there I had another strange experience. Maybe it was simply due to pure grief, or the enormity of the whole moving occasion, but as we sat during the service, I sensed his strong presence and visualised him as a self-conscious young man before me holding a muddy football and wearing a baggy tracksuit with white sandshoes. It appeared as if he was really just wishing the whole thing was all over so he could get away for a practice game with the lads. After the service he smiled to an unaware Mum, told her he'd be waiting and then vanished.

One of the final requests Dad made was for his ashes to be scattered over the Gallowgate End of St James' Park, and so a few days later it was arranged for the immediate family to respect his wishes behind closed doors. Regrettably, some of the TV and press chaps were informed of this and accordingly turned up at the ground, though admittedly did ask permission to film. Within ourselves, it made each of us feel uncomfortable and when later shown on TV, we were pictured standing around the centre circle holding hands and saying a prayer. Sadly, it appeared somewhat like a charade, which was without doubt never the family's intention. It was simply an extremely private moment that was lost.

# 1

# The Early Years

To play for Newcastle and to score goals out there on St James' Park was a dream come true for me. You have to actually come from Newcastle to appreciate that and I'm sure Jackie felt exactly the same.

Alan Shearer

On 11 May 1924, just a few days after Newcastle United lifted the FA Cup, John Edward Thompson Milburn was born in the upstairs flat of his grandparents' house, at 14 Sixth Row, Ashington. Also sharing the flat were his mother Nance and father Alec. Little could they have known at the time the significance of the initials they had him christened with: JET. He would be better known as Jackie.

As a youngster, he would wave to his miner father from his bedroom window as he crossed the back lane to the pit yard just a few yards away. 'I used to shiver as he disappeared into the deep shaft leading down to the coalface,' he later said. Even at that early age, he just knew he did not want to spend his own life down that black hole.

Alec was well known as one of the best coal-cutters at the colliery, and because of that ability, the family probably lived a little more comfortably than many of the other 30,000 folk in the town. Being on piecework, he was prepared to break his back to earn enough for the essentials the family needed to get by, and then some more for a few little luxuries.

By the time he was six, Dad was kicking out a pair of shoes a fortnight, even though he knew it meant a walloping from his father. One night though he felt as proud as punch as he overheard his parents talking. 'He must be getting better, Nance,' whispered Alec, 'he's using two feet now. Both shoes are worn out.'

Although he could barely afford the shoe repairs, Alec wanted his son to do well, maybe even to live out his own dreams of a life on the pitch. Alec had a cracking left foot and was a hard hitter of the ball himself, and he'd once been offered a trial with Tottenham Hotspur. At the time though he was about to marry Nance, so not wanting to be parted from her he declined their offer. Who knows what the alternative outcome might have been – possibly a cockney-born Jackie Milburn? 'Aar Jekky'?

During this time Dad was too young to be involved in any organised football matches, but was thrilled to bits when Willie Chambers, the lad next door, offered him his first pair of real football boots, even though they were not new. 'Willie was a year younger, though fortunately for me he had big feet for his age. They fit perfectly.' The Chambers family were fortunate in having four elder brothers earning their keep and as a result could afford to splash out on a new pair of boots for Willie.

As Dad grew older, Nance, who wanted him to look really neat and smart on his first day at school, busily knitted him a little uniform consisting of a woollen top with a matching pair of woollen pants. As he donned it on that all-important morning he felt extremely proud, that is, until he crossed the boundary of the school gates and gawped open-mouthed at every other lad running happily about the playground in 'proper' shorts. A horrified Dad clung desperately to the railings and bawled his eyes out for an age before his mother was able to calm him down. 'I felt like a real Jessie with my knitted stuff on. I thought they were all laughing at me.'

Even though Dad's parents allowed him to carry on living at his Granny Thompson's, they insisted he spend every Christmas with them, and at last, when he was eight years old, he was given his first brand-spanking-new pair of football boots. There was nothing by his bed as he excitedly clambered in on Christmas Eve, but when he woke from a restless sleep at 3.30 a.m. and grabbed his new flashlight to shine it round, he discovered there were now a dozen gifts lying about him. When he eventually spotted the new football boots at the foot of the bed, he let out an enormous yell of delight. 'Christmas was a time of magic for me. My parents always made sure of that.'

There was no stopping him now and even though it was only 4 a.m., he quickly dressed, donned his new boots and pelted down Sixth Row where he knew for sure all his pals would be – that is, if they too were lucky enough to have received new boots. 'When I got there it nearly broke my heart. There were already dozens of lads playing by torchlight. With tears streaming down my cheeks, I had to wait a full ten minutes before I could join in the game.'

From that day on, football dominated his life, and out of school hours during the week, he practised on a piece of green at the end of the row and then on Saturday mornings at the Peoples Park. Most weekday mornings he would jump up at 6.30 a.m., grab a quick breakfast and afterwards play football from 7.30 a.m. until 8.30 a.m., then run two miles to school, dash back for lunch, kick around once more, dart back to school and then after the final lesson it was football once more. To help with his ball control, he even kicked the same stone the eight miles to and from school each day, before finally losing it after three years.

On the academic side, Dad only ever came top in one school exam and that was in history. 'I sat next to a very bright lad called Joe Morton. I always wrote with my left hand and Joe wrote with his right. Strange how we both ended up with exactly 73 marks each!'

Dad and his pals were a canny bunch of lads and, with their

rugged outdoor lifestyle they were fairly hardy, too. As a nipper, he only recalled ever having to spend just one day in bed, and that was due to playing a reckless game of football on a pond covered with thin ice, which he suddenly crashed through. His mother confined him to bed simply as a precaution against developing a chill.

A few of the housewives in Sixth Row noticed he could run considerably faster than his chums and therefore singled him out to fetch their errands as required, and for his troubles he would earn around a penny a time. Soon his pockets jangled with the cash: 'Though for all of that I was never too keen as it kept me out the game.'

During that period, a chap called Cyril Brown became Dad's big hero. Cyril was an Ashingtonian who played for Irish League club Glentoran, and it was always a great occasion when Cyril returned home for a close-season holiday. Ever keen to involve the youngsters in sport, the kindly Cyril would organise races among them and it was during one of those that Dad won his first ever prize. 'For being first "man" around the block, I received a little box of paints.'

With the passing of time, and his love of football and the desire to be involved in it at every opportunity, Dad developed a tremendous interest in Ashington FC and became a regular ball-boy behind the goals. However, to ensure he was able to take part in a match, he had to be at the Portland Park ground before 11 a.m., often having to queue with 200 other eager beavers just for the privilege. If for any reason he were to miss his chance and happened to be penniless at the time, he would simply tunnel under the fencing to watch the game. The Ashington ground could thrill spectators with the quality of the football on display and one of Ashington's 'guest' players was none other than Stan Mortenson himself, the Blackpool and future England star.

In Ashington, the Milburn footballing roots go back a long way, in fact as far back as 1886 when Dad's great-grandfather 'Warhorse' Milburn played in goal for Northumberland, Ashington and Morpeth. After that, his cousins, Jack and George, played at full-back for League side Leeds United, while their brother-in-law, Jimmy Potts, stood between the posts. Later, the legendary World Cup-winning Charlton brothers, Jackie and Bobby, who were Dad's second cousins, would follow the tradition.

For Dad, one of the most thrilling days of the year was when the eagerly awaited Cup final was broadcast over the radio. For their first ever listening, he and the other lads eagerly marked out a pitch on the asphalt of Sixth Row, and then broke it into squares so they could follow the game by moving a ball from square to square once the game had kicked off and his granny had carried the radio to the windowsill. It was their way of 'watching' the game.

'Arsenal's Joe Hulme was my hero,' Dad said. 'As the commentator ranted about his terrific bursts of speed I vowed to my pals that one day I was going to be a fast winger just like him.'

Dad adored his Granny Thompson and she him. She just knew from when he was a toddler that football would dominate his life and encouraged him in every possible way, even allowing him to stay out practising after most of his pals were tucked up in bed at 7 p.m. He always appreciated that.

Quite understandably, the majority of the mining dads would enjoy a glass or three of beer in the Ashington clubs, mainly to rinse the clinging coal dust from their throats, but come each Sunday, they always made sure their offspring attended church in the morning and Sunday school in the afternoons, when each and every one of them would be given a penny to place on the collection plate. 'And that's precisely where it ended up,' Dad affirmed.

As a growing lad, Dad was always brim full of confidence, especially playing football or whenever running competitively, but on one particular afternoon an event took place which was to change his outlook forever. 'In my heart I know I've always possessed an inferiority complex. To some folk I may appear to be shy and retiring but that's not really the case. I really do have an inferiority complex and I'm certain it stems from a triumphant afternoon during a school sports day.'

He had already won the 80 yards sprint, long-jump and high-jump and been a part of the winning relay team, when his father Alec arrived at the ground, just in time to see him run and win his final event, the 440 yards. The second Dad threw himself over the finishing line he collapsed flat on his face – he was completely shattered from taking part in far too many events. He wasn't prepared for the thunderous look on his father's face as Alec glared down at him, nor the reception he was to receive as he later entered the house. His father looked up from his chair and said, 'What's the matter with you, lad, got a big head or something?' Before a confused Dad had time to reply, Alec proceeded to give him a severe hiding.

Later in life, Dad declared that it was probably due to that one incident that he always kept both his feet firmly on the ground. 'Maybe my father's intentions were the best in the world and I've certainly never had a big head, but that thrashing laid the foundations for an inferiority complex I have fought all my life to overcome.'

It was a while before Dad was quite ready to begin chasing the girls. One afternoon he had returned home from a kickabout with his pals, to find his sister Jean sitting in the yard with a few of her friends, and so began to annoy them by kicking his football at them. One of those girls, Joan (née Wallace), who was later to marry a great pal of Dad's, Ronnie Coulson, remembers: 'I didn't really think Jackie was too nice on first impression and as for being used as a practice 'target' . . . well, that wasn't very kind. Nevertheless, in later life we became good friends.'

At the age of 12, Dad was selected to play for the Hirst East Senior Boys School, on the right wing – the position of his great hero, Joe Hulme. After excitedly spotting his name on the team sheet pinned to the school notice board during the lunch break, his concentration during the afternoon lessons was lost and he found himself severely ticked off by the teacher on more than one occasion. As soon as the end-of-day bell rang, he pelted home to tell his mother the good news. He knew his father was on the late shift and wouldn't be home until 1.30 a.m., but still pleaded with Nance to be allowed to stay up to tell him of his selection, though she strongly recommended he wait until morning.

Dad lay wide awake on his bed until his father came home, but decided to heed his mother's advice and wait until breakfast, though found he simply couldn't sleep. After hearing his father slip into bed, he got up and dressed himself in his red-and-green-squared shirt, blue shorts and football boots, and sat in front of the dying ashes of the fire to while away the hours that loomed before him and his first game against Linton School.

'The match wasn't due to kick off until 10 a.m., but I arrived there at 8 a.m., just to stand on the pitch that I would make my debut on in my first proper game. There was no one else to be seen.'

Eventually his mother and father and two sisters, Jean and Mavis, arrived, his father promising to give him a penny for each goal he scored in the future. 'I earned tuppence that morning after our 6–4 win.'

Further games saw him shuffled to inside-forward and also into defence at left-back, though he didn't really care where he played as long as he was on the field. Always standing on the touchline to encourage the team were the school's headmaster, Jack Denton, and sports master, Phillip Wood. Dad never forgot Jack Denton's words of advice: 'Toe down and heel up, and you'll score.'

Although standing at below five feet, Dad soon found himself selected to play for East Northumberland in the English Schools Shield, and his team made it to the semi-finals to be played at Maine Road, Manchester, against Lancashire. Sadly, through his work, Alec couldn't be there to witness his son's proud moment, but Nance and a few of her friends actually hired a taxi to take them all the way.

Even though the Geordies were ultimately defeated 3–2, Dad notched a goal and was thrilled to read a report of the match in the *Newcastle Football Chronicle* that mentioned his name. He carried the cutting with him for years, particularly during matches, considering it as his own lucky mascot, though when eventually it became too worn he swapped it for a white handkerchief, which he clutched rolled up in his right hand throughout his career.

At 13, he changed to Bothal School and found himself under the guiding wing of headmaster, Jack Gray. Although academically Dad wasn't too bad, he already knew his career lay in the sport that dominated his life. A year later, and due to leave the school, Dad was asked by Mr Gray, in front of a full classroom, what he would like to do with his life. The headmaster, fully expecting Dad to reply, 'To be a footballer, sir', was somewhat staggered when he received the mumbled words, 'To be a butcher, sir.' The old inferiority complex had once again reared its head.

Mr Gray looked a little puzzled. 'Are you quite sure?'

Dad blushed and grinned sheepishly. 'Well, sir, I had thought about playing football, but . . .'

Mr Gray's eyes twinkled. 'I thought as much. Well we shall see, shan't we?'

Dad certainly felt no desire at all to follow his own father's weary footsteps down the pit in search of the black diamonds. In reality, he much more than anything wanted a life above ground in the fresh air, and also felt the urge to travel and spread his wings, praying that one day he'd actually realise his boyhood dream to become a professional player. He and one or two of his pals considered themselves the 'revolutionaries' of their day by declaring their disinterest in going down the mine.

After a lengthy family discussion when Dad was 14, during which he made clear his claustrophobic fear about going down the pit, Alec quite understood and told Dad to follow his own star. But Dad simply followed his pal Eddie Main instead and plucked up the courage, after failing three times, to knock at the door of the local agent who had found Eddie a job in service down south. Right away, the agent informed him there would be a position waiting for him with a Captain Evelyn, down at his home in Dorking, Surrey. So, one

Saturday night during August, he packed his toothbrush and one and only best suit and amid a flood of tears from both him and mother Nance, apprehensively clambered the high steps of the overnight bus to London. Alec was working the night shift.

Also on the bus sat a dejected-looking school friend, Lance Richardson, who was travelling south to join a riding stable in Beckhampton, Wiltshire. The pair comforted each other and tried to make light of their plight, though with each passing mile they began to feel very much alone in the frightening big wide world.

On his arrival, Captain Evelyn sensed Dad's unrest and did his utmost to reassure him that everything would be fine once he'd had time to settle in, but after giving him a tour of the house to explain his duties, he then showed him his room and was taken aback when Dad burst into uncontrollable tears. The radio he had kindly placed next to the bed was identical to the one in the living room back home.

All night Dad wept buckets. Then at 6 a.m., when finally he could stand it no more, he crept out of bed and packed his bags, scampering blindly down the road to anywhere, but after a couple of miles, the captain drew alongside in his big car and gently persuaded him to return to the house. 'I spent all next day polishing silver and washing dishes through sopping red eyes.'

In bed that night, he felt so ashamed – although that didn't stop him absconding once more on the Tuesday after returning from watching a game of football in Dorking that was supposed to make him feel more at home. This time his mind was positively made up: he was going home to play football with the lads, even if it meant going down the awesome pit when he reached the qualifying age of 16. 'I silently packed once more and escaped in real commando style.'

Then he hopped on a train to Waterloo Station where he carefully counted his pennies before jumping into a taxi to Eton Mews, where his mother's sister, Aunt Bella, worked as a housekeeper. She was all too sympathetic, wiped the tears from his eyes and kind-heartedly gave him the train fare back to Ashington, where the next day he discovered that Lance had also returned home too, making him feel not quite so bad. 'I suppose my mother and father should have expected it, as I'd done it all before and ran away on a local camping trip with the lads.'

Anyway, soon after his return, a job became available at the local Ideal Store, where he mundanely filled flour and sugar bags and stacked shelves for eight shillings (forty pence) a week, of which he gave his mother seven shillings, feeling prouder than ever with a whole shilling burning a hole in his own pocket. 'It was the first time in my life I'd owned a shilling of my own.'

Football was still his main aim, though, and for a time he played for the East Hirst Old Boys – though he still yearned to link up once more with his Ashington pals. The opportunity to do so came one Saturday afternoon when his team were without a game and the Ashington YMCA were short of a player. Dad was invited to play and scored a hat-trick, but then, for the one and only time in his life, found himself suspended. After the game, the officials of the opposing team protested at his inclusion in the YMCA side and so he was summoned to appear before the League officials, who then cautioned him before suspending him for two weeks. 'Quite a sentence for a lad not yet 15 years old.'

After that, he and a few of the lads he'd grown up with decided to form what was to become a none-too-successful team of their own, a team that was eventually accepted into the Ashington Midget League. 'I'd like to be able to say that we were a tremendous success. However, just the opposite was the case.'

Defeat after defeat followed, sometimes 16–0 or 18–0, and a great result would be a mere 10–0 thrashing. With Dad playing at centre-half, he always had a pretty hectic time of it. As he explained later, 'I learned to endure defeat in a sporting manner.'

The following year, 1939, Dad attempted to join the Royal Navy, though found himself rejected simply because he was just an inch too short, though over the following nine months he did manage to sprout another nine inches – but by then he had joined the Air Training Corps (ATC) instead.

Now turned 16, to his great relief he was offered an apprenticeship as a fitter at the pit, now a reserved occupation for the duration of and certain years after the war. He had 'pestered' the Ashington Coal Company for ages and finally they relented 'simply to keep me quiet'. He began work in the saddlers shop, making kneepads and belts, while also oiling the harnesses for the pit ponies. 'At last I was happy.'

Now playing football for the ATC, he made good progress on the pitch, firstly as a winger and then as an inside-right. His speed was improving too and he used to spend a lot of time training at the Ashington 'Rec' (recreation ground), with ex-school pal and house captain Ronnie Coulson, whom he'd met at Bothal School. Their birthdays were just one day apart and they also shared the same love of athletics, though were frustrated by the lack of a club in the area for them both to join. As well as both serving their time together at the pit, they played in the same ATC side that for three whole seasons lost only a single match, the final one of the third season.

Ronnie remembers Dad's shyness whenever they attended the local dances: 'Jackie was too shy to ask the girls up for a dance, so, whenever he spotted one he quite liked the look of, it was me who invited her onto the floor just so he could 'buzz' [cut in] me off. He did that for three years.'

Dad and Ronnie took up sprinting seriously and began to enter handicaps all over Northumberland and Durham, competing for the £10 first prizes – an awful lot of money in those days. Dad was successful in a handicap at Ashington's Portland Park and immediately went out and bought an engagement ring for his current girlfriend, though the engagement itself didn't last too long; however, he soon met another girl and repeated the very same exercise in order buy her a ring too. Ronnie was dumbfounded.

Later, Ronnie and some friends travelled down to Stoke with Dad to watch him compete for a £200 first prize. It was the only time ever

Ronnie saw Dad break down in tears. A local Potteries lad called Haldcroft beat Dad to the finishing tape, but it wasn't that fact which bothered Dad so much; it was simply that his own pals had bet on him to win and he felt he'd let them down so badly.

While in the ATC, four nights a week were taken up at the 'Rec' training like commandos, always preceded by rigorous sessions in the gym, but the best part of the night was the hectic free-for-all of 20-a-side football using trees as goalposts.

Some of the lads did not even possess a decent pair of shoes, never mind football boots, and many would play with just a piece of wood, shaped like a shoe, strapped to their feet by a piece of string. 'Many of those lads were much better footballers than me, but never had the opportunity to show their ability, many of them disappearing below ground to work the rest of their lives down the pit.'

One afternoon, when turning out for the ATC team, Dad was given the word that a Newcastle United scout was coming to watch the team perform. Everyone played their best and they won 8–3, with Dad netting five goals, but to everyone's bitter frustration, the scout failed to arrive. Before the end of the game and the sad discovery, Dad's confidence was sky high and he was fully expecting a summons to the hallowed St James' Park. 'It was a bitter pill to swallow.'

All the lads lived and breathed football and saw it as the escape route from the mine – if only they could be spotted. Even during their lunch breaks they managed to have a game. Typically, they started lunch at 11.50 a.m. to resume work at 12.30, rushing home to gobble down a full dinner in 15 minutes and then pelting back to play a quick match organised by Cyril Brown, who now worked at the colliery and acted as their coach.

Dad himself was training in earnest, starting work at 7 a.m. and finishing at 4.15 p.m., before heading straight for the local ground where a key was always left for him and he would then put in a quick spell of training before going home for his tea. 'After tea, I would spend three nights a week sprinting and two learning ball control, then on a Saturday morning I would prepare for the afternoon match by going for a five-mile hike with my heaviest boots on to strengthen my legs. Then on a Sunday it was back to sprinting.'

The progress made by the ATC team did not go unnoticed by the county and when the Northumberland XI met Yorkshire at Gateshead's Redheugh Park, Dad found himself selected at outside-right. Northumberland won 3–0 and watching the match was Wilf Taylor, a Newcastle United director and member of the Football League Management Committee. The impressed Taylor handed the Northumberland team his card and invited them to St James' Park to watch United play Darlington. This greatly excited Dad, as Cyril Brown now 'guested' for Darlington: 'I'd never been to St James' Park and my only previous visit to a League game had been to watch Sunderland play Blackpool in 1936.'

Dad travelled to Newcastle with his left-half pal Raymond Poxton, though had to admit after the match that he was not the slightest bit impressed with the United inside-forwards that day. He genuinely felt he could play just as well, so on the bus home, he and Ray talked about nothing else but the poor standard of play and long before they had reached their destination, their minds were firmly made up to answer the club's annual advertisement in the *North Mail* for prospective players.

Not too long after, they actually found themselves invited for a trial after Raymond, who had the better handwriting, wrote to the club, but as Dad had no proper boots, he had to borrow a pair from another pal, Joe Smith. He and Raymond weren't due to arrive at St James' Park until 2 p.m., but nevertheless, due to their great excitement, they arrived four hours early, and so to kill time, went to a café and ordered a couple of meat pies and then went to the ground to sit, in the pouring rain, on the steps and wait.

In due course they were allowed into the dressing-room where another of their great heroes and then-current United centre-forward, Albert Stubbins, patted the awestruck duo on the back and wished them the best of luck.

Dad did not play in the first half of the United team versus 'the rest' trial match, although was given the opportunity to show what he could do after the interval and thankfully managed to bang in two goals. As he walked from the pitch, club director and stand-in manager Stan Seymour told him he'd done very well and would like to see him return the following week. Sadly there would be no place for Raymond. 'Raymond had played just as well as any other trialist and I felt terrible as he came close to tears. After all, he was the one who'd written the letter to ask for the trial.'

Once back home, Dad blurted out to his father and Uncle Tanner about being asked back the following week, but the pair warned him not to sign any contract until they had checked it over first, and his father's tone of voice told him there would be mighty big trouble if he did not heed his advice.

Word soon spread and the whole of Ashington seemed to want him to do well, apart from a few jealous former school friends, who made some wisecracks after reading about his two goals in the *Sunday Sun*. Dad ignored the jokers and threw himself into an even heavier training routine for the rest of the week.

On the day of the second trial, he finished work at midday, having been told there was no chance of having the day off, and then caught a bus through to Newcastle. Possessing something of a superstitious nature, he went back to the same café and ordered two of the very same meat pies. However, after a poor first-half display and with his confidence waning, Joe Richardson, a trainer from Bedlington, grabbed Dad's arm and told him to snap out of it. Suddenly realising it might be his last chance, he forgot all about his inferiority complex and the large crowd and did just that. He now found the ball being pushed through to him in the centre-forward position – he had taken over from Albert Stubbins – and from through-runs beginning almost at the halfway line, soon found himself banging in six goals. 'I was as surprised as the next man when the ball kept flying in the net.'

After the match, the seed was planted in his head that it was not really his own ability or Joe Richardson's sound advice that had enabled him to play so well, but rather, it must have something to do with the two meat pies. 'This, in fact, became my routine lunch before a match for many seasons to come.'

Club directors Stan Seymour and Wilf Taylor came into the dressing-room to offer him their congratulations, with Seymour adding: 'A really wonderful display. Will you sign pro for us? There's a place, you know, in the first team for you next week.'

Dad was gobsmacked, but staggered Seymour with his nervous reply, 'Sorry, sir, but I promised my father I wouldn't sign any forms until he had seen them.'

Used to having his own way, Seymour persisted, no doubt worried that he may lose his young prospect to another club, so he sighed with relief when Dad agreed to sign an amateur form. As Seymour left the dressing-room he stressed one thing: 'Don't forget to bring your father along to see me here on Monday. If you bring him we'll all be happy.'

He returned with the form, which he handed to Dad. 'I'd like you to give this to your father to let him see what you've signed. I don't want anyone to think we're pulling a fast one.'

Dad was walking on air as he strolled from the players' entrance of St James' Park. He was now a fully signed amateur and a colleague of the great Albert Stubbins himself, who now accompanied him down the steps. 'All my schoolboy dreams had come true.'

Suddenly, hundreds of boys descended on Dad and Albert, asking them both for their autographs. 'My day was then made.' Dad spent almost an hour obliging the youngsters and the fact that he missed his bus didn't worry him in the least. He now felt like 'one of the boys'.

In the Milburn household, it was unthinkable for Alec to miss a shift at the pit, so he must have been as thrilled as Dad was as he accompanied him to St James' Park on the Monday. Although Alec took the day off, Dad went to work as normal and had to rush home to get himself ready for the bus trip to Newcastle.

Unbeknown to Dad at the time, the wily Seymour had actually

driven over to Ashington on the Sunday morning to speak with his Uncle Tanner in an attempt to make sure no other club manager sneaked in to secure his signature. After the pair spent a day in one of Ashington's social clubs there was no need for any further doubt about Dad signing for Newcastle.

They hopped on the bus from Ashington to Newcastle's Haymarket then walked to the ground, arriving at 5.45 p.m. to be ushered into the deified boardroom. 'My father,' Dad remembered, 'could not have been given a bigger thrill, even if the prime minister had invited him into 10 Downing Street.'

In his time, in all kinds of weather, Alec had stood on the terraces of St James' Park to cheer on Newcastle United and in particular former left-back Stan Seymour himself, who played in Alec's own favoured position, so Dad sensed the thrill he must be feeling at meeting him in this most Holy of Holies room. Seymour crossed the floor to Alec with an outstretched hand, saying, 'Welcome to St James', Mr Milburn and it's nice of you to come over to see us. Would you like a glass of whisky?'

On their way to the meeting, Dad had agreed to allow his father to carry on all the negotiations with Seymour, but the chief was direct and got straight to the point. At the moment, all we can offer is 30 shillings (£1.50) a match, plus expenses to and from the ground. As you'll appreciate, this is purely a wartime measure and when League football is eventually resumed, you can leave the pit to become a full-time pro. Your income then will be very much higher than some may believe.'

Dad and Alec nodded at each other, knowing Dad had nothing to lose but everything to gain by signing on the dotted line now.

David Halliday, a former Sunderland and Arsenal player, was a visitor that evening and when the time came to sign the form he said, 'Give me the honour of letting Jackie sign with my pen.' As Dad signed, Halliday looked over at Seymour and grinned, saying, 'I guess you've got one of your best ever signings.' Dad was now a part-time professional at the age of 19.

Before the pair left the boardroom, Alec had gratefully toasted Seymour's health several times and Dad pocketed the statutory £10 signing-on fee; Seymour had been flicking and fingering it temptingly behind his own back. Dad never forgot that. 'I'd never seen, let alone owned, so much money in my life.'

As he stored it carefully in his right-hand trouser pocket, Dad was already planning how to spend the money, and on the bus back to Ashington Alec joined in with a few ideas. Finally, though, without any help, Dad decided to give £5 to his mother for a new dress, keep £4 for himself to buy a badly needed new suit. The remaining pound would go to his father for a few pints and some tobacco.

'Back home in Ashington that night, almost all the entire 73-member Milburn clan celebrated well into the wee small hours.'

# 2

# Pro at Last – But Still Down the Pit

He used to remind me of a wave breaking. He'd just surge past defenders with his incredible pace. Everybody loved watching him. Wor Jackie. Wey aye!

Sir Bobby Charlton

Dad's career began under the shadow of the Second World War. The Football League programme had been suspended and at this time only friendly matches were played.

The Wednesday following Dad's signing a card arrived for him instructing him to report to St James' Park on the Saturday, ready to travel with the first team to play against Bradford City at Valley Parade on 28 August 1943, though before that he had to return in the evenings for training. 'I'll never forget the thrill of my first entrée into the ground as a fully fledged pro,' he recalled. That evening, Albert Stubbins, the current fast man of St James', invited Dad to train with him and when they raced over 100 yards, was surprised when Dad got his nose in front. A few other eyebrows were raised too. Andy McCombie, who helped with the training, seemed to be very impressed.

While Dad lay in the bath after training, Andy came in to

introduce club trainer Norman Smith (Norman would be associated with Newcastle's great post-war run of success), to discuss Dad's turn of speed. Dad clambered out the bath, dried off, dressed and donned spikes to give Norman a one-man show.

After the performance, Norman beamed, saying, 'I like your style, Jackie, and it's obvious you have studied this important side of football. We'll make a player out of you here.'

Dad was given another bonus when Seymour invited Alec to accompany him and the team to Bradford for his debut match that Saturday, even booking them into the County Hotel in Newcastle on the Friday night so they wouldn't miss the train. Dad reckoned Alec didn't know whether to laugh or cry. 'You see, my father couldn't afford the luxury of even the saloon bar of our local clubs, let alone visit big hotels.'

As the starry-eyed pair travelled from Ashington to Newcastle, Alec confided to Dad that it was indeed the first occasion he'd ever stayed in a hotel. 'But for goodness sake, son, don't let us oversleep and miss the Bradford train.'

After clambering into bed, they suddenly panicked as both of them realised that neither had brought along an alarm clock, so for the rest of the night both son and father tossed and rolled about so much they finally dragged themselves from bed at 4.30 a.m., lit a fag and kept their eyes firmly focused on the Central Station clock across the way . . . just in case. They were not going to miss the 8.15 to Bradford.

Lo and behold, and with plenty of time to spare, the hotel staff knocked on their door as per instructions. Dad and Alec hadn't reckoned on that. After breakfast, an excited Alec made another confession: it was to be the first time he'd travelled anywhere further than Newcastle.

Under the clock in the station's main hall, Dad met for the first time the players with whom he was to make his debut later that day. At centre-half would be big Tot Smith, whom Dad had 'roasted' when he scored six in his trial game.

As they sat on the train, Dad noticed his agog father watching the world flash by the carriage window: 'For the first time in his life he was really living . . . and enjoying every second of it.'

At Valley Parade, the management and staff went out of their way to be courteous to Alec. 'My father was really made to feel like an important person and I gloried in his happiness.' Then, as the team sat down to lunch, Dad sneaked himself off and bought a couple of meat pies, which he ate in the privacy of the bathroom so no one would see him and rumble his superstition.

On the pitch just prior to the kick-off, Dad was a bundle of nerves, so Jimmy Mullen, who went on to play for Wolves and England, walked over to him and whispered, 'Don't worry, Jackie, I'll do all I can for you by keeping on running.'

Newcastle lost 2–1, thanks to two goals scored by a tall, dark, strong and very fast inside-right by the name of Joe Harvey, the man who in later years would go on to captain Newcastle from the Second to the First Division and to two Wembley Cup final victories.

Dad reckoned his own game was not so good and he missed a couple of easy chances with his head, so was just thankful that Stan Seymour didn't mention them after the match. All he said was, 'Well played, son. You'll be in the side again next week.'

The following week Newcastle faced Bradford again, though at St James' Park this time. There were no nerves for Dad this time and after just two minutes, he achieved the ambition of every footballer by scoring with his first kick of the game. From that moment, he had the honour of scoring in the first and last games at St James' for four successive seasons.

Dad felt he was playing within a happy team of youth blended with experience and as more players came back home on leave from the forces, Seymour drafted them into the side to give them more experience. Slowly but surely, names like Bobby Cowell, Bobby Corbett, Charlie Crowe, Tommy Walker, George Hair, Ernie Taylor and Charlie Wayman became familiar to the United fans and when Wayman became the obvious choice at inside-left, Dad found himself once more at outside-right, declaring, 'I must make it quite clear that for the 30 shillings I receive per match, plus half a crown [12.5p] for my tea and a further half a crown for my bus fare, I consider Newcastle have the right to play me in any position.' The first game he and Wayman played in those positions, Newcastle trounced Middlesbrough 8–2. 'I suddenly got the feeling that I might just be starting a long career running the right flank,' said Dad.

Many more games after that brought a stream of goals and against Bradford again United won 11–0. Joe Harvey must have done enough to impress Seymour, though, and in June 1945, he signed for the Magpies for £4,500 while still a sergeant-major in the army.

The beginning of the 1945–46 season saw Newcastle United building up to the return of League football the following season.

Joe Harvey had come in as the first big post-war signing, though he now played at right-half. Established players like Harry Clifton, Doug Wright, Jim Woodburn, Jimmy Gordon, Ben Craig and Tommy Pearson, plus the young squad of eager local lads produced during the war years, were all keen to fight for their places.

During one of the early games, two of the local lads, Corbett and Crowe, helped blot out the soccer master himself, Stanley Matthews, as United trounced Stoke City 9–1. Although Dad did not score, Stanley Matthews singled him out after the match and told him, 'I watched you this afternoon and would like you to know I think you have a bright future if you continue to play like that.' As a mere youngster, Dad was delighted to be told that by one of football's all-time greats. He never forgot it.

The following week Newcastle again faced Stoke, though this time on their home territory, and it proved a completely different ball game. 'Stanley Matthews made us all realize what a treat we all missed at St James' last Saturday. He made the ball do everything but unlace itself and name its maker. And after that superb display, I felt I should go home and burn my boots, for as a footballer, I realized that I could never, for all my natural speed and great enthusiasm, hope to be in the same class as this distinguished player.'

During the war years and just after, Dad never felt he was really tested by many solid full-backs, mainly because of their lack of availability – until he came up against one George Hardwick of Middlesbrough and England, that is.

George never allowed Dad a kick of the ball or a clear view of the goal and during one match in particular, completely knocked him off his stride. With the score level at 2–2, Newcastle were awarded a penalty kick and Dad was told to take it, even though he knew his confidence was rock-bottom after his tussles with George. He protested, but was told to just get on with it. He missed, saying after the match, 'There is no excuse for missing the penalty, but it taught me something I shall never forget, namely that you should never ask a player to take a penalty if he is having a bad game. It is only asking for trouble and is unfair to both the player and his team.' A vital lesson learned by him.

During that first post-war season, Newcastle played in front of a total of 882,980 home spectators, with centre-forward Albert Stubbins notching himself 43 goals and Dad 17 from the right wing. The nucleus of a very useful team was now in the moulding.

In his first ever Cup tie, played against Barnsley, Dad took particular notice of their eye-catching Chilean-born inside-forward, George Robledo. Although Newcastle beat them 4–2 in the first leg in front of 60,000, with Dad grabbing two, it was in the second leg that George did something to make Dad's eyes pop.

After George had agreed to take a penalty, he only took three short steps before cracking it hard towards the bottom-left corner of the goal, but United's keeper, Ray King, somehow threw himself full length to get a fist to the ball. Dad never forgot what happened: 'As if jet-propelled, the ball flew from King's fist like a bullet high into the air, way over the grandstand and out of Barnsley's ground. I gasped, but so did Ray King, because as he made the save, he broke his wrist.' Barnsley won 3–0.

Little did Dad know at the time, but George Robledo was destined to become a United player – for a £26,500 joint fee along with his brother Ted – and a close friend.

While touring Norway with the club on a close-season tour, the players were told that big Frank Brennan, the renowned Scottish centre-half, had been secured for £8,500 and then a few weeks later Roy Bentley joined from Bristol City, for the same fee. Things just seemed to be getting better all the time.

The 1946–47 season saw the Football League resume for the first time since 1939, meaning that promotion and relegation would be factors once more. Newcastle United resumed their pre-war status as a Second Division club.

United's first game was to be played in London on 31 August against Millwall, also known back then as the 'dour fighters', so the Magpies knew that it would not only be a tough test for them but also a preview for all the exiled Geordies living in the south. The players desperately wanted to do well.

After checking in to the hotel, Dad discovered he was to share a room with Frank Brennan and Roy Bentley, though on entering it realised the hotel had dropped a clanger and there was not the double and single bed as expected, but only one single. After speaking to the management, they were told there was not another spare bed in the entire building, so simply had to get on with it. 'So never one to make a fuss, I shared the bed with expensive Frank [£8,500] on one side and costly Roy on the other [£8,500] with me in the middle [£10] . . . needless to say, I never slept a wink. How those soccer stars snored.'

This was Dad and Frank's first visit to London, so they found the bustling city a little daunting. However, Roy claimed he knew the big city well and so offered to show them the sights, but as they sauntered among the sea of people, Roy suddenly disappeared. Panic set in and with the game only an hour away, the pair became really worried. 'So that we wouldn't be parted, we grasped hands as we made our way through the crowds and down the Underground escalators. Many folk stared at us two hefty lads running hand-in-hand, but I can assure you we had to, just to stick together.'

United beat Millwall 4–1, with Dad scoring one. As he looked around the dressing-room after the match, he suddenly realised just what a good squad of players he had around him. They were a side that had every chance of going places. The team that day consisted of: Garbutt; Cowell and Graham; Harvey, Brennan and Wright; Milburn, Bentley, Stubbins, Wayman and Pearson.

Back home, out of the blue and for reasons only he really understood, Albert Stubbins made his decision to ask for a move and was immediately snapped up by Liverpool, leaving a huge gap in the front line. Seymour, though, had the perfect answer. Newcastle forked out £13,000 and a penny to Bradford City on a player called Len Shackleton. He was soon to earn himself the title of 'The Clown Prince of Soccer'. 'Shack' slotted in at inside-left and Wayman was moved to centre-forward.

In Shack's first match against Newport County at the start of October, having missed a first-minute penalty, he went on to slam in six of the goals in the 13–0 United win, just to show everyone he was worth every penny of the mammoth figure forked out for him. He even had the audacity to knock the last one in with his backside, causing great delight to the fans. Dad got two of the goals and reckoned at the time: 'We now looked set to bid for some of the game's honours.' So proficient did United's attack become that even talented wee Ernie Taylor couldn't get a game.

Seymour's reward for his players were occasional special training stints away to places like Blackpool or Brighton, where they could relax in the evenings at the amusement parks and forget about football for a few hours. Dad reckoned this policy paid dividends and it certainly seemed so, with Newcastle topping the Second Division at Christmas. Then, though, came the 'big freeze', and as the temperatures plummeted, so did United – down the table.

This left only the FA Cup to play for. Hopes were raised when they got through to meet Charlton Athletic in the semi-final and to get there they had defeated Crystal Palace, Leicester City and Sheffield United. Newcastle were now hot favourites to reach the final. However, to everyone's great surprise, Seymour unexpectedly announced that he was dropping Charlie Wayman in favour of George Stobbard. Very quickly, rumours began to spread about a split camp, but the squad were just as surprised themselves as the fans and press boys, so everyone remained tight-lipped about the whole situation.

On the day at Elland Road, Newcastle were smothered and defeated 4–0 by Charlton, who had obviously done their homework well, and it was a gloomy United squad who sat in the dressing-room at 4.40 p.m. that Saturday afternoon. Everyone was fed up. To make matters worse, on the following Monday, Joe Harvey and Len Shackleton announced that they would not return to Tyneside from their Yorkshire homes until they could move into the club houses they had been promised. 'So one way or another, we were a pretty dejected side after that semi-final defeat,' Dad recalled.

At the end of the season however, Newcastle's average home gate was calculated at 56,350, the biggest in the world, as a season total of over 1,000,000 supporters squashed into the ground, proving that the bread-and-butter fans were not too disgruntled with their team. They had finished fifth.

Promotion became paramount and everyone's sights now focused on First Division football the following season. Stan Seymour stepped down and George Martin was brought in from Luton Town to manage the team. A new goalkeeper, Jack Fairbrother, was then signed for £7,000 from Preston. The biggest surprise though, as the 1947–48 season got underway, came with the sudden departure of Charlie Wayman to Southampton. Dad made it known in later life just why Wayman left the club: 'We had over 70 pros at the club and shared two dressing-rooms. Charlie couldn't find a peg to hang his clothes on and that was it. He asked for a transfer. Simple as that.'

The whole of a stunned Tyneside now had the same question on their lips: who would be the next man to wear the revered No. 9 shirt?

In October Dad found himself summoned into George Martin's office for what he thought was a routine chat. 'Sit down, Jackie, and listen carefully to what I have to say. Mr Seymour and I have decided to play you at centre-forward against Bury on Saturday as George Stobbard is injured. We both believe you'll settle down and be a big success down the middle.'

Dad's stomach filled with butterflies. He had only ever once played a full match in that position for his school team and had been a complete flop. He explained that to Martin, but was told not to worry and that if things didn't work out he could go back out on the wing. 'For two nights before the game I never slept a wink.'

Just before the teams took to the pitch, Shack sidled up to him, 'Don't worry, Jackie, I'll look after you.' And he did. Largely due to his unselfishness, he fed Dad a stream of passes and when the Bury keeper was unluckily carried off with a broken leg, their defence was hastily reshuffled and Dad notched himself a hat-trick, even nodding one in with his head, which a lot of folk thought had always been his weakest point.

'Len Shackleton was a master craftsman and thanks to him I got among the goals. I clicked with him because I expected the unorthodox. If he ran one way, I ran the other, and sure enough the ball always found me. On the other hand, Len's quick-witted humour often caused me to laugh outright and lose control of the ball.'

Mid-way into the season gone, Newcastle were well on target for promotion. Odd as it may seem, one of the key players, Roy Bentley, found himself transferred after complaining about the state of his bath in the flat he lived in, which belonged to the sister of a club director. George Martin inspected it himself, but could see no real problem, though Bentley still thought differently. A couple of months later he found himself playing in the blue of Chelsea.

Due to his reserved occupation (an occupation considered by the

government to be essential in war time and in the following years),
Dad still worked at the pit, though now at Hazelrigg Colliery where
Shack was his assistant. Unable to afford a car of his own to get back
and forth to training, he bought himself an old boneshaker of a
motorcycle and he and Len, still dressed in full pit gear, raced to the
ground after work. It wasn't long though before United put the
blocks on him travelling anywhere on the bike – especially when
they got wind the pair had tumbled off after the front wheel wedged
into the tram lines on Gosforth High Street – so it was back to
Shanks's pony or the bus.

During that November of 1947, Dad prepared himself for the most
significant match of his life.

As he gawped, starry-eyed, at the beautiful décor of the swanky
lobby of a Letchworth hotel in which United were staying for a
week's special training, he couldn't help but whistle under his
breath at another fine spectacle.

In the corner, with her back to him, perched on a pair of
wavering stepladders, as yet quite unaware of his gaze, teetered my
prospective mother, 19-year-old silver service waitress, Laura
Easton Blackwood.

He grinned, admiring her curves as she stretched awkwardly to
pin Christmas decorations to the ceiling, and then as she descended,
she turned to face him, finding herself drawn to return his gaze. 'We
both glowed as the "electricity" flowed between us . . . we were
hooked. Simple as that,' Dad recalled fondly.

Although bashful, he promised himself to find the courage to ask
her out during his stay. Likewise, she hoped he would.

The following morning, as she emerged from the kitchen to serve
his table's breakfast, he impatiently nudged his roommate, United's
goalkeeper Jack Fairbrother, somewhat startling him by announcing
that the waitress was going to be his future bride. Fairbrother
smiled dryly and said, 'At least hang fire until we've finished our
breakfast.' But Dad meant it.

That evening, knowing dinner wasn't served until 7 p.m., he coyly arrived in the dining room at 6.30, knowing she would be busy laying the tables. He asked if it would be all right to take an early seat.

As she finished preparing his table, he sat fidgeting and blushing, struggling to find the self-confidence to introduce himself, but then suddenly he just blurted out his name and said he played football for Newcastle United. He had to laugh though, as she politely apologised for having heard of neither, but was surprised by her soft Scottish accent, expecting her to be a southern English girl.

After a little small talk, he finally managed to ask her if she'd care to join him for a walk around the grounds the following afternoon and was thrilled when she agreed – although she said she would have to get permission from her mother, Molly, who also worked there as a waitress. After speaking to Dad, and although quite shy herself, Mum was puzzled as to why such a confident-looking, tall, handsome young man should feel so uncomfortable, even if she did find it a major part of his charm.

Noting the great excitement on her daughter's face, mother Molly agreed to their rendezvous and the next day, as the pair strolled arm in arm around the pleasant gardens, she peeped out from behind the hotel's lace curtains.

Mum was curious and asked Dad about his shyness, but he simply dismissed it as an 'inferiority complex' more than anything else, reckoning it affected him in most of life's situations. That is, until the second he donned the black and white of Newcastle United and was given the freedom of the pitch, the one place his confidence in his own ability grew as high as a skyscraper. The couple walked on, now beginning to realize just how at ease they were in each other's company and before heading back to the hotel, Dad asked her to accompany him to the local picture house to see the new movie, *Mrs. Miniver*, the following evening. Molly gave her blessing.

The next afternoon, an excited Mum and a waitress friend spied discreetly from the kitchen windows as the players trained in the hotel grounds.

Later, as the film flickered above them, the young couple held hands but shuffled nervously in their seats, not really watching the screen and then all too soon it was over. Slowly they made their way back to the hotel. Halfway back, Dad stopped to light a cigarette and as he did, edgily shuffled his feet.

He was suddenly compelled to tell her of his totally unexpected feeling toward her, and so he did. She heaved a sigh of relief and quickly confessed to feeling the same. 'We both put it down to the old maxim: love at first sight . . . aided a little by the hand of fate.'

Dad though, admitted he still had another confession to make – a huge one. He was already engaged to a girl back home in Ashington, but deep down knew it wasn't meant to be. It was his intention to break it off as soon as he got back home, and to prove it, vowed there and then to marry Mum if she would have him. She was stunned and burst into tears, yet knew he meant it. 'There was just no stepping back now.'

The next day, after training, Dad, bearing in mind Mum's Scottish heritage, aptly bought her a little silver Scotty dog brooch. He then confirmed his feelings. She knew she felt the same.

Friday came and as the team checked out, the pair bade a cheerless farewell, but very soon Dad's first letter arrived, explaining that he'd broken off the engagement and repeating his promise to marry her if she would care to join him up in the Northeast.

Before too long, Newcastle United had a match to play in London, so Mum's father took her along, which gave the pair the opportunity to meet up briefly. It was at this meeting that Dad formally proposed and she accepted. Then, just after Christmas 1948, he invited her up to meet his folks and once there wanted her to stay for good. For their part, Alec and Nance knew their son must be head over heels, so therefore offered to put Laura up, and in January Mum worked her notice, packed her bags, and set off for Newcastle.

As she sat on the train for the long journey north, Mum had time to reflect on her life and my father's words about fate dealing them a hand, realising just how easy it would have been for them never to have met. It was a complicated path that had brought her to her meeting with Dad.

Born in Glasgow in November 1927, she lived there with her parents and older sister, Betty, for just a year before the family uprooted and emigrated to Australia, where an aunt had settled a few years before. The family stayed for four years until Molly contracted tuberculosis and it was thought a wise move to take a ship back to Glasgow.

As soon as the Second World War broke out in 1939, Mum and Betty found themselves evacuated to the little village of Penman, near Fraserburgh, but after just a year, homesick Betty wanted to return to Glasgow, so left Mum alone. Still, Mum was quite happy to move to a nearby farm, where the kindly folk taught her a little about milking the cows.

The snow was particularly heavy the next winter and she took advantage of it, though barely avoided what might have been a really nasty accident while sledging speedily down the steep village hill. As a low bough loomed before her, she only just managed to avoid cracking her skull by swerving at the last second, but then careered into a stone wall instead and crushed her left ankle between it and the sledge. It was many months before she could walk properly again, but that incident alone was not to be her only fortuitous escape.

The farming family had set off on a shopping expedition to buy their daughter a pair of new shoes, though instead of heading directly to the shoe shop, decided to window-gaze other shops first. As they walked down the main street, Mum looked up and saw dozens of spiralling black objects falling speedily earthward, at first not realising they were German bombs.

Fortunately someone shoved her into the lobby of a hotel, where she threw herself to the floor and covered her ears. After what seemed like an eternity the bombs ceased, so she dragged herself to her feet and out into the street, discovering the frantic family conducting a search for their charge. Now reunited, they simply wanted to head for home, so hurried to the shoe shop to quickly purchase the shoes, but as they approached it, soon realised their lucky escape. It was nothing but a pile of rubble.

Hitler's bombs, raining havoc again, later forced Mum out to Kirkfieldbank, just outside of Lanark, where during the summer she developed green fingers while working for a market gardener.

Unfortunately, during this time, her parents formally separated and her father, John, moved down to London where he set up his own hairdressing business. Mum missed him, so at the end of the war followed him down and took a job working in a large store near his home, before being hired as a nursemaid. However, it wasn't long before Molly moved down too and found employment as a waitress at the Letchworth Hotel, inviting Mum to join her there.

Meanwhile, Mum's sister, Betty, who was now settled in Canada with new husband Roy, wrote and told her what a beautiful country Canada was and that she felt sure she would really love it there too. Almost immediately, Mum made up her mind to emigrate and if the hand of fate and Dad hadn't intervened, that is undoubtedly where she was bound.

Dad drove to the Newcastle Central Station to collect Mum, having learnt to point and steer a motor car. In those days there was no compulsory driving test to be sat, so Dad felt confident enough to borrow an ancient Austin from a pal of his Uncle Fred. 'I had it drummed into me not to dare slam the passenger door as the flimsy window was liable to drop out.' The couple met on the platform in excitement, then went to the station café for a cuppa. 'I slipped an engagement ring on Laura's finger and we just gawped at it for ages,' recalled Dad.

After a rickety journey back to Ashington, they drew up outside his parents' home, where he proudly threw open the back door to introduce his love to the impatient sea of curious faces. Mum was almost sick with nerves. With over 70 members of the Milburn clan living in the area, she felt sure she must be meeting them all at once.

One enquiring family member gave her a solid 'grilling' into the wee small hours to find out everything about her, though it wasn't long before they discovered for themselves what a canny lass she was, and quite understood just why Dad should want to marry her so soon. Later in the evening, Mum found herself squirming and could no longer fight off the desperate urge to use the bathroom, but was surprised to be led to the back door and pointed across the dark back lane before being handed a torch and told the 'netty' was straight opposite. As she fumbled back out from the 'ice-chamber', a whistling pitman hurried past in the opposite direction armed with a candle and newspaper tucked under his arm, smiling cheerfully as he unsnecked the adjoining 'quiet room', enquiring, 'Y'all reet, bonny lass?'

Just three weeks later, the happy pair stood side by side before the Registrar at Willesden Green in London, near to Mum's father's home. As neither wanted a big fussy wedding, nor really could afford one, they invited only a small party of 20 guests and then after the reception, journeyed down to Folkestone to spend three days honeymooning by the sea.

On arriving back in Ashington, my parents began to search for a place of their own. Although more than grateful to Alec and Nance for putting them up thus far, space in the little terraced house was becoming a little precious. So, with just £17 in the bank, they were overjoyed when Newcastle United offered them a club house in Gosforth, Newcastle, but there was just one slight snag – it wasn't yet free.

Len Shackleton was by now on his way to Sunderland, probably spurred by comments made by Joe Harvey to manager George Martin. Shack was developing more into a crowd entertainer rather than a team footballer and seemed to be getting more of a kick out of beating four or five men than passing on the ball when it mattered. Joe declared that Newcastle would never win anything with him in the team and United listened.

Both clubs had agreed on a fee, and now the only stumbling block remaining was that Len simply couldn't find a suitable Wearside home and so was staying put in the Gosforth house that my parents wanted to move into. However, he invited Mum and Dad over and showed them around the house, as well as offering to sell them a huge oak table for £3 – what would be their very first piece of furniture – so they were cock-a-hoop as they hopped on the bus back to Ashington. From then on, they could hardly contain themselves at the prospect of the impending move, though Len was still unhappy with the accommodation he'd been offered, so dug his heels in and sat tight.

Each day grew to be a week for the desperate duo and each week a month, until at last Len found precisely what he was after and upped sticks. 'We went mad, hopping about and walloping the air, never dreaming I would ever be glad to see the back of my pernickety old buddy,' Dad remembered. Soon they were in, scrubbing the linoleum and furnishing the house with oddments graciously donated by friends or bought on hire purchase.

It was around this time that Dad broke the superstitious habit he'd carried with him for about five seasons. He stopped eating the two meat pies he always ate before each match and settled instead for a small piece of grilled fillet steak on two slices of toast.

In early 1948, along with Shack and Roy Bentley, Tommy Pearson had also left the club, so new replacements had to be quickly drafted in to the forward line. They came in the form of Welsh international George Lowrie from Coventry and Frank Houghton from Ballymena; in addition little Ernie Taylor was now coming into his own and there was also Willie McCall.

The promotion-deciding match of the 1947–48 season came against Sheffield Wednesday at St James' Park in front of 66,483 on 17 April, and a win was crucial if the Magpies were to gain promotion.

In later years, Dad declared that during the game he'd never heard the roar of the Geordie faithful so deafening, and that even included Cup finals at Wembley. 'The players' ears thumped the whole time.' But it had done the trick and they were spurred on to score four goals to Wednesday's two. Frank Houghton notched the fourth, but at the same time ran on to crash into the goalpost and break his arm. Houghton then found himself carried from the pitch, though he still managed a brief smile in the knowledge that his goal was enough to seal the game and promotion was secured.

For all the great glory of that promotion-winning season, Dad still had to work at Hazelrigg Colliery, albeit he was now required to work only above the ground.

He often felt embarrassed about the way he secured that privilege, but knew he had to, simply to keep up the standard of his game. Before he was transferred from the Woodhorn Colliery, he would often begin his shift at midnight on a Friday and not finish until 7 or 8 a.m. on the Saturday morning; then he'd have to dash straight home and scrub up, before joining the queue for the bus with the United supporters and play in front of 60,000 of them at St James' Park. 'Often they would yell at me to get to the front of the queue, but I waited my turn like the rest.'

When I asked Alan Shearer how modern players would respond to the pressures of working down the pit the night before playing a match, he told me:

> I don't think they could cope with that at all, and to be honest, we've got it cushy – there's no doubt about that. We train for two to three hours a day and we play ninety minutes on a Tuesday and Saturday and get paid for doing something that is a pleasure. There might be one or two – but there wouldn't be a lot – who could work eight hours and then go out and play.

Under no circumstances did Dad favour being down the dark hole in the ground, never mind being down there all alone, which to his complete horror, is precisely where he found himself one night. 'This time I'd had enough. I was finished.' The pawl had broken on the diamond coal cutter, leaving it jammed in the cut along a seam just 18 inches high and he was the only fitter available to do the repair.

Most of the night he worked at it, after crawling in on his back to work flat out as lumps of stone, dripping water and choking dust dropped onto his face as the pit props creaked eerily about; nevertheless, after hours of cussing and knuckle scraping, he finally got the job done. 'In just a few hours, I had to get myself into shape to play in front of 60,000 screaming Geordies against West Bromwich Albion at St James' Park.'

Dad eventually mentioned his exhaustion and worries at not being able to play football to his best ability to a chap called Mick Bell, who was then in charge of the Mechanics' Union. Mick in turn spoke to the colliery manager and threatened all-out strike action if Dad wasn't given a Saturday off and every single electrician, fitter and engineer unanimously backed him by agreeing to down tools, so the disgruntled boss reluctantly agreed.

Dad also mentioned it in passing to an auctioneer friend, a fervent 'black and white', while visiting his Gallowgate salerooms. 'He agreed wholeheartedly that the whole state of affairs was ludicrous, but he told me not to worry. He went off to speak with a doctor friend of his.' After being sworn to secrecy, Dad met up with the doctor, who told him to keep poking and prodding at the inside of his ears, with a clean matchstick, to such an extent that they wept. 'I just sat in a chair at home and did as I was advised.' In the meantime, the doctor arranged for him to undergo a medical at the Royal Victoria Infirmary, Newcastle, after which, due to the weeping, he was diagnosed with external otitis – inflammation of the ear. From that day on, he never set foot down the pit again, though still remained certified to work on the surface in the fitting shop.

Dad later discovered he was not alone using the tried-and-trusted ear-picking ploy and felt a little less guilty. 'Even though my ears never really ran at all, it got me out the pit.'

I discovered a little about mining conditions for myself during that period after a friend of mine, Joyce Crass, told me about her own father's distinguished unbeaten record. He was a chap called Jim Marley, who grafted hard at the East Walbottle Colliery in Northumberland where he dug coal by hand from a narrow seam just three feet deep. After that particular pit was asked to increase its output, Jim quickly found himself in the *Guinness Book Of Records* and stunning the world by cutting a staggering 218 tons in just a single week – and 47.5 tons of those took him only six hours! During that entire period he ate nothing, drank only water and lost a full stone in weight. For all his backbreaking effort, the coal bosses boosted his wage packet by a mere sixpence (2.5p), but nothing could diminish Jim's pride at holding the world record.

With all the underground shift pressure behind Dad, a blissful marriage and a new home to settle into, he not only started hitting the back of the net more frequently in 1948, but there was also newspaper speculation of an England call-up – a dream for Dad, who hoped to be able to do it for his country too. Then came the icing on the cake: his new bride announced she was expecting their first child. Strange as it may seem, with all the happiness in their lives, it was around this time they had their first 'huffy' row.

At that time, Dad was receiving anything up to 2,000 fan letters a week, many of which were sent by doting females. Certainly never one to brag, yet without realising the effect it would have on Mum, he thought it would be amusing to read out a few of the messages of enduring love and lines like 'if you ever get tired of her, you always know where to find me'. Green-eyed and positively in a 'pregnant mood', Mum retorted she was packing her bags and heading back to her mother's in Letchworth, quickly storming up the stairs to do so. Dad followed, realising the error of his teasing way, and apologised copiously through the keyhole of the locked bedroom door. But there was no reply. After a while he had to leave for training, so he pushed a written apology under the door and left her alone. However, on his return he found only an empty house and the suitcases missing. Frantic, he dashed from room to room but found neither hide nor hair of Mum and then thought of ringing Molly at her hotel to see if Mum had been in touch. He ran downstairs to head for the telephone box, but while fretting in the doorway heard a muffled sneeze from the bedroom so darted back upstairs. Throwing open the large wardrobe door, he revealed a tearful Mum huddled on the packed suitcases. Never again was either of them so daft.

There was one incident in the 1947–48 season that saw my father consider a move away from Newcastle.

On the ferry home after playing for England against Northern Ireland at Windsor Park, Belfast, Dad's attention was grabbed. 'I listened absorbedly to the craic of a few of soccer's "wise boys", and their tales of great jobs to be had outside of football down in the prosperous south. But something else pricked my ears, something they called programme money.'

Programme money, he was led to believe, was a 'share out' among the players from the sale of 'surplus' programmes on match days, something he felt Newcastle United boss Stan Seymour would never consider, even though many a rumour abounded about the 'directors' gates' at St James' Park.

With just £12 a week wages, hire purchase commitments, a wife and young baby on the way, Dad's head whirled with all the possibilities the much-needed extra cash might bring. 'It had never crossed my mind to take on a mortgage before . . . until now that is.'

Once back home, he and Mum discussed the whole idea and were thrilled at the notion of being able to afford to buy their own home and not having the worry of being 'turfed out' of a tied club house once Dad's playing days came to an end. The couple paced the floor and laboured over the decision for days, until Dad decided it was time for action. He came up with a spurious excuse – that his wife was suffering from bronchitis since arriving in the smoggy Northeast – and decided to put in for a transfer. 'I arranged a meeting with the club directors to officially request a move.'

During the uncomfortable, smoke-filled gathering, he blurted out his request and the room fell silent. Asked if he was adamant, he nodded and without further ado was given the unanimous thumbs down. The old 'inferiority complex' and lack of confidence caused him to back down straight away, 'Though I discovered later it was much to the great relief of the directors.'

Back home, he told Mum what had happened and, in the clear light of day, he confessed that 'easy money' probably wasn't really his cup of tea and that his conscience would have found it difficult to live with it. Sadly, it meant a house move would not now be on the cards.

At the end of that season, Newcastle found themselves promoted to the First Division, albeit in second place. However, the players and the Geordie public didn't care about that; at last, they were back in the top flight where they belonged. The Northeast was in heaven – if your eyes were black and white, that is.

Dad ended the season, his first as centre-forward, after scoring 20 League goals and got a further 8 during a short close-season tour of the Emerald Isle, including 4 during the 4–0 drubbing of his future club Linfield. On the eve of his 24th birthday, he also grabbed a hat-trick in the 6–0 defeat of Shelbourne.

Prior to the kick-off of the 1948–49 season, Dad's, the club's and the supporters' feelings were running high. After their promotion, everyone felt sure United had the nucleus of a strong team, good enough even to finish near the top of the First Division.

They were right – they finished fourth, though only after a somewhat shaky start. The first game against Everton at Goodison Park ended 3–3 and the second against Chelsea at St James' Park

2–2. Then came a 2–5 home defeat at the hands of Preston, before Newcastle found their form with two away wins: 2–3 at Chelsea and 0–3 at Burnley, followed by a 2–1 home win against Aston Villa, in which Dad notched his 5th goal. Two goalless draws, a 1–0 defeat and then a 1–1 away draw against Sunderland saw the tide turn, as they went on to win the next six games with Dad banging in a further five.

Among the crowd at St James' that season was a young Bobby Robson:

> I used to watch Newcastle back in 1948 when I was 15 and so Jackie Milburn meant a lot to me. Wor Jackie was one of my idols. Why did I love him? Well, when you look at a player, sometimes just something about him appeals to you. He was tremendously quick, as you know. He really could catch pigeons could Jackie.
>
> He was a good taker of a chance and I liked his energy. He was a good individual player, but also a team player and he worked hard for them. He would chase defenders too and try to recover the ball and then go on the re-strike. He had tremendous pace, always robbed the ball from behind defenders, and, boy, could he beat a man with a ball. He started playing outside-right but could also play centre-forward and it was hard to decide just which was his best position. I think I preferred him through the middle, because through the middle, once he got clear of centre-halves, no one could catch him – he was a mean goal-scoring machine.

Making his St James' Park debut for United in the 1948–49 season derby match against Sunderland on 5 March was the 'King of Dribble', Scotsman Bobby Mitchell. He thrilled many a fan that day with his fancy footwork and accurate passing and proved himself the perfect feeder for Dad and George Robledo, who already had a great partnership going. If Dad belted in long-range efforts that failed, George was always ready to pounce on the rebound. Played in a heavy blizzard at St James' Park, the match resulted in a 2–1 win for Newcastle, with Dad and George grabbing one apiece.

The FA Cup, though, would have to wait for another season. A quick exit came at the hands of Bradford City on 8 January and United were left to concentrate on the League campaign. During the final run in, they suffered a 5–0 hammering from Portsmouth at Gallowgate, though bounced back by winning 4–2 at Derby and 1–0 against Middlesbrough at home the following week, where Dad got the winner. Three draws and two defeats completed a season in which Dad managed to grab himself a total of nineteen goals.

Early in 1949, Newcastle United had announced the squad were to tour Canada for several weeks during the summer break, as a team-building exercise, although there was never any question of the players' wives being allowed to join them.

Mum was thrilled for Dad, but she also knew just how much she would miss him. She appreciated how good an opportunity it was for him to visit another part of the world so she tried to keep her sadness to herself and never did let him know exactly how she felt for fear of putting a cloud over his trip. However, she made a huge blunder in letting the news slip to an overbearing neighbour, who immediately rattled off tales of 'slack' Canadian girls and alluded to how Dad couldn't possibly remain faithful while on tour. At this point Mum knew she had to find somewhere else to live and jumped with joy when Dad arrived home and announced that a club house would soon be available in High Heaton, a couple of miles away; they could move there in early March. Soon after settling in, Mum gave birth to a daughter, Linda, and looked forward to a serene life of relentless nappy washing and sleepless nights.

Although he knew that she was much happier in Heaton, Dad was worried that with Mum having no Northeast roots, she would still feel isolated when he was away. He reckoned she would fare better having the Milburn family around her. He was also looking further ahead to the following summer of 1950 and the possibility of him taking part in the World Cup in Brazil, which would mean yet another lengthy stay away, so he vowed there and then to save enough money to put a deposit on a little house back home in Ashington. Mum agreed on that as the most sensible course to take.

In the June of 1949, having bid a tearful farewell to Mum and baby Linda, Dad boarded the *Queen Mary*. As the ship steamed its way out of Southampton, Dad felt he 'had to nip myself just to see if it was all just a dream'. He remained in absolute awe of the beautiful surroundings for the entire voyage to New York – especially the first-class cabin accommodation the team were honoured to be enjoying.

Skipper Joe Harvey had kicked up a fuss after discovering the Scottish national team were travelling first class and therefore demanded the United players be upgraded from tourist class, threatening that otherwise the team would refuse to kick any leather in Canada. To his great surprise, the club directors unhesitatingly agreed, and so for three unforgettable days, the squad were pampered and entertained until they finally disembarked in the USA. They then hopped on a north-bound train for Niagara Falls and the beginning of their grand Canadian tour.

Newcastle easily won all of their ten matches, which were played over the next six weeks, and demonstrated some fine exhibitions of English-style soccer, banging in a total of 79 goals, of which Dad managed to bag 31.

United defeated Montreal 4–1, Ontario 8–2, Saskatchewan 13–2, Vancouver 5–2 and 8–1, Washington 11–1, Winnipeg 7–4, and Kamaterna 4–0 and 3–0, but the one match that stayed with Dad was when he popped in 5 goals against Alberta. That game featured an awesome, pony-tailed, spirited Native American, who, though he had never before kicked a football in his life, was purposely drafted in to try and curb Dad's speed. He could run like the wind all right, but their ploy failed to work and Dad ran circles around him as Newcastle went on to win 16–2.

After the tour and on the return journey home, now onboard a different ship, *The Empress of France*, the voyage proved more than just a tad choppy for the passengers and during one particularly ferocious storm, several players suffered from excruciating bouts of sea sickness as the liner bobbed around on the troubled Atlantic, with many of the lads even fearing for their lives. After what seemed like an eternity the rage subsided, the ship finally docked and their grateful legs were at last able to wobble down the gangway onto terra firma. 'I was just really pleased to be on the last leg home to Newcastle,' recalled Dad.

For Dad, his extremely enjoyable trip to Canada flew by, but for Mum, with a new toddler underfoot and everywhere else, it was just the opposite; nevertheless, when Dad was safely back that was all that mattered.

Before the end of the year, Mum had another happy announcement to make: she was expecting once more, so now they could look forward to yet another chaotic new year.

The 1949–50 season got off to a disappointing start with a run of defeats for Newcastle, but a 4–0 home victory over Everton on 31 August, in which Dad scored one, provided a much-needed fillip. It was clear new recruits were needed, though, and two fine players joined from Linfield: full-back Alf McMichael and inside-forward George Hannah. In front of 58,142 jubilant supporters, they helped United to a 4–2 victory over Manchester City in mid-September, with Dad scoring again.

Halfway through the season though, Newcastle languished at 15th in the table so 5 more changes were made to the team for a match against Stoke City. The attendance of 49,000 was notable given how poorly the team had been playing. However, United pulled their socks up and won 4–1, with Dad, who was really into his stride by now, scoring a goal.

His opposite number that day was his England teammate Neil Franklin, who after the game was asked what he thought of

England's centre-forward, to which he tersely replied, 'He's not a Tommy Lawton.'

England were due to play Italy and Dad found himself excluded from the team, so set about banging in as many goals for United as he could to stake his claim for a place once more.

Newcastle built up the supporters' hopes by recording a resounding 7–2 victory over Oldham in the third round of the FA Cup; however, Chelsea, in front of a record 65,000 crowd at Stamford Bridge, then knocked out the Magpies, winning 3–0. Nevertheless, United showed the promise of a strong team knitting together, and finally ended up finishing fifth in the League, with Dad scoring eighteen goals. Dad then received the great news that he was to be included in the England World Cup squad bound for Rio.

This was also a busy time in my parents' personal lives, with the birth, in July 1950, of their second daughter Betty. Early in the following year, 1951, Dad kept his long-term pledge and slapped a down payment on a little terraced house in Ellington Terrace, Ashington, just a few doors from his sister Jean and her husband Jack, who had a little boy called Stanley. There were plenty other small children living in the street too, ideal company for Linda and Betty to grow up with, and the house also had the luxury of a long, safe back garden just across the back lane.

# 3

# Cup Glory

Joe Harvey and I were saying, 'He's not going to shoot from there!' . . . In my book, it was the best goal that's ever been seen at Wembley.

Charlie Crowe

Newcastle began steaming their way toward the 1951 FA Cup final with a coasting January third-round victory over Bury, winning by 4–1 at St James' Park. 'The delightful way the whole team played convinced me we only had to keep our form to stand an excellent chance of reaching Wembley,' Dad remembered.

After the next round was drawn, Dad would rush out and buy a newspaper to find out who Newcastle's next opponents would be and then the team would meet and sit down to discuss their foe's strengths and weaknesses, probably in more depth after the return of someone from a 'spying mission'. To keep the winning momentum going, Stan Seymour reckoned the ideal thing was to pack them all off to the seaside for 'special training' sessions. 'Where we would live and breathe football almost every hour of the day and often far into the night,' Dad recalled fondly.

His theory appeared to have reaped the dividends after Newcastle beat Bolton Wanderers 3–2 in the fourth round. Next, they fixed their eyes on Stoke City at the Victoria Ground and after defeating them 4–2, suddenly found themselves hailed as firm favourites to lift the Cup. Dad never liked being favourite for anything: 'Favourites, you see, have a nasty habit of coming unstuck.'

Sir Bobby Charlton remembers the quality of football Dad was playing at that time:

> We used to go to watch him at Newcastle and he was always the focus of attention. I loved him as a player and always got excited when he got the ball. I used to say, "Give Wor Jackie the ball!

The team was knitting well together and were said by most to be a power to be reckoned with. Most supporters had every confidence in them and when they were drawn at home to Bristol Rovers in the sixth round, United were considered as good as in the semi-finals. Bristol, however, had different ideas and proved themselves to be a strong, determined side that deserved the hard-fought goalless draw to take the replay down to the West Country. 'They never gave us an inch and their attack was always troublesome.'

Dad was to hail the replay as the 'Battle of the Songs'. With Newcastle trailing 1–0, and the sound of the Rovers anthem 'Good Night Irene' ringing in their ears, the frustrated Geordie supporters quickly got behind their team and roared out 'The Blaydon Races'. The game shifted: tackles that had been lost were now won as United's players dug in and gritted their teeth. Dad always swore the singing fans won the day for them: 'The men of Bristol tried to drown out the Geordies but our men have tough throats, and as they roared, so did it have a remarkable effect upon our team. It was as if we were given a tonic.' Newcastle battled on to win 3–1.

The Magpies soon found out that their next semi-final opponents were to be none other than Billy Wright's mighty Wolverhampton Wanderers, FA Cup winners over Leicester City just two seasons earlier. Billy Wright was known as one of the hardest and most accurate tacklers in the business and an awe-inspiring leader, so United's nerves jangled a bit as they faced Wolves at Hillsborough. The match ended goalless. 'We were rather fortunate,' Dad mused.

Nevertheless, victory was clinched at Huddersfield's ground and Newcastle won 2–1 after a gruelling game. Dad never forgot the minutes that followed them reaching the final: 'A disconsolate Billy Wright shook hands and wished me well, then an emotional Stan Seymour thanked everyone, congratulating us on a wonderful performance and declaring there was no need to worry about who would play in the final as all the team that day had secured their places.'

However, the players' form in the League matches that followed made a lot of folk wonder if Seymour would have to swallow his words and make changes, as Newcastle suffered eight defeats in nine games.

Dad had his own views on this. 'Although none of us ever thought of holding back from a tackle for fear of being hurt, or taking a chance which may have brought us an injury, I'm confident that, quite consciously, every man who is going to play in a great match doesn't put everything he possesses into ordinary League games before the great day. I'd like to see the Cup final played a fortnight or so after the semi-final, so no one would suffer. It is a very big ordeal.' With this in his mind too, Seymour stuck to his guns and Dad was soon to realise his boyhood dream of playing at Wembley.

On the eve of the final, United were booked into the luxurious Oatlands Park Hotel, Weybridge, where he and teammate George Robledo, regular roommates on away trips, soon found themselves to be the brunt of the other players' jokes by having to share a double bed in the 'Bridal Suite'. Many times that evening their door pounded and the phone rang constantly as the rest of the squad enquired if everything was just quite to their liking. However, once the comedians had finished their fun, the pair tried to settle their pre-match nerves by settling down to a good book at about 11.30 p.m., but after fruitlessly attempting to read the same paragraph of their respective novels what felt like a million times, they all but gave up and just tried to get some sleep. But then the phone rang once more, only this time it was Mum.

She'd rang in an attempt to try and take his mind off the game. She spoke for an hour about the kids, the new sitting-room curtains she fancied, a holiday and anything else that sprang to mind other than the looming match, and for a short while after she'd hung up it worked. However, in spite of that, every 15 minutes or so Dad would nudge George or vice-versa, each checking if the other was still awake to discuss tomorrow's match tactics. Most of the night this went on, until they finally dropped off around 5 a.m. – only to be woken a couple of hours later by some excited United fans outside their window, howling 'The Blaydon Races'.

After breakfast, to get them in the right frame of mind, the players were entertained by United's own travelling comedian, Harry Goodfellow, and pianist Benny Needham, and it seemed to work a treat as they boarded the team coach with a 'let me get at Blackpool' attitude – that is, everyone except George Robledo, Bobby Cowell and one of the trainers. George simply couldn't travel by bus as it made him feel travel sick, so he and the other pair hopped on a fast train from Weybridge Station. 'I remember saying to George, I really hope we see you later.' He did.

Meanwhile, on their journey to Wembley the players' wives simply accepted their lot and travelled to London unceremoniously by third-class rail, several carriages behind the directors up in first class, with the Newcastle squad having already left the previous week for the special training at Buxton. But after the wives were offered tickets for the Wembley paddock, Joe Harvey's wife Ida quite rightly stirred up a mini uprising and insisted the wives be given decent seats as, after all, no single black and white would have been there if it wasn't for their husbands. The sheepish United directors quickly backed down and granted their wish.

Arriving at Wembley with around 90 minutes to spare, a nervy Dad and a relieved-to-be-there George strolled onto the pitch to soak up the superb atmosphere and then stood quietly in the players' tunnel to listen to the crowd sing 'Abide With Me' – something that had always been an ambition of theirs. Sadly, at that precise moment they were called back into the dressing-room and though they did as requested, they felt bitterly disappointed.

Now changed for the game, nerves got the better of Dad, so he sneaked into the bathroom for a sly smoke, smiling as he discovered four other players who'd had the same idea.

Due to another pre-match superstition of his, Dad slotted into fourth place in the line and it seemed an eternity before the players were called onto the pitch, but the second both teams trotted out into the brilliant sunshine, their ears were almost burst by the fans' echoing roars. 'There was simply no comparison with the tepid reception offered at an England international,' Dad recalled.

The previous night whilst talking to Mum, he had promised to give her a wave where she sat just behind the Royal Box and so did, also spotting his own mother, Nance, sitting next to her, sporting a huge, proud grin. That gesture made his mother's day.

Newcastle lined up as follows: Fairbrother; Cowell and Corbett; Harvey, Brennan and Crowe; Walker, Taylor, Milburn, Robledo and Mitchell.

Just prior to the kick-off, as the spellbound team were presented to King George VI on the pitch, Dad could not help notice just how pale and frail the King looked and actually felt extremely sorry for him. 'He looked a very sick man,' said Dad, yet at the time did not realise just how ill the King was. It was to be George VI's last duty at a Cup final.

The captains were called to the centre of the field for the toss of the coin and then Joe Harvey, 'looking like a shaggy sheep dog with a fierce expression on his granite face', strode back to the players and summoned them round him, snarling, 'Right you lot, this is the big chance we've all been waiting for. Don't anyone forget you were selected six weeks ago, now get out there and prove the guv'nor right!'

The match itself had been hyped-up across the country as the 'Stanley Matthews final'– except, of course, by the United players, the ecstatic horde of travelling Geordies and, not to forget, all those cheering back at home. But it was not to be Matthews' day and he was completely cut out of the first half by the shadowing Charlie Crowe.

Dad had a perfectly legitimate first-half goal disallowed after chesting it down and cracking it into the back of the net when, to his annoyance, the referee decided he'd handled the ball. Not one to normally argue the toss, he barely managed to check himself, and only just in time remembered Stan Seymour's changing-room warning: 'On no account are you to question the referee's decision.' As the game to and fro'd, Bobby Cowell desperately managed to save Newcastle's bacon by kicking a Stan Mortenson header off the line to keep the score level at half-time, though the United players' confidence remained sky high. The experience for Dad and the other players 'was like watching an exciting film and then suddenly finding yourself in it'.

In the half-time dressing-room, hawk-eyed trainer Norman Smith told the lads to go for the longer ball, reckoning they might just catch Blackpool out and after the re-start, they set about doing just that. From within his own half, George Robledo glanced up to see Dad waiting just inside the Blackpool half and slotted the ball forward. Dad gratefully took it and raced past Eric Hayward – Blackpool's centre-half – to find a huge chasm of open space between him and goalkeeper George Farm, who appeared to Dad to be a mere a dot in the distance.

Sprinting on for what seemed like an eternity, Dad finally reached the 18-yard line, now quite positive the entire world was snarling down on his heels. Then, for a brief moment, he forgot all about the eyes of the King, Queen and the crowd and even the hounding defenders, concentrating only on whether he should belt the ball or slot it toward the goal.

The Blackpool goalkeeper bobbled to his front, but then Dad noticed he'd left a narrow gap to his right and decided to chance on gliding the ball home. For a soundless, split second he was worried he hadn't struck it hard enough, until the humungous roar of the Geordie section of the crowd quickly told him different. Newcastle led 1–0. No kissing, no hugging, no prancing or well-rehearsed diving sequences, just a quick handshake and a determined, 'Come on lads, let's get on with it.'

The Blackpool attack tried their best, but soon weakened as Charlie Crowe successfully continued to blot out Stanley Matthews and Bobby Corbett refused to give a single inch to Stan Mortenson.

Then, in a flash, Newcastle's Tommy Walker broke down the touchline and cut inside and just as he did so, little Ernie Taylor ran on to the wing to collect the likely pass. Dad screamed at him to back-heel it, but Ernie held on to the ball for a fraction longer than Dad expected, hence Dad connected with the ball much lower than he'd anticipated and was amazed when it still flew into the back of the net. 'My first reaction was to run and join our cheering supporters behind the goal, so great was my elation.'

It was all but over then until the final whistle, even though Stanley Matthews and Stan Mortenson tried every trick in the book to get their team back in the game.

Later, in the dressing-room, Dad told the lads he'd never struck a ball harder in his life, though nevertheless shyly declared it as only a 'freak goal'. Many thousands of folk who witnessed it and have seen it since on film totally disagree, pronouncing it one of the finest goals ever scored at Wembley Stadium. I myself wonder if he was simply speaking modestly because of all the attention his wonder strike received. Anyway, straight after the game he quickly hailed 'wonder-stopper' Charlie Crowe as his own undisputed man of the match.

Dad felt on top of the world after he climbed the famous steps to collect his medal from the Queen. He then quickly and excitedly glanced over her shoulder and saw Mum and his own mother sitting just a few rows behind, both now wiping away tears with their handkerchiefs – a never-to-be-forgotten sight he may possibly never have seen had it not been for captain Joe Harvey's wife, Ida.

An ecstatic Dad waved at Mum and Nance, before beginning his proud descent down the steep steps to the pitch, when suddenly, from out of the mass of faces around him, a disgruntled, fiery-eyed so-called Blackpool 'fan' leaned over the barrier and grasped his shirt collar, twisting it viciously. Dad stared into a contorted face absolutely satiated with hatred and struggled frenziedly to free himself before he choked, barely able to splutter at him to leave go, or words to that affect – 'But the maniac's cast-iron grip merely tightened.'

Strange as it may seem, no one around appeared to notice his sorry predicament, possibly due to all the ballyhoo, and not even after a teammate walloped the delinquent to free him, but the sorry episode almost ruined Dad's big day and it took him a long, long time to get over it: 'Later, I made a few discreet enquiries, but never did find out just who the frenzied culprit was. That awful memory, seconds after a moment of glory, remains.'

He pushed it to the back of his mind as best he could though, as Joe Harvey rushed to the touchline and held high the Cup for the Geordies, yelling, 'It's yours! It's yours!'

Dad felt emotional, hot and drained, so left the field first and was absolutely amazed at the huge cheer he received from the sporting Blackpool fans standing above the tunnel leading to the dressing-rooms. 'In the quietness of the dressing-room, I looked unbelievingly at my Cup medal, placed it in my jacket pocket and then to cool down, went straight into the bathroom, and still wearing my shirt, shorts and boots, plunged headfirst into the cold bath. It was wonderful.'

Five minutes later the rest of the team came into the dressing-room. 'There were tears of laughter, jokes, shouts and songs. Only Bobby Mitchell and George Robledo, who are two strong silent men, showed little emotion. They just sat to watch everyone else's reactions. Then came the greatest moment of all, when the Cup was filled with champagne and I had my first taste of it. For someone who usually only drinks milk, "bubbly" was new and exciting, but only one sip made me dizzy.'

Dad wondered how different the team might have felt had they lost, and paused to reflect on the half-smiling face of Stanley Matthews as he was handed his runners-up medal. 'What a pity it is, after reaching the Cup final, there has to be a loser,' Dad mused.

Back home in Newcastle, all the players felt the unbelievable wild reception they received at a packed St James' Park was magnificent, to say the least, and in front of the main stand Dad was handed his turn on a microphone to say just a few words. Because he'd never really spoken in public before, Dad, for the first and last time ever, made a regrettable attempt to 'talk posh', but the side-holding, finger-pointing crowd to his fore simply couldn't believe the words he spouted and rolled about in hysterical laughter, yelling, 'Howay, Jackie lad, just taak proper . . . you're only one of us, man!'

Now as if that wasn't bad enough and to make matters worse, 'it was all clearly caught on the newsreel cameras, giving many a regional cinemagoer a cracking belly laugh between the main features for quite a few weeks to come.' Dad never forgot that.

As a thank-you gesture and in celebration of winning the Cup, the directors invited the team and their wives to a dance at the packed Oxford Galleries.

At the interval, all the players' wives were invited up on stage to receive a 'special' presentation. For a while, there had been a buzz of anticipation among the players and wives alike, as Seymour himself had made the earlier pledge to the team: 'You lads do your bit on the field and I'll look after the groceries.' The blushing ladies lined up to step onto the stage, and each was furnished with a copiously 'stuffed' handbag. Could they really be crammed with pound notes as a huge thank you to the lads for bringing home the Cup? Suddenly there was a ripple of mirth as the handle snapped from one of the players' wives' gift as she stepped down from the stage.

The simple fact that the handbags were made from synthetic leather was positively ignored in the increasing excitement to get back to their expectant men. However, once thoroughly rummaged through, they were found to be stuffed with nothing other than old crushed newspapers to help keep their shape. Later, the players discovered that some spendthrift at Newcastle United had purchased the bags as a job lot of 30 . . . for a mere £17.

Nevertheless, the lads had been victorious and to all concerned it was really the pride of winning that counted, and anyway, it kept them out of the pits and shipyards.

'To win the FA Cup is a great strain, but to try and retain the trophy is an even greater strain, as we discovered the following season.'

Before the third-round tie against Aston Villa, the team were of the general opinion that they had developed into a useful side and saw no real reason why they couldn't go all the way once more. So, after hearing they had been drawn at home against the Midlands team, there were a few smiles around St James' Park; however, with only eight minutes to go during that match, United found themselves trailing 2–1. Thousands of disgruntled supporters streamed from the ground, already quite sure that Newcastle were about to make an early exit, only to find out they'd jumped the gun.

Bobby Mitchell gritted his teeth, put his head down and with his own particular brand of magic, banged in two fine goals to put United in the lead, before George Robledo netted an unbelievable fourth. 'They gave us on paper a much more convincing victory than we had in reality achieved,' explained Dad.

If nothing else, Aston Villa's gritty display had the effect of doing United a power of good. 'It made us realise that we might not be as good as we imagined and that every future match was going to be a fight.' Those words were proven after Newcastle were drawn out of the hat to play Tottenham at White Hart Lane.

Whenever the two teams had met previously, the matches had been exciting: 'This cup-tie proved to be no exception and ranks among one of the best I've ever taken part in,' said Dad. After a hard-fought game, Newcastle left the pitch eventual 3–0 winners and suddenly the sports pages were full of it, pronouncing them once again as budding Cup finalists.

'Our old confidence, call it cockiness if you like, swiftly returned.'

As though to put their feet back on the ground though, Swansea, at Vetch Field, were next on the list – never an easy assignment for any team – and it was only after a tremendous battle that United scraped through 1–0, with a Bobby Mitchell goal.

Now the Geordie supporters feared the worst after the sixth-round draw threw up yet another tough match, this time against Portsmouth – and on their home territory at Fratton Park. As Dad remembered, 'Jimmy Scoular, Jack Froggatt and Jimmy Dickinson, their international half-backs, were feared throughout the football land.'

In the past, Dad was only too well aware that Pompey had always put up a good fight against Newcastle, so had no doubt they would be more determined than ever to secure their own semi-final spot. 'However, Newcastle, as the record book proves, are always at their best when faced by class opposition, and at Fratton Park, we enjoyed one of our best afternoons out, while I considered it to be the finest game I ever played for Newcastle United. Every move I made seemed to bear fruit and I notched three goals.' George Robledo scored another as United romped home 4–2 winners and the semi beckoned.

For that Hillsborough semi-final, the Black and Whites were somewhat relieved to be paired against Second Division Blackburn Rovers, and not Arsenal or Chelsea, the other semi-finalists, but after a surprisingly tough goalless draw, Blackburn proved to the nation their record as magnificent Cup fighters. As Dad remembered it: 'When you consider that Charlton Athletic had previously given us a mother and father of a hiding at the replay venue of Elland Road, it was quite obvious to us that Rovers were a much tougher obstacle between us and Wembley, but then any side with such a dynamic skipper as Bill Eckersley could be expected to fight all the way.'

Thankfully George Robledo scored first for United and the supporters all breathed a little easier, but then Eddie Quigley notched a Blackburn equaliser to put them right back in the game. Suddenly all the pressure was on the Newcastle goal. 'Fortunately skipper Joe Harvey steadied our defence and our attack once more got weaving.'

During a sustained attack, Newcastle were awarded a penalty and Harvey shouted at Dad to step up and do his stuff. 'As I was the current "penalty-king", Joe nearly collapsed when I told him, not this time. I had just received a knock on the knee and felt I may not do myself justice.' As they argued the toss, Bobby Mitchell stepped up, placed the ball on the spot and slammed it into the back of the net. The goal proved to be the winner.

Now they had set a new Wembley record by being the first ever Cup holders to return the following season to defend the trophy.

Because of his own superstition, Stan Seymour decided the team should, once more, prepare themselves in readiness at the Royal Albion Hotel, Brighton. He wasn't going to take any chances.

During the week's stay, quite a few of the lads developed something of a penchant for swallowing fresh oysters, enjoying two or three dozen per session – none more so than Bobby Mitchell, 'Though amazingly not a single player reported any feelings of sickness,' marvelled Dad.

There were four changes to last year's winning side, including Chilean Ted Robledo, who'd now joined his brother George; the pair would become the first foreign brothers to play alongside each other in an FA Cup final. Ted had proved a little injury prone during his earlier Newcastle days, though happily thus far had enjoyed a good run.

The full Newcastle line up consisted of: Simpson; Cowell and McMichael; Harvey, Brennan and Robledo (E); Walker, Foulkes, Milburn, Robledo (G) and Mitchell.

Before the kick-off, the team were introduced to Winston Churchill, who, when it came to Dad's turn, smiled and asked if he was going to grab the headlines again this year. 'It really impressed me that a great man like that should take notice of a mere pit lad. I considered it a compliment of the highest order.'

Opponents Arsenal had defeated Liverpool in the final two years before and were one of the most-feared sides in the land, so just as with Blackpool in '51, most folk fancied them to hoist the silverware. Again the Newcastle players had other ideas. 'During the pre-match build up, our confidence did not slip one iota.'

During the first half, as Dad chased Arsenal's Welsh international Wally Barnes in the hope of making a tackle, the right-back's studs caught in the thick grass as he tried to twist with the ball and he collapsed screaming, badly injured. He bravely, though briefly, managed to play on after some treatment, but was soon forced to retire, and with no substitute players allowed, Arsenal were down to ten men.

These days it may seem a little odd, but the Newcastle lads were actually disappointed for the Gunners at their loss of a key player and it certainly affected the game. Soon the Arsenal players were well out of position and chasing all over the pitch. They ran themselves ragged, but in the end, Newcastle's extra pair of legs made the solitary difference and when George Robledo headed a Bobby Mitchell cross against the upright and the ball glided over the line, it was all over.

The much-relieved Geordie supporters went wild, because until that moment, neither side had really looked like scoring; however, when the game ended at 1–0, many unbiased folk reckoned that Arsenal had scored a moral victory. At the end of the day, though, United were the ones to climb the famous steps to raise the Cup.

It was an immensely proud moment for Dad: 'We gratefully received the Cup from Winston Churchill, the greatest hero of my life, a man whose bust has occupied pride of place in our house since 1948.'

Even though Newcastle had secured the Cup once more, Dad publicly declared that 'the absence of Wally Barnes made what should have been a colourful match fade into a colourless one'. After that he and many other players appealed to the FA to allow substitutes in Cup finals, though their pleas fell on deaf ears for many years to come.

Newcastle's Cup success was not to be repeated in 1953 or 1954, so by 1955, the supporters' hopes were not too high. It seemed far-fetched to think that Wembley's Twin Towers might beckon a third time in five years.

Dad explained that at the time 'few folk gave us very much thought as potential Cup winners. This was quite understandable as we looked anything but a good side.' With Dougald Livingstone recently appointed as manager, the team suddenly struck up the kind of winning Cup run that every soccer boss dreams about. They even surprised themselves.

In the third round of the Cup, United were drawn away to Plymouth Argyle and so had to make the long wearying journey to the West Country. 'Fortunately it wasn't wasted and after a Vic Keeble goal, we won 1–0,' remembered Dad.

Brentford were next in a home tie at St James' Park and after another close struggle United won 3–2. 'Even then, no one visualised us as a possible Cup side.'

Worse was to follow and Newcastle had to scrap it out three times before finally scraping through 2–1. 'I played at inside-left for those games – one of the positions I filled when I originally joined United – but I did not altogether enjoy the experience, although I'll be honest and say I was glad just to play in any position as long as I was in the first team.'

Dad remembered previous Cup ties in former years as a pure joy to play in, but in 1955 they became something of a nightmare. The sixth round saw Newcastle eventually beat Huddersfield 2–0, but only after being held to a 0–0 draw. 'Now folk were saying we played so badly and with such consistency we were sure to win the Cup.'

By the semi-final everyone sat up as Newcastle drew lowly, Third Division York City. It seemed a great chance for the Magpies to reach the final.

The semi was played at Hillsborough and Dad was moved to inside-right. The game itself was the third Newcastle semi-final to be played in Sheffield and the third to result in a hard-fought goalless draw; however, in the replay at Roker Park, and much to their relief, United went on to victory, winning by 2–0. 'At last we had reached Wembley and it was recognised that we stood a chance of winning the Cup for the third time since the war.' Newcastle would face Manchester City in the final.

As a footballer, Dad had always given his best for Newcastle United and the supporters, but not once, from the third-round tie to the semi-final, did he think the team were good enough to reach Wembley itself. 'The old zest and power which had been such a feature of past Cup triumphs just was not with us. We rarely had a settled team and with some of the old stars disappearing, to be succeeded nearly every week by new faces, no fewer than 17 different players helped Newcastle along the Wembley trail. Now, having helped them to Wembley once more, I, like my colleagues, wondered whether or not I'd get into the team for the match of the season. In previous years, Stan Seymour had assured us that the side that did well in the earlier rounds would represent the club at Wembley, but Livingstone never gave any of us that assurance.'

After the stomach-muscle injury he'd been plagued with all season flared up again, Dad found himself sidelined and cursed his bad luck. Even though he had played in every previous cup-tie, the forward line of White, Davies, Keeble, Hannah and Mitchell were knitting together so well, that Dad now genuinely feared for a place. However, once fit enough to play again, he thankfully found himself thrown another lifeline as Livingstone shunted him from centre-forward to inside-forward, then out to the wing, until finally, just three weeks before the final, he was told to concentrate on the role of centre-forward. Now he knew only too well how brilliantly Vic Keeble was playing in that position, so deep down Dad expected the worst; however, once more he was given a swift reprieve when inside-left George Hannah suffered an injury and Dad was told to adopt that position for the next League match. He was left with a slender ray of hope.

By now, most of the other players were fed up with being mucked about by Livingstone and not having a clue as to their Wembley fate, so after a tactical team talk at the County Hotel in Newcastle prior to the final mid-week League game, they insisted on being told the final Wembley line up. Livingstone reluctantly agreed, and so left the room to speak with the directors in an adjacent room, himself returning an apparently very unhappy chap just a short while later. He blurted out the selected names, but then stated categorically that the final selection was certainly not of his own personal choosing. Dad 'sighed with relief when my name was read out, though felt extremely sorry for Len White, whose place I had secured'.

It was not until after the Cup final itself that Dad discovered had it been left up to Livingstone alone, he, beyond a shadow of a doubt, would not have played. An irate, grim-faced Stan Seymour, who had led the 'Newcastle don't play in Cup finals without Jackie Milburn' campaign, had ripped up and chucked Livingstone's selection into the waste bin.

'I'm glad I didn't know at the time of Livingstone's plans to drop me, as it would have left a deep mental scar and done nothing to help my inferiority complex.'

Soon after, Livingstone was relegated from his big office to a tiny space formerly used as the referee's changing room, before eventually being sacked in 1956.

So, once more it was off to sunny Brighton and the Royal Albion Hotel, though Dad felt the rousing atmosphere of their previous two visits was missing, and so were the likes of Joe Harvey, George

Robledo and big Frank Brennan, who had all moved on. Yet more forced changes were to come when a devastated Charlie Crowe became injured – to be replaced by Tom Casey – and then, ironically, Reg Davies went down with a sore throat and stepped aside for Len White. This would now mean Dad being handed Reg's role of inside-right.

Charlie Crowe recalled Dad's words to him after he discovered he was injured. Knowing just how disappointed Charlie would be, Dad said, 'Just say you're OK to play, Charlie, and we'll carry you.'

A stunned Charlie replied, 'It's a bloody Cup final, Jackie, remember?'

The training sessions were intense and not many of the players felt able to relax, as even at this late stage they still wondered whether more last-minute changes might be afoot.

In spite of this, the big day arrived without any changes being announced, so the much happier squad boarded the London train to Wembley. In the Wembley dressing-room, a resolute Stan Seymour pulled Dad to one side, and told him, 'Get out there and show them what you can do, Jackie.'

As both teams lined up on the Wembley turf, Dad confessed later that he'd been as 'nervous as a kitten' when presented to the Duke of Edinburgh and then just after the captains made the toss. He described the way he felt as 'a greater tenseness than I've ever experienced before'. He put it all down to the fact that he felt the need to justify his inclusion in the team and didn't want any single person to think he'd only been included for services rendered in the past.

The final team selection was: Simpson; Cowell and Batty; Scoular, Stokoe and Casey; White, Milburn, Keeble, Hannah and Mitchell.

Just 45 seconds after the kick-off, Seymour's decision to include Dad was proved right. 'I won a corner on the right and Len White ran over to take it. Manchester City's captain, Roy Paul, was standing next to me as Len placed the ball, but he suddenly yelled, "Bloody hell, I should be marking Keeble," so off he darted to find big Vic, who was more widely noted for his prowess in the air. Len fired the ball in my direction and there was I standing all alone like Grey's Monument. I headed the ball past their keeper, Bert Trautmann and that was it. I'd proved my point.'

It was clocked as the fastest goal ever scored in an FA Cup final (the record stood for 42 years) and it happened so quickly that up in the stands Mum and many others missed it as they adjusted their coats after taking their seats.

Later in the game, as fate would have it, City's right-back, Jimmy Meadows, went down painfully on almost the same spot as Arsenal's Wally Barnes had in 1952 and just as Barnes had, tried to resume his game until forced to leave the field for good. However, City gritted their teeth and managed to get themselves on top, pulling back a much-deserved goal before half-time.

During the break, Dad nipped into the bathroom for a smoke, not only to steady his nerves, but also to take his thoughts away from the agony of the stomach muscle he'd pulled again after just ten minutes. He found sitting around only aggravated it. Captain Jimmy Scoular then decided United should switch tactics for the second-half to avoid the midfield crowding, so plumped for the use of the long ball, and it worked a treat.

Newcastle went on to beat Manchester City 3–1, with the other goals coming from Bobby Mitchell and George Hannah, becoming the only club to win at Wembley Stadium each time they'd played there and the first to play in ten FA Cup finals, equalling the record of Aston Villa and Blackburn Rovers. Once again though, during the after-match post-mortem, the subject of using substitutes was raised, but seemed to fall on unresponsive FA ears.

Three extremely proud United players picked up their third Cup-winner's medals that afternoon: Jackie Milburn, Bobby Cowell and Bobby Mitchell.

For his part in helping United win three FA Cup finals, Dad received a grand total of £73 16s and 'no groceries'. Not much of a chunk from Wembley's overall gate receipts which exceeded some

£120,000 . . . but then, if he didn't have the money, he had the glory.

The players' reward for winning the Cup for the third time was a silver-plated bon-bon dish. 'It was the final bitter insult,' said Dad. 'We were sickened.'

In those days, the winning clubs held the FA Cup for a year and were allowed to proudly display it at various local functions. Occasionally, if a player specifically needed it, he would seek permission to keep it at home, possibly overnight. There is a little Milburn family story that one of my potty-trained sisters took the FA Cup out into the back garden when no one was looking and made mud pies with it. She didn't – they weren't mud pies at all. Anyone for champagne?

# 4

# Playing for England

I played with him for England. For a big fellow he was
extremely fast, a sprinter almost. We would have sprints in
training and he would always win.

Sir Tom Finney

Dad felt extremely proud that someone from 'England's forgotten
backwater' was chosen to play for his country. Although he played
in only 13 full internationals, he himself reckoned that because of
injury he was unable to participate in a further 20 games.

With no Under-23 side to encourage younger international
prospects, the FA selected players to play for the Football League
against other League representative sides and for one such game,
against the Irish League at Liverpool in September 1948, Dad found
himself included in the team along with Len Shackleton.

Dad was fortunate to have a cracking game and managed to score
a hat-trick, self-effacingly putting his goals down to the assistance
of Len. 'Len gave me such great service I couldn't help but score.'

Just a few days later Dad, along with Shack was included in the
England squad for the match against Denmark in Copenhagen,
though as reserve he never got to play. He and Shack travelled to

London together and met up with the rest at the Great Western Hotel.

Dad was thrilled to meet some of the great men of football, such as Stanley Matthews, Tommy Lawton, Neil Franklin, Frank Swift, Jimmy Hagan and, to top it all, Billy Wright. It was Billy Wright who suggested the pair sit together on the Viking aircraft, as Dad had told him he'd never flown before and was a little nervous, though Billy soon put his fears at rest by talking all the way there. 'I remember looking around at my companions on that plane. Stanley Matthews, always so cool, simply lay back, closed his eyes and went to sleep, while others like Tommy Lawton, Jimmy Hagan and Frank Swift laughed as they cracked jokes. Ever watching was manager Walter Winterbottom. He was always ready to chat about the forthcoming game with anybody. He was a great manager and a magnificent tactician.'

Later, during the pre-match discussion, Winterbottom brought a lump to Dad's throat when he asked him if he had any views or angles on the game. 'You see, a little touch like that makes you feel that you're a member of the party,' Dad explained. 'That you're wanted and that your opinions are respected.'

The match itself turned out to be something of a damp squib and Denmark were unlucky not to clinch it when their last-minute goal was disallowed as offside.

At the post-match reception, after accepting a toast from the Danes, England team captain and acting choirmaster, Frank Swift, called over the party to return the compliment by singing them a song after the game. He chose 'When Day Is Gone', but blushing Dad, not knowing the words, could only mutter sounds; strangely, Stanley Matthews mouthed the correct words, though not a solitary sound came forth from his lips. Dad joked that Mathews 'proved he was the quiet man of football'.

Although he didn't take part in the game itself, Dad still put a huge grin on his own mother's face by returning home with her first-ever pair of nylon stockings.

Not long after, Dad was intrigued when he spotted an *Evening Chronicle* poster that read: 'United player capped for England'. He ran over and bought a copy, wondering just who the lucky man could be. When he saw his was the player's name he 'nearly jumped over the Tyne Bridge with delight. The stop-press column said it was me who was to play in a forthcoming full-international match against Northern Ireland on 9 October at Windsor Park, Belfast. I read and re-read the paper. What more could I wish for?'

As yet, no selector had phoned or written to inform him personally, but after a few frantic phone calls he was given confirmation. 'In those days, the newspapers were always the first to know. We never found out until we'd bought the 2 o'clock edition.'

Before Dad left to join the rest of the squad in Liverpool, Mum presented him with a little ebony elephant she'd always carried in her handbag, promising it would bring him luck. Before the game he slipped it into the pocket of his football shorts, though still his nerves were jingling. He was the only player present earning his first cap.

England's team that day was: Swift; Scott and Howe; Wright, Franklin and Cockburn; Matthews, Mortenson, Milburn, Pearson and Finney.

In the dressing-room, first-time captain Billy Wright patted Dad on the back and told him just to play his natural game, while wishing him the best of luck. 'Frank Swift did too, and then the rest of the team, but the one man I wanted to come up and speak to me didn't – Stanley Matthews. I felt so disappointed. But as we lined up for the national anthems and stood to attention, Stan came waddling over and told me he preferred not to make a fuss in the dressing-room and wished me the very best of luck. He then told me that when I saw him running down the wing I had to get to the far post and wait on the edge of the six-yard box then he would cross the ball. He said he always put a lot of top on it to fool the keeper, to make it hang, so that would give me time to close in. The great man was true to his word and I headed in my first international goal from his inch-perfect cross. He was a genius. The greatest.'

England easily won the match 6–2, though Dad typically responded to pats on the back with regard to his goal with 'The missus could've scored that one.' But as he made his way back to the centre circle, he tapped his lucky ebony elephant.

Stan Mortenson, who Dad used to idolise when he was a ball-boy at Ashington's little ground where Stan 'guested', banged in three himself. 'Little then did I ever think I would be playing alongside my hero in an England shirt.'

Dad's next international match against Wales proved to be a disappointing one for the whole team, even though they won 1–0. He reckoned the team never clicked because of injuries and the fact that certain players were asked to play out of their customary position.

However, the selectors reckoned he'd done enough in the game to be chosen to play against Switzerland on 9 December at Highbury. After leaving their training base at the Grand Hotel in Brighton and boarding the train, the squad suddenly came face to face with a blanket of fog on the outskirts of London. The FA announced that the match would have to be postponed, but then as irony would have it, a glorious sun burst through the vapour. It proved too late, but instead of returning to Brighton, the team stayed overnight in London at the Great Western Hotel and were treated to a visit to the Drury Lane Theatre Royal to see the musical *Oklahoma*.

First thing next morning, Dad rushed to the bedroom window to check the weather and it was fine. He sighed with relief and knew the game would be given the go ahead.

The England line-up this time was: Ditchburn; Ramsey and Aston; Wright, Franklin and Cockburn; Matthews, Rowley, Milburn, Haines and Hancocks.

Dad deemed the game to be a great England success as they cracked six goals past the Swiss and he even notched one for himself. Others were scored by debutants Haines, Hancocks and Rowley.

'Every trick we tried seemed to work. The ball just flowed for us, while England's shooting was a dream. I remember one of Jack Rowley's shots in particular though. He struck it so hard that had I not ducked in time it would have knocked me into the net and I'd have come out like chips.'

After the match, Dad publicly sang the praises of a certain debutant – a contemporary full-back called Alf Ramsey. 'So much self-assurance had Ramsey that he even dared yell at the great Stanley Matthews to hold the ball after sending him a meticulous pass. But he was right. Alf's passing was as accurate as any man I've played with or against, and that includes Wilf Mannion. I can pay him no greater tribute than that.'

There was now a four-month break until the next international, when England would face the Auld Enemy at Wembley on 1 April 1949, which for Dad meant that he 'was, for a time at least, spared the worries of thinking I'd be dropped'. However, Dad once more found himself selected to pilot the attack against Scotland, something he had dreamed about since he was just a lad.

Once more, the team stayed and trained at Brighton, though this time Dad found himself subjected to four days' intensive shooting and heading practice by manager Walter Winterbottom, who reckoned Dad's heading ability to be his one weakness. Dad had mixed feelings about this regime: 'Anyone who has ever headed a heavy leather-case ball with its attached lace will know exactly just how much it can hurt. By the end of the fourth day I was suffering from nasty headaches. But I reckon my skill improved somewhat.'

Dad said before the game he felt like a youngster attending their first dance: excited but uncertain. Reality was to kick in the second the England team stepped onto the Wembley turf: 'Instead of the roof-blowing reception I was used to at St James' Park, we received only lukewarm applause from our supporters, yet the Scots were given a thunderous welcome by their own travelling hordes.' It always puzzled him as to why the England team nearly always received the same tepid reception.

In the first 15 minutes, England piled on the pressure, but Scotland keeper, Jimmy Cowan, somehow blocked everything that came his way. Then the tide turned and suddenly Scotland were 3–0 up, sending their fans into raptures. Dad pulled one back and the English fans politely applauded 'like an audience having tea at an afternoon matinee'.

He felt that he'd learned something from the game though – that simply throwing 11 top-class players on to a pitch doesn't mean they will suddenly click together. He became a firm believer that the national side should play several practice games together just to build an understanding. However, on the day in question, 'England were beaten by a much better and purposeful side'.

After the 1948–49 season ended, Dad requested he be released from the proposed England tour of Norway, Finland, Sweden and France. He later explained his reason: 'Really, it was because of the lack of urgency among the team and supporters alike.' Although he had been selected, he preferred instead to venture on the ten-week tour of Canada with the Newcastle United squad. So, Stan Seymour obligingly contacted the FA on Dad's behalf, though much was made of the situation in the press. Some said that Dad was snubbing his country. 'The truth is,' he said, 'I never received the kind of service I should have as England's centre-forward. At least not the kind I did at St James' Park. It seemed to me that a lot of the England players were simply out to impress as individuals, just to secure their place for the next game. I worried about the unhappy experiences I had in the England team and discussed them with Mr Seymour. One or two of them were outright snobs. Then I became selfish myself and plumped to go to Canada with my pals. It was then that Mr Seymour contacted the FA and requested they did not consider me for their tour; they agreed.'

The World Cup beckoned in Rio de Janeiro, Brazil, in 1950 and the top two teams in the home championships would automatically qualify to be there. England's first opponents were Wales on 15 October 1949 and as the current League top scorer with ten goals, Dad was in contention for the No. 9 shirt. Other candidates included

Lawton, Bentley, Pye, Rowley and Lofthouse, though many reckoned Nat wasn't quite yet ready.

Much to Dad's relief, he picked up a newspaper the following week and read 'Milburn and Shackleton for England' – he was playing. However, some newspapers expressed their surprise at his inclusion as, in their eyes, he'd previously 'affronted' the FA on their Continental tour. He'd also been passed over for England against Eire, a match that they had lost.

The entire defence was retained but the sole forward line survivor from the Eire defeat, Tom Finney, was switched from the left-wing to his more familiar right.

That day England fielded: Williams; Mozley, Aston, Wright; Franklin, Dickinson, Finney; Mortenson, Milburn, Shackleton and Hancocks.

Dad and Shack teamed up at the Seabank Hotel, Porthcawl, for the Cardiff game. 'We had a good laugh as, after his £20,000 transfer to Sunderland, he was the most expensive player in England. I had cost United a mere tenner.'

Shackleton had a brilliant game as England trounced the Welsh 4–1. Dad scored a hat-trick and laid a goal on for Mortenson. 'I was particularly pleased with two of my goals because I scored them with my head.' Because of the high stakes, however, the intensity of the match was such that five England players received injuries. Dad was one of them: he'd broken a bone in his wrist.

Dad described the match reports as 'very encouraging'. One of them read: 'Milburn has come to stay'; and another: 'England has solved her centre-forward problem'.

Sir Tom Finney recalls playing with Dad at this time:

> He did have an inferiority complex. He never thought he was as good as he was. Prior to a game he'd be talking himself down and saying the feller he was playing against was a great player. I used to say to him: 'Well you're a great player – you've been selected for your country!'

> I remember a match against Wales. Jackie was playing against T.G. Jones of Everton, who was a good player. He said, 'I never play well against this feller,' but promptly went out and scored a hat-trick!

Against the advice of the club doctor Bob Rutherford, Dad, sporting a plaster cast, took to the field against Bolton just two weeks later; but he had good reason to want to play: 'Nat Lofthouse, a contender for the England No. 9 shirt, would be playing, so I had to go out and prove myself still worthy of a place.' Both centre-forwards shared the honours with a late goal apiece, but it was to be Jack Rowley who would step in against Northern Ireland, managing to bag five of the goals in England's 9–0 win.

England's next match was against Italy on 30 November at White Hart Lane and when the side was announced, Dad found himself chosen only as first reserve – although as a consolation, he was picked to play for the Football League against the Irish League at Windsor Park. He would play alongside his cousin Stan, who played for Chesterfield, and United captain Joe Harvey. Dad clocked up another hat-trick in the 3–1 win and suddenly the papers were full of 'Milburn for Rio'.

Nevertheless, Dad found himself passed over once more for the remaining matches of the home internationals, but then was surprised to find himself selected for a short tour of Portugal and Belgium. 'I saw it as my last chance to get on the plane to Rio.'

Prior to the tour, the England team were issued with a brand new lightweight boot to try out while practising at Wembley Stadium. 'I always wore a size-six football boot even though my feet were size eight, so I used to 'break in' a new pair by wearing them without socks and soaking them in cold water to mould them to my feet. I always preferred heavier soles to put some clout in my shots. Those new lightweights weren't for me.' Most of the team were quite happy with their new footwear though and quite happily took them to Lisbon.

The Portuguese government had spent a fortune on building a

vast new National Stadium near Estoril and had imported lush Cumbrian turf for the pitch, so they expected their team to do well. Both sides stayed at The Hotel do Parque and during dinner, found themselves in the unusual position of sitting opposite each other. Dad remembered the scene: 'In the heat we sweltered in formal blazers and ties as the Portuguese relaxed in very casual tracksuits.'

In their last meeting, England had trounced Portugal 10–0, but they now had an English coach, Ted Smith, who knew the English game and things were expected to be a lot tougher this time round. Dad was in his favoured position on the right-wing, and though he failed to get among the goals in the 5–3 win, he reckoned he may just have done enough to find himself picked for the next game against Belgium in Brussels at the Heysel Stadium. This was to be England's last game before the squad was chosen for Rio.

He was right. Again he found himself out on the wing and as the game went on felt he was doing OK, but then tragedy struck as he pelted down the line and he thudded heavily to the ground as his right foot went over. 'I thought I'd broken my ankle as I was carried from the field. All I could think was goodbye Rio. I cursed my luck.' Jimmy Mullen, England's first ever substitute in an international match, hurried on to take Dad's place, but soon after Belgium went ahead. Ironically, within ten minutes Dad was able to sprint without any sign of trouble.

In a dogged fight back, goals from Mannion, Mullen, Mortenson and Bentley gave England a comfortable win. 'I was convinced that the only place I'd be going that summer would be Ashington.'

However, the following week Dad spotted 'England team for Rio' on a poster, so he sped to buy a newspaper. When he read the selection he was stunned: 'I could hardly believe it, I was in the final squad.'

The players were summoned to Dulwich Hamlet for a few days of training and received their dreaded yellow-fever injections. On 9 June 1950 the England squad boarded the plane to Rio from London Airport.

After a sapping 31-hour Pan Air journey via Paris and Dakar, the plane and team, on touchdown, were sprayed by a hostess with a pungent anti-mosquito mix: 'Just as a precaution, gentlemen, to make sure you haven't brought any mosquitoes from Africa with you.' The immigration authorities then held them up because Tom Finney was missing a small piece of documentation. Hasty negotiations took place and eventually the exhausted team were allowed to pass through customs and take a cool shower in the airport.

The South American press hailed them on arrival as 'The Kings of Football' and bombarded them with some of the most ridiculous questions almost the second they touched down.

'Where were your fathers born?'

'Do you have any sisters?'

They checked into the luxurious Luxor Hotel just 20 yards from the sun-kissed, yellow Copacabana beach and the only thing separating them from the rolling Atlantic were streams of bright, speeding American motors filled with flamboyant 'beautiful posers'. Dad was amazed at what he saw, failing to draw a single comparison with his little hometown of Ashington, and commented later: 'I knew precisely where I'd rather live out my life . . . Ashington'

Something else really left him astounded. 'I was amazed at the incredible skill of the hordes of young boys over on the beach playing "keep ups" and "headers" with just ordinary oranges . . . yet without bursting them.'

Over the next couple of days, a lot of the players suffered sickness problems as they struggled to adjust to the local water and oily food – that was until manager Walter Winterbottom crossed the threshold of the hotel kitchen to give the bemused chef a few pointers.

Alas, the English nation were soon to wonder if their team should really have bothered going all that way. They did get off to a decent start by beating Chile 2–0, although this was a match that Dad sat out. His arm was hugely swollen after his yellow-fever inoculation and, besides, the England selectors wanted to keep faith with the same forward line that had netted four goals against Belgium.

The next match has become infamous in England's international history. It was supposed to be a stroll against the USA and England stuck with the same line up, with Dad again forced to watch helplessly from the sidelines. What followed was the nation's most humiliating defeat ever, as the side went down 1–0. 'I reckon I was just glad to have sat out that game,' Dad mused, 'but then again I always wondered . . . what if?'

For the vital third game against Spain, a now fully fit Dad found himself selected, although he was extremely annoyed to have a perfectly legitimate header somewhat surprisingly disallowed for offside. This was later validated by photographic evidence, but sadly that proved of no consequence.

Spain won 1–0 in a match where England got their first taste of continental unsportsmanship. The Spaniards continually handled the ball and when the referee wasn't looking they spat, kicked and took digs at the astounded English players. For long periods of the game the infuriated Brazilian supporters had been right behind England as the Spanish tricksters tried every one in the book – and then invented some more. After a Stan Mortenson shot, one of their defenders had even dived full length to catch the ball 'with all the skill of a Surrey slip-fielder'.

Oddly, the Italian referee seemed to have forgotten his much-needed glasses. Once the overjoyed defender realised he'd got away with it he 'laughed his head off' at the disappointment on the English players' faces. 'Many more passes through to me were halted by the Spaniards who must have thought they were playing basketball.' It was an end to England's high hopes.

England flew home the very next day, not even waiting to see the eventual winners, Uruguay, beat favourites Brazil 2–1 in the final.

Dad had a valid point to make after the event: 'Once a long English League season is over, there's nothing left in a player, and it doesn't matter how willing you are, you're exhausted. Believe you me, when you've played nine months on some of the pitches we had to, you've had enough. At our first training session in Rio, the boss left us three bags of balls when he went to speak to the press. Normally you'd be lucky if you got one . . . but we opted to play cricket instead. What does that tell you?'

Dad did have one thoroughly memorable moment to take home with him, though. As he and a couple of teammates strolled through the winding Rio streets after dusk, a booming, welcoming Geordie voice hollered down at him from a balcony way up in a block of flats, 'All reet, Wor Jackie?'

Dad was pleasantly surprised to be recognised halfway around the world in the semi-dark and bounded straight up the stairs to shake hands with the jubilant Geordie. He was warmly invited inside for a coffee but shook his head. 'Lad, it doesn't matter where you go in this world you'll always find a Geordie,' declared Dad.

Apart from England's results, there was another thing about Rio that Dad found very upsetting and that was the staggering amount of genuinely disabled or deprived people begging scraps from the 'beautiful', but very indifferent, affluent folk. 'Being an Ashington lad, I'd never seen that before.'

There was one final significant episode in World Cup adventure on the return flight. Dad, with his engineering background, noticed there was something amiss with one of the engines on the port side. So, not to disturb his dozing companions or cause mass panic, he had a discreet word with the pilot, who on closer investigation discovered the engine had completely packed up. As luck would have it they were thankfully still over Brazil and not the middle of the Atlantic, and were able to land for emergency overnight repairs at Recife.

Back home meanwhile, a beady-eyed Mum scrutinised not only the match reports in the newspapers, but also stories of how bronzed, handsome and fit the players looked.

Jack Fairbrother's wife, Belle, had arrived to stay with Mum for a few days and after the pair read the articles they vowed not to be outdone. So, whenever the sun shone they lay tanning in the back garden and even on cooler days lay wrapped under a warm blanket with just their faces exposed, even though Mum was expecting a baby any day. When Dad did return home, he had to laugh at the motley 'rare steak' waiting on the doorstep to greet him.

On 7 October 1950, Dad was considered by many as a certainty for another cap against Northern Ireland at Windsor Park, but the selectors plumped for Derby's Jack Lee instead. Dad was named as reserve.

Stan Seymour needed Dad for a vital League game against Aston Villa and thought that was more important if he was to be just sitting on the England bench, so therefore applied to the FA for his release. This was the second time Newcastle had requested that a player be freed from international duty – and both times it was Dad.

Many ears in other clubs' boardrooms suddenly pricked, as most of them believed the FA should not have the divine right to call upon their players as and when they liked. They were looking for a precedent and thought this might just be it.

Newcastle even offered to fly Dad straight over to Birmingham if he found on the morning of the game he wouldn't be playing for England, causing one sensational newspaper headline to state: 'Milburn to be the First Flying Footballer'. Quite something in those days. However, the FA were not amused and so flatly refused United's appeal.

While Dad sat out the England match on the bench, Villa beat Newcastle 3–0 and United lost their place at the top of Division One. Seymour was not a happy man.

The next international was to be played at Roker Park against Wales and after some good League performances, Dad discovered he was to spearhead the attack this time. In a pulsating game England ended as victors, winning 4–2. Dad scored with just a minute of the game left and once more he was tipped to hold his place for the next match against the touring Yugoslavians. 'I was pleased with my performance,' he said.

Once more though, the FA selectors proved hard to predict and Dad was dropped. This time some of the press boys were not enamoured and one of them wrote:

> Most surprising is the omission of Milburn of Newcastle United, who needs only a little more confidence to be one of the greatest centre-forwards to lead an England line. This is a fine way to increase a lad's confidence. Anyone who was at Sunderland and thought Milburn a failure must have been blindfolded.

There were then mutterings that Dad had probably only been selected for the Wales match at Sunderland because of its proximity to Newcastle.

Dad soon found he was to be ignored again by England against the Irish League and Nat Lofthouse, who was making the No. 9 shirt his own, notched six of the seven goals.

During the 1950–51 season, Dad did manage to get back in an England shirt and scored a further three goals, one against Argentina in a 2–1 win and two against Portugal in a 5–2 win, though he drew a blank against France in a 2–2 draw. There would now be a gap of four years until his next call-up – against Denmark in Copenhagen, on 2 October 1955. Nat Lofthouse became England's first-choice centre-forward as he regularly played in that position for his club, while Dad found himself playing in every forward position at Newcastle except outside-left.

Newcastle had won the FA Cup that year and Dad had been playing well in the League, having just notched himself a hat-trick against Charlton Athletic. As it happens, Stanley Matthews was injured, so therefore England needed a competent winger. 'I'm thrilled,' Dad said. 'I made it quite clear I didn't care where I played on the field as long as I was in the side. I only hope this first international of the season proves successful.'

The England team to line up against the Danes were: Baynham; Hall, Byrne; Clayton, Wright, Dickinson; Milburn, Revie, Lofthouse, Bradford and Finney.

Mastermind Don Revie stole the show for England in their convincing 5–1 win, grabbing two of the goals for himself in the process. Centre-forward Nat Lofthouse netted two more and Bradford a fifth. Alas, some of Dad's attempts on goal were simply wild and desperate, and in all probability he tried too hard. 'In spite of being moved into the middle late in the game, I'm afraid I left my shooting boots at home. I just so desperately wanted to do well.'

After an international career spanning eight years, it proved to be his final game.

# 5

# Looking to the Future

My old man told me that people used to say he wasn't great in the air, but when he had to head the ball he could, and I've seen that from the footage.

Alan Shearer

The 1950–51 season, which would be remembered for Newcastle's FA Cup triumph, started with a win against Stoke City – Dad managing to score both goals, with one a penalty. This led to a great run of ten games without defeat, including convincing victories over Burnley (2–1), Huddersfield (6–0 ) and Arsenal (2–1). Dad felt that his 'confidence on the field was growing all the time'. In spite of his league form, he found himself offered only the role of reserve for the next international against Ireland. 'A hornet's nest was certainly stirred around that particular game,' he recalled.

At this time, United manager George Martin had quit the club to manage Aston Villa and Stan Seymour had again taken the reins. Martin had never really enjoyed full control over the team's selection or tactics.

It wasn't all plain sailing in the League now either and newly promoted Spurs cracked seven goals past United in front of a whopping 70,000 supporters at White Hart Lane to top the table. However, Newcastle enjoyed the welcome distraction of the FA Cup.

Though they only won one of their last eight games, the Magpies still managed to finish a credible 4th in the table with Dad netting a total of 18 goals. During the '51 summer break, United enjoyed a short seven-day tour of Belgium and during it managed to thrash the Belgian League champions 5–1.

Now carrying the burden of a new mortgage, an extra child and lower 'off season' wages only, Dad enthusiastically accepted the offer of advertising Quaker Oats, taking over the mantle from Dennis Compton – at the time the most famous cricketer in England. He also made a record for the Royal Society for the Prevention of Accidents, urging car drivers to be more safety conscious; then he was offered a part-time representative's job with William Crook's, a local boot manufacturer based just over the Tyne Bridge in Gateshead.

The second an ecstatic Mr Crook had secured a confirmatory signature, he placed an advertisement in the press, displaying Dad recommending the 'Jackie Milburn Own Design Sports Shoe'. Mr Crook reckoned Dad could easily earn £20 a week – double United's paltry summer wage of £10 – and also declared he may even progress within his company to become a full director.

Needless to say, the Newcastle board soon got word of all this and summoned Dad before them, immediately informing him that their policy of not permitting players to take up part-time work elsewhere was still very much in force, and he was certainly not going to be an exception to the rule. 'I didn't even bother to stand my ground and caved into their ludicrous demand. I quit Crook's before I'd even made my first call.'

After the board meeting, it was announced by the club secretary, Ted Hall, that Dad had left it on friendly terms and had not resigned from the football club. He wasn't the only disappointed United player though, as the club were simply refusing to release Joe Harvey, thereby denying him the opportunity to manage Carlisle United.

Just after this episode, Mum, now something of a creature of habit, declared herself to be once more with child, and at 5.10 am on the 24 March 1952, she produced this time an eight-and-three-quarter-pound son, yours truly, Jackie junior.

Before the start of the new season, Newcastle involved themselves in a lucrative English–Scottish Cup-Winners match against Celtic, and surprisingly three of the players who had helped them to lift the trophy at Wembley were excluded: Charlie Crowe (Dad's man of the match), Ernie Taylor and Bobby Corbett. They voiced their annoyance, but Seymour refused to budge. Taylor was one of the mainstays of the team and although Joe Harvey strongly protested the club's actions, Ernie Taylor soon after found himself transferred to Blackpool for £25,000.

Next to go was Bobby Corbett, after squaring up and swearing at captain Joe Harvey during an incident in a later game. Seymour was not happy and Bobby quickly found himself playing for Middlesbrough.

Charlie Crowe, who had been replaced by George Robledo's brother Ted, then slapped in a transfer request, though Seymour refused it and also refused to even discuss it with Charlie. He ended up playing most of the season in the reserves.

Having finished the previous season on such a high note, Newcastle now had to begin rebuilding their team. 'I always said the 1951 Cup-winning team was priceless. It was a sad time.'

Dad missed a few of the early games with a pulled leg muscle, but United still got off to a good start and in the first four home games they banged in twenty goals, conceding just three. 'After I recovered from my injury I thought it unfair that the forward line should be changed just to accommodate me, so I asked Mr Seymour if he would play me in the reserves and he agreed,' Dad explained.

His appearance in the Central League match put an additional 10,000 on the gate, though he soon found himself back in the first team.

In the November of 1951, as a PR exercise and to encourage folk to participate in sport, Dad, George Robledo, Frank Brennan and Bobby Mitchell, plus Sunderland's Watson and McLain, took part in 'Spotlight on Sport', which the Central Council of Physical Recreation staged before a packed audience at the Newcastle City Hall. They were there to demonstrate various training techniques, and United's trainer, Norman Smith, acted as commentator.

Pat Hirst, the 1950 British champion, was among other ladies offering a display of gymnastics, the first ever of its kind shown in the Northeast.

Harry Whittle, British decathlon champion and captain of the British Empire Games team also took part, as well as weight-lifting champions Tom Oliver and Ted Hodgman. Jack Flaherty, former captain of the British Olympic team and Jim Semmence of Hebburn, at the time the Northeast champion, performed men's gymnastics.

Local lads, Tony Craig (Newcastle Boys Brigade) and the up-and-coming amateur gymnast Tommy Dawson (Vickers), a future champion and Olympic contender, accompanied them.

A couple of months later, on 20 January 1952, Dad notched his 100th Newcastle goal, though the side were still beaten 2–1 by Burnley. For one of their goals, Cummings, the Burnley centre-half, ran all of an amazing 75 yards before hitting the back of the net. 'I reckoned it to be the best goal I ever saw,' Dad marvelled.

With their Cup run underway and going well, Newcastle were looking for the same consistency in the League. Before a home match with Charlton, Charlton's jovial manager, Jimmy Seed, joked, 'I don't suppose Jackie Milburn is off with a cold or something?' He wasn't and banged in two of the goals in a 6–0 United win. The final game of the season ended with a 6–1 victory over Aston Villa and United finished in 8th position. For the first time in five seasons, however, Dad was not the club's top scorer – that honour went to Chilean George Robledo, who notched up 33 goals. His partnership with Dad helped the team to net a total of 98 goals by the end of the 1951–52 campaign. Charlie Crowe remembers: 'Jackie was a better centre-forward when George Robledo came. They were the perfect pair.' In four matches of that season the Magpies scored six times and twice they banged in seven.

Now they were on their way to meet the mighty Arsenal in the FA Cup final at Wembley, but before then, Newcastle found themselves in a little spot of bother. United were fined 50 guineas by the FA on 9 April 1952 for giving their players too much spending money while away from home: they had each been receiving £2 a day when FA regulations stated that £1 was the maximum. It was immediately reduced to that amount plus a packet of John Player's fags. Dad considered himself lucky as his new roommate, George Robledo, was a non-smoker and always handed his over.

Soon after the final, as a team reward, the United squad were taken off on a ten-week tour of South Africa, having been given special permission by the FA to take with them the Cup – the first time it had been allowed to leave the country. For the first five weeks of the tour Dad underwent intensive treatment for an injury he sustained from a kick by Arsenal's Don Roper during the final and was forced to remain at the team's base camp. 'I just want to be back home with Laura and the family,' he said at the time.

Even with Dad's injury, the tour proved to be a resounding Newcastle success and the team lost only one match, 5–3, to South Africa. To some of the players' disgust, after that particular match, there followed a gripe of a report in the *Johannesburg Daily Mail* from their columnist and former Newcastle player, Eric Litchfield. Litchfield absolutely slated the Magpies, suggesting they were all simply suffering from 'delusions of grandeur' and certainly not much good either, signifying that the Newcastle board would surely have to offload quickly and find a much better class of player. He concluded with a firm suggestion that South Africa should never again invite Newcastle United back to their country.

After a sorry start to the team's 1952–53 League season, rumours began to spread of a Jackie Milburn transfer.

The saga had begun during a general meeting of the executives of numerous League clubs. One official from Portsmouth lightheartedly asked Lord Westwood, who had only recently found himself appointed to the United board, about a price for Wor Jackie and was, without further ado, advised the bidding would need to start at £30,000. The watching Stan Seymour noticed a few raised eyebrows and, never being a one to stand in the way of hard cash, suddenly decided to test the water, without showing the slightest regard about any outcome.

Soon the back pages of the newspapers were full of transfer speculation, which upset Dad greatly – it was the first he knew about the situation. 'I went straight to the club to speak with Stan Seymour and challenged him to get to the bottom of it. I asked him outright if he was expecting me now to request a transfer. He said yes and that I must put it in writing immediately. So I did.'

With a reeling head, Dad headed straight back to Ashington and in a short time found his house under siege by bands of ravenous journalists, desperate to find out the real reason why he should want to leave. 'I could only reply in truth, and that was that I had no desire to move on, but I now felt there was no longer a future for me at St James' Park.'

The £30,000 price-tag proved too high though, and when not one solitary League club placed a bid on the table the wily board decided to declare publicly that it was indeed they who had turned down Dad's self-instigated transfer request.

To Dad, the whole situation had now developed into a complete farce, especially as Seymour had always told his players to simply ignore newspaper transfer gossip, as most of it was 'simply claptrap'. Anyway, according to Seymour, 'It was, after all, Milburn who had asked me outright for a transfer, so therefore I'd requested he put it in writing'. Lips were forcibly sealed and eventually the hullabaloo calmed down.

Around that time, due to mounting players' protests, the Newcastle United board finally relaxed their decree that any employee should not be allowed to take up part-time work elsewhere, so Dad, now having several hungry mouths to feed, jumped at the opportunity when a close friend offered him the chance to 'front' a fireplace shop on Station Road in Ashington – a good opportunity in those days. It was a time of great modernisation in the mining town, when everyone wanted brand new, modern tiled fire surrounds with which to replace their old black ranges. And to top it all, the job included a free, three-bedroomed flat above the shop, so he and Mum promptly sold their little house in Ellington Terrace to offload the crippling mortgage payments.

Dad managed to secure a huge contract with a builder who was helping create Cramlington new town, so after that cracking start, reckoned it might just be an excellent business move. Mum too thoroughly enjoyed busying herself about the shop, even though she had to endure three screeching kids gnawing at her ankles all day. All too soon though, it became very clear that the demand for the fireplaces was far outstripping supply and after finishing his training stints at Newcastle, Dad would often return to the shop just to spend laborious hour after hour on the telephone in a desperate effort to chase up non-forthcoming orders. In due course, this took over his life even more than football.

Once more he was forced to take stock of his life. He felt extremely frustrated and embarrassed at being unable to fulfil understandably irate customers' needs. 'When I had to face the consequence of that on the shop floor, I knew it wasn't worth all the frustration and aggravation. The same day a complainant started hammering on the door of my flat after hours, I knew it was time to go. So, without further ado, I packed it all in to concentrate solely on my football.'

Luckily, a club house became available at the top of Benton Park Road in Newcastle, so the pair jumped at the opportunity. The family settled easily into the new surroundings, even if it was never quite a tranquil house. Having said that, however, many happy family evenings were spent at home, especially when Dad prised open the lid of the old piano he tinkled at, while at the same time craftily switching on the microphone of the new-fangled tape-recorder gifted him by an Ashington shop. Some nights we kids would howl along to Doris Day or Nat King Cole 78 rpm records, then cover our ears with horror as he replayed the tape. Mum and Dad were different – they could each warble a pretty tune just as well as many a good crooner. With time though, all good things come to an end, and thanks to the introduction of more children's programmes on the little black and white TV which he'd bought especially for Queen Elizabeth's Coronation, we kids became more interested in gawping at the corner of the room it now dominated, firmly glued to the likes of BBC's *Rag Tag and Bobtail*, *The Woodentops* and *Andy Pandy*.

I remember catching a bus into Newcastle with my mother one day back then – she was taking me to a professional photographer to have me snapped. These days that might seem a little extravagant, but considering the quality of some of the little box cameras that most folk could afford then, it was deemed the done thing to leave it to the professionals. However, being forced to sit and pose with a phoney grin, for what seemed like an eternity, led to shenanigans, so I suppose the chap was just glad to see the back of me when it was all over.

On the return journey home, just as Mum dragged me from my seat as we approached our stop, something or somebody forced the driver to brake hard just as we walked up the aisle and Mum plummeted face down on the deck. I was somewhat luckier as someone grabbed and held onto me. Luckily, Mum was able to pick herself up and she wasn't really hurt that badly, though the knock to her nose caused it to bleed nastily. Fortunately though, she always carried a handkerchief, but it quickly became saturated with blood and the poor conductress could not apologise enough as Mum and I stepped down from the bus.

Just as Mum pushed open the back door of the house, Dad arrived back from training in his car and looked horrified at seeing the blood-soaked handkerchief pressed to her face. He raced up the back path, but in his hurry stumbled awkwardly over the back step and yelped as he landed on his knee, jumping quickly to his feet to hop around the back garden. Mum followed him out with her bloody hanky in one hand, while the other pinched her bleeding nostril, only to be confronted by a host of inquisitive neighbours alerted by the yelling. The pair swiftly scrambled back inside and left them to make up their own minds.

It was also at this time that Dad felt proud and privileged to be approached by the local newspaper to write a weekly football column. The extra income would come in more than useful, though at first he'd struggle to find the right words and the floor of the house would be littered with screwed-up paper balls. One day a week, the United players would enjoy a round at a local golf club and often Dad would sit jealously in the clubhouse to finish his column if he hadn't got it right at home. However, he was quickly learning to love being involved in the world of sports journalism.

Not long after, he was offered the opportunity to become involved in the coach-touring business, after Bob Armstrong, a good pal of his with a thriving coach business, offered to help him all he could as a reward, not only for the pleasure he'd given him on the football pitch, but for the extra business his company had enjoyed during Newcastle's three Cup runs. He could hardly believe it when Bob, who had already given him a motor car, gave him the full loan of a 29-seater 1949 Bedford coach, and as if that wasn't enough, allowed him the use of all the facilities of his workshop if he needed them for any servicing or repairs. 'I was speechless when Bob went on to say he would even guarantee me my first summer bookings with pre-booked trips to places like Seahouses in North Northumberland and Blackpool, Leeds, Glasgow and Edinburgh.' Dad proudly renamed the coach 'The Ashington Flyer'.

Straightaway he sat and passed his public vehicle licence test and then got cracking, even giving a hand to paint the bus in his own chosen colours of maroon and cream. 'As well as having the summer excursions, I was fortunate enough to secure a winter contract with the General Post Office to deliver their Christmas parcels, eventually becoming successful enough to acquire a second 35-seater. I was thrilled.'

There was one other opportunity in the early '50s that appealed to Dad when he almost went into business with Albert Stubbins. Together the pair discussed opening a restaurant in the centre of Newcastle and even chose a name for it — 'The Goalmouth'. However, nothing ever came of it, due to financial problems.

The next couple of seasons were uneventful ones for United, with disappointing League campaigns in both 1952–53 and 1953–54. Season 1952–53 was also a frustrating time for Dad's personal playing career: he managed to net only five goals, mainly because of injury — niggling knee problems that eventually led to a cartilage being removed — and played in just 16 League games.

In spite of Dad celebrating his 250th United appearance in 1954–55, he found he just wasn't banging in the goals like he used to, scoring 16 in 39 League matches — low by his standards. There was significant news on the financial side at this time, however, when his weekly wage, along with that of the other players, was increased from £14 to £15.

When Dad's dip in form in 1953–54 led to him being dropped from the team for a match against Middlesbrough, other clubs were once again alerted to the possibility of signing him. In particular, United's great rivals Sunderland, who had recently sold their own centre-forward, Trevor Ford, to Cardiff, made discreet enquiries about Dad, but Stan Seymour would hear none of it.

Dad looked back on those times:

> That season I suffered the only serious injury of my career, as a result of which I had to have a cartilage operation, but believe it or not, I was playing again in less than six weeks. I wouldn't have done, only director William McKeag asked

me to have a run out in the third team at Wallsend and promised me 'a little something' for supposedly adding a bit of glamour to the match. As it happened, I got nothing, not that I'd wanted anything in the first place, but my appearance caused more than a spot of bother. Twelve thousand folk turned up to watch us at a little welfare ground designed to only hold twelve hundred. We won 2–1 with me scoring one of the goals, but this sparked off violent protests from the opposition who would have won the League title but for that defeat.

Mum began to notice a considerable change in Dad's frame of mind. He suddenly became easily irritated and would snap at the most trivial things, something he had never done before. If we kids stepped out of line we were for the high-jump and, being bawdy little horrors, I'm sure we must have broken the world record for it several times, but we were just kids and simply didn't understand the outside pressure he was feeling. Like most youngsters, all we really understood was me, me, me. Generally speaking, Mum was never a one to discuss football with Dad at all, something he always appreciated, but this time she wisely changed tactics and decided to probe deeper to source the cause of his problems. He soon confided in her.

In 1954, Stan Seymour had taken a back seat once more after the Newcastle board appointed a new full-time manager, a dour Scotsman named Dougald Livingstone. He was a former trainer at Sheffield United and carried a bit of a reputation as a coach on the Continent and in Eire. From the very day of his arrival, he had instructed every player, no matter who they were, that each of them now had to fight tooth and nail for their places, and not one of them would be guaranteed a game. They soon discovered him to be true to his word.

Livingstone himself was the instigator of one of the most acutely embarrassing moments of Dad's life, and many years later, as he tried to boost my own flagging resolve after an upsetting incident involving athletics at my school, he told me about it.

The incident occurred just before a United home match, as Dad stood naked in the centre of the crowded dressing-room preparing to don his strip. After throwing open the door, a sullen Livingstone enquired of him just what he thought he was doing and an embarrassed silence fell over the other players as they glanced in the direction of Dad who, with a scarlet face, replied he was simply getting ready to play. Livingstone frowned and told him not to bother, as he wouldn't be playing at all that day.

Feeling totally humiliated, Dad covered his blushes as best he could, before quickly throwing his suit back on and leaving the changing room, but he was absolutely positive about one thing: that particularly discomforting moment and the manner in which it was handled would live with him for the rest of his days.

Charlie Crowe remembers: 'The dressing-room just went silent and we bowed our heads in embarrassment.'

Livingstone's arrival also caused cliques to form in the camp. Dad recalled: 'Some of us were hard-bitten pros when he arrived and you expect a new boss to be, well, the boss. But he was a school-teacher type and some of us found it very difficult to look up to him at all.

'Joe Harvey had left the club and cliques of three and four formed with this lot ignoring that lot. We had never known that before.'

After the third Wembley experience, the Newcastle board arranged a ten-day tour of Germany during the close-season, leaving on 23 May. In the first rough-and-tumble match, Dad managed to net two goals in the 3–2 win over a Berlin 11, with Vic Keeble scoring the other. The second game, against FC Nuremburg, proved to be even tougher and signalled the end of three-times-Cup-winner Bobby Cowell's career. As Bobby arranged a wall for Ronnie Simpson, the frustrated German left-half, Uckow, who'd been having a running battle with Newcastle's tough captain Jimmy Scoular, lunged at his calf with both feet, and Bobby was carried off the pitch. It was the last game the 33 year old ever played for United or anyone else. Four more games were played, two wins and two defeats, but the tour had lost its edge.

In the July, Livingstone, who still lived in a city-centre hotel, was given the biggest of hints about his future when the club house he'd been promised was given to Bob Stokoe instead. Not long after, club chairman Wilf Taylor held a press conference and stated: 'Newcastle United and Dougald Livingstone have parted company by mutual consent – and that's all there is to it.'

Livingstone later added, 'It was because I'd been told four days after the Cup final that I would no longer select the team. All my duties had been taken from me and there was nothing for me to do.'

After the pre-season Charity Shield final, in which Chelsea beat Newcastle 3–0 in front of a crowd of just 12,802, Stan Seymour called for the fixture to be done away with. After turning in a good performance, Dad was singled out by his good friend and journalist, Ken McKenzie, as a 'giant among pygmies'.

His good form continued into the new season, 1955–56, and during September in London, he managed to bag a hat-trick against Charlton Athletic, prompting the selectors to pick him for England's forthcoming match against the Danes. United then completed a brilliant Christmas programme, collecting maximum points from their three games, including the 6–1 thrashing of Sunderland. 'As we eased off during the second half I yelled at my teammates, remember the 9–1,' Dad recalled, referring to Newcastle's record 9–1 hammering by Sunderland back in 1908.

Newcastle drew Sheffield Wednesday in the third round of the FA Cup and shared with them the honour of being the first clubs to take part in a floodlit Cup tie. Dad grabbed one as United won 3–1. Next United were drawn away at Fulham whose team included the young Durham-born Bobby Robson. Within 40 minutes Newcastle had cracked three goals past their keeper, Dad having notched the first one himself, and most folk thought the game was wrapped up. However, Fulham gritted their teeth and stunned United by coming back with four goals of their own to make it 4–3; nevertheless, Vic Keeble saved Newcastle's blushes by scoring another two to make the final score

5–4. Also playing in the Fulham side that day was a young Jimmy Hill.

The fifth round was drawn and Newcastle found themselves facing Stoke City. In front of a 61,450 crowd, United won the game 2–1. Who should they draw next but bitter rivals Sunderland? It was the first Cup meeting between the two sides since the First World War.

The atmosphere was tremendous, with 61,500 crammed into St James' Park for the game and many more watching eagerly from the roofs of nearby Leazes Terrace. Sadly for Newcastle they were beaten 2–0 and Sunderland went on to the next round only to be beaten 3–0 by Birmingham.

It proved a sad season for Dad, first with the departure of Joe Harvey to manage Workington Town, then a not-so-good England performance, losing to Sunderland in the FA Cup and, finally, Newcastle losing nine out of ten of their final League games. Vic Keeble finished the season as top scorer with 26 goals. 'I seriously began to think about hanging up my boots,' Dad said.

Dad's confidence really began to slip as the 1956–57 season got underway. Alex Tait, a Bedlington youngster, was beginning to overshadow him, even scoring a hat-trick as Newcastle hammered Sunderland 6–2. He took Dad's place in an exciting third-round Cup-tie replay against Manchester City and scored a superb goal from a run that began well inside his own half. United won 5–4. However, in the next round they were knocked out by Millwall at The Den.

Jack Charlton, who with brother Bobby had marvelled at Dad's speed as a child, saw how far Dad's style of play had changed:

> I only remember playing against him once at Newcastle, in my early days at Leeds. We played at St James' Park and I had a good game against him. I got to the ball first and thought, 'He's not as quick as he used to be.' I tackled him a couple of times and he fell down. He finished at Newcastle that year. There was a one-year crossover between us.

There was another player emerging at the club at this time who always impressed Dad. In later life, Dad reckoned Len White to have been the best uncapped centre-forward in England. Others reckoned that had Len been a couple of inches taller than 5 ft 7 in., then, even in those days, he would have commanded an £80,000 transfer figure. After moving to Tyneside from Rotherham for a modest fee of just £13,000, Len was amazed at the comparatively palatial club house he was offered. He and his wife Joyce had been living in a Rotherham United club house that was so damp they couldn't even use two of the rooms. His more relaxed home-life must have benefited his play on the field too, as he developed into a formidable goal machine, becoming the club's top scorer over five consecutive seasons, scoring 13 goals in 1956–57, 25 in 1957–58, 25 in 1958–59, 29 in 1959–60 and a further 29 in 1960–61. Sadly, Len picked up an injury after a crippling tackle by Tottenham's Dave Mackay during that last season and without his goals, United found themselves relegated to the Second Division. Dad had travelled to White Hart Lane to watch the game, commenting later, 'I reckon that Mackay's tackle was the worst I've ever seen.'

Ironically, Len may just have pipped Hughie Gallagher's 1926–27 record of 36 goals in a season, as there were still nine games to play. However, even though Newcastle banged in a staggering 86 goals during the season, they had failed to keep them out at the other end, letting in 109. United's manager Charlie Mitten found himself sacked and then soon after, Len left for Huddersfield Town.

In what was to become his last season playing for Newcastle, it would be an understatement to say that things were just not going right for Dad. He was also aware that he was losing a bit of pace too, wondering whether being a smoker might be affecting his stamina, and being gifted packets of un-tipped John Player's by the directors may not have helped either. At just 33, he was beginning to feel like a much older man.

For the first time in his career, he endured a lengthy spell of poor games and could now sense the fans and press alike were slowly turning against him. 'It seemed I could do nothing right and I began to lose sleep, lying in bed and staring blankly at the ceiling.

'I relived every kick of the last match and then began worrying frantically about the next. My confidence had completely gone and I thought seriously about chucking in the towel for good.'

After winning his third Wembley medal, his frame of mind had improved dramatically and the Milburn household became quite a serene place to live, but the pressure was now beginning to tell once more. We kids were now all at school, but as soon as we arrived home and began to squabble, his short fuse, returned after a short absence, would blow and he would yell at us once more, triggering Mum to say her bit – something that was always followed by long stony silences.

Normally arguments between Mum and Dad were a rarity: they simply eyed each other after a disagreement and uttered not a word until one of them caved in and then they would laugh at their own stupidity. This time it was different and Mum knew it . . . Dad was totally strained, drained and stressed out.

Oddly enough, all that seemed to change the day he came home with a book on Yoga tucked under his arm and sat down quietly to fastidiously study it. He was astonished to discover it proved to have an almost immediate, 'magical' effect on his temperament and football. He apologised profusely to Mum and us kids for his outbursts and then the night before the next game, he clambered between the bed sheets and began muttering words over and over to himself. Although Mum was a trifle puzzled, she thought it best to simply let him get on with it, though she did listen carefully to his mumblings as he drifted off to sleep: 'I must score tomorrow . . . I must score tomorrow . . . I must score tomorrow.'

Next afternoon, just after the kick-off, although Dad still suffered a belly full of butterflies, he realised it was now or never, so instead of making the usual short passes he had fallen into the trap of playing when given the ball, he looked around him first and then pelted like a steam train a full 60 yards towards the goal. He unleashed a belter that flew just wide. 'Fair enough, I missed, but that wasn't the issue. It was the old familiar roar of the expectant crowd flooding my ears that suddenly brought back my lost confidence. I scored later in the game and at long last, I had the crowd on my side once more.'

That match proved to be the turning point that prevented him from hanging up his boots forever at the end of that season. Although he scored just 12 goals and Newcastle finished their season in a lowly 17th position, he realised that, with his wealth of experience, he could still play a valuable part in a match. So too did Linfield FC.

At the end of the 1957 season, to keep every option open, Dad attended a training course which would guarantee him a position as a physical instructor with the local authority and better still, a secure pension (though he knew his heart would always remain with football) so when Belfast club Linfield approached United with a view to offering him the job of player/coach, Dad was sorely tempted. Their ultimate dangling carrot was the prospect of eventually taking over as manager when his playing days were over.

He looked over to Workington Town FC, where former Newcastle captain Joe Harvey was doing an excellent job, and reckoned that with his own sound football knowledge, he too could do the same over the Irish Sea. And who knows, maybe even one day, once he'd gained enough experience, he might just receive a call from his beloved Newcastle United to take over the reins? But if he had learned nothing else thus far, it was never to employ any of the insulting tactics he'd witnessed Livingstone use on several of the Newcastle players – such as the day he scratched a chalk mark on a precise spot of the great Bobby Mitchell's boot, simply to enable him to pass the ball more accurately. This treatment appalled Dad, who later remembered how 'Bobby could precisely flight a 50-yard ball and drop it perfectly on the little toe of an ant's right back leg'.

With all that in mind, Dad discussed his dilemma thoroughly with Mum, and, as usual, she gave her assurance that she would back him all the way – whichever direction he decided on. He plumped to head for Belfast, so in June 1957, Newcastle United formally announced to the press world that Jackie Milburn was about to leave the club, though most readers simply dismissed it as, 'Aye, heard it all before'.

They remembered back to 1948, when he'd been on his way to London and then 1951, when Hunslet tried their best to lure him to make the big switch to rugby with an incredibly generous offer of £3,000; also, there was 1952, when other clubs were told the bidding started at £30,000 and, of course, in 1953, the 'old enemy' Sunderland AFC almost achieved the unthinkable as they attempted to lure him to Roker Park to play in their famous red-and-white shirt.

This time though, it was for real.

– 6 –

# From Black and White to Blues

Your Dad told me, 'Never mind the coaches who want people
to get back and defend. There's ten others to do that! You do
it all in the last third.'

Malcolm Macdonald

The whole Linfield FC transfer saga actually began when Newcastle
United accepted an invitation to play a friendly against the Irish
side at Windsor Park, on 10 October 1956, to celebrate the
installation of a new £17,000 floodlighting system. On the day,
35,000 fanatical Irish spectators turned up for the huge occasion.

Dick Keith, a recent United signing from Linfield, and also now a
great friend of Dad's, light-heartedly asked him how would he feel
about playing in a blue shirt in front of a rousing Irish crowd like
that every week. Dad replied that he really wouldn't mind at all – in
fact he'd be delighted. 'Unbeknown to the two of us,' Dad
explained, 'an eager Linfield director overheard our conversation
and very quickly tentative wheels were set in motion.'

Shortly after returning to Newcastle, Dad, and now Mum too,
found themselves invited back to Windsor Park to be further
sounded out by the Linfield officials. While there, he also played in

two benefit matches to show just what he was still capable of, and as he ran onto the pitch during one he heard a proverbial Geordie voice boom, 'Gan on, Jackie, show 'em what ye can dee!'

It turned out to be that of a British soldier doing his national service in Belfast, a lad called Ray Brotherton, who, by coincidence, also hailed from Ashington. Dad suddenly felt at home and ran across to Ray and his pals to shake their hands, even offering to give them a full tour of the ground after the game and, true to his word, that is just what he did. At the end of the walkabout, he asked them to hold on to a big secret – he was just about ready to sign the papers to join Linfield. The soldiers were over the moon.

After enjoying 14 great seasons at Newcastle, Dad, sad though he was, knew his time there was at an end. He also knew the once brilliant dressing-room morale had all but gone since Joe Harvey left, and in truth, felt sure it would never get any better. Not only that, but he clearly remembered the words of his father, Alec, 'Never outstay your welcome, son', and really, he didn't want the United supporters to remember him simply as a has-been. Now, at the age of 33, he was well aware that the rigours of many a long tough season in the First Division had taken their toll.

A somewhat reluctant Stan Seymour accompanied Dad on the ferry to Belfast to thrash out terms with the Linfield officials. It proved a long, strained 15-hour journey for the pair, and during their time on board football never entered into the conversation once.

Once back home though, Seymour admitted to the press that he'd secretly hoped Dad wouldn't sign; but the offer of a five-year contract, £1,000 in his hand, a huge detached four-bedroom club house, a £1,300 salary and the enticement of eventually taking over as manager proved just too tempting for Dad.

Dad simply loved the ambitious Linfield attitude. The club aimed to top the Irish League and win every available piece of silverware, and the board of directors were absolutely convinced that Jackie Milburn was the final piece in their jigsaw. But now, all of a sudden, there loomed a snag – a very large snag.

Knowing Linfield had swallowed their bait hook, line and sinker, Newcastle United quickly pulled a stunning flanker by demanding a massive £10,000 transfer fee, plus a player in exchange – a totally unexpected gambit that would most certainly empty the coffers of Ireland's once richest club. The injustice was not lost on Dad: 'The day I learned of Newcastle's demands, I was taught a very valuable lesson and that was that football was not just simply the sport I loved playing, but also a big, greedy business too.'

He was absolutely furious with United, who tried desperately to hush up the whole scenario for fear of upsetting further their own loyal supporters by selling the club's most loyal servant for such a vast amount in the twilight of his career. 'After all, back in 1943 I'd only cost them ten quid,' Dad said.

He had felt it only right to expect to be allowed to leave for free, especially as he was now getting on a bit. Nevertheless, the Linfield board thought he was worth chancing their remaining money on. So on 13 June 1957 pen was put to paper and Dad officially became a Blues player.

Dad was reflective about his transfer. 'To mark the grand occasion, a private room was booked in a Belfast hotel and the press were invited to a cocktail party. We then moved on to a grand civic reception at the Belfast City Hall. I stood in awe amid the beautiful surroundings and my mind couldn't help but drift back to what I might just be doing that day if I had not been fortunate enough to have made the grade as a footballer. Probably sweating down a deep dark mine at Ashington Colliery, repairing a broken cutter on the coal face.'

After Dad received a magnificent welcome from the civic dignitaries, Stan Seymour, who had returned for the occasion, took to his feet to make an extremely flattering speech, declaring Dad to be the greatest player he'd ever signed for United and wishing him every success with his new club. He then good-humouredly waved a fist at Mr Mackey and Mr Lunn, the two Linfield officials responsible for the transfer.

Meanwhile, back in Newcastle, hundreds of letters were pouring into St James' Park from disgruntled United fans who still felt that Dad had a lot to offer, but it was too late – the transaction was done. 'I don't expect anyone will ever know how much sorrow I felt the day I actually walked from the players' entrance of St James' Park for the last time.'

Mum, by now an expert packer, busied herself cramming tea chests in readiness for the removal men's arrival. Many tearful farewells were bade to family and Tyneside, though for us kids it was definitely more than just a bit exciting to be setting off on this mammoth new adventure.

Once across the Irish Sea, the furniture van rolled off the ferry and on to the fine-looking club house in Belfast Road, Holywood, just on the outskirts of Belfast.

Our jaws dropped at its size. After the cosy little three-bedroom semi-detached in Newcastle it stood like a whopping mansion, comprising four huge bedrooms, an attic playroom, three reception rooms, kitchen, pantry and large lawned gardens. It even boasted its own garage. As anyone who has ever moved home knows, tempers are easily frayed during the bedlam of shuffling furniture and unpacking, so we overexcited kids were shunted out into the back garden to explore and to our great delight, discovered a magnificent tree full of juicy apples.

'Last one to the top branch is a cissy!'

The three of us clambered towards the high branches, but halfway up Betty's foot slipped and she found herself snagged and left dangling by the thick elastic of her navy-blue knickers. Of course, Linda and I slid back to earth to point and shriek at her plight, but then thought better of it, so climbed back up to set her free, both being too frightened to go and tell Mum and Dad for fear of being given a right rollicking.

Unable to release her, we descended once more and with typical children's logic, determined that the only way to get her down would be to pelt apples up in the hope of dislodging the elastic.

Several throws later, one of them bounced from her and straight through the tall hedge, smashing a pane of the new neighbour's greenhouse. As panicking Betty thrashed, the offending twig snapped and she plummeted to earth with a bump.

Suddenly, a shrieking, irate woman's voice boomed over the hedge in a broad Ulster brogue. 'It's those bloody Milburn kids! I told you that family would bring nothing but trouble when they moved here! They haven't even been here five bloody minutes! You . . . get round there and sort them out!'

Linda and I quickly dragged Betty behind the body of the tree in a desperate attempt to hide, but then a docile-looking man padded up the front path to meekly complain to a much-embarrassed Mum and Dad. Thankfully, he turned out to be a soccer fan and the sorry situation calmed quickly after he was compensated, though we kids were hastily rounded up and given an extremely early bath. Welcome to Holywood.

Not long after settling in, Dad drove into Belfast to discover the streets around the Lisburn Road area chock-a-block with cheering, flag-waving folk. He stopped the car, absolutely flabbergasted that the kind Irish folk should display such a warm welcome for him. 'Admittedly, I had heard plenty about their fine displays of hospitality, but this greeting simply took my breath away. And then someone pointed out that it was in fact 12 July.' Never quite such a big date to celebrate back in England.

His first match loomed against Distillery FC at their Grosvenor Park ground and, after the entire hullabaloo that surrounded his signing, he certainly felt the immense pressure of having to play to his best. 'By the time I ran on to the pitch that day, I was an absolute bundle of nerves.'

The majority of the jubilant, travelling Linfield supporters fully expected him to crack in goals left right and centre, though unfortunately for all concerned, that never happened. 'All I did right was toss the coin as captain.'

He made no excuses at all, quickly succumbing to the fact that he had quite simply just played a stinker, but deep down, he knew he had been completely marked out of the game by big Joe McKinstry, a six-foot policeman. Thankfully though, the other ten face-saving Linfield players knuckled down to secure a draw.

After the match, Dad was able to take some heart from the words of Distillery's manager, Maurice Tadman, who told him not to over-fret as he himself had suffered the same tough baptism and it would probably take at least a couple of months for him to settle into the different style of play.

In spite of those reassuring words, shamed Dad still came home in a paddy and then virtually hid indoors for four days until the next home match at Windsor Park. 'Thankfully I scored a simple tap-in to restore my confidence,' said Dad. The crowd went absolutely wild and their huge ovation showed him they were ready to at least give him a chance. 'My five-year-old son could easily have scored that one,' joked Dad.

In fact, unbeknown to Dad, his utterly naive five-year-old son was managing to give his Mum a very scarlet face that day at Windsor Park.

Up the hill behind the new house, lay a large housing estate that boasted its own little play park containing a roundabout, slide, monkey-puzzle and seesaw, so naturally it was where all the local youngsters would congregate. After discovering who Dad played for and that I was to attend his home debut with Mum, some of the local lads educated me with a selection of 'essential Linfield supporters' chants' full of special 'Irish words' that I *must* yell at the top of my voice during the game. 'You have to give your Dad all the support he needs in his first home game,' I was urged.

I listened intently to them and later memorised the 'chants' by mumbling them over and over again, so desperate was I to spur Dad on.

At Windsor Park that day, Mum and I were shown to our seats in the directors' box just before the kick-off and for the first time, I sniffed in deeply the bracing atmosphere of fags, burnt match sulphur and liniment. I looked up at Mum and smiled excitedly, absolutely confident in my ability to remember all my proudly learned, well-rehearsed supportive words. I just knew I was going to thrill her with my newfound 'football expertise'. The crowd roared, the match started and I let fly.

'Kick him in the fucking air! Tackle the silly shit! Come on, you useless bastard!'

All around us, folk gasped and Mum cringed, hastily slapping my leg and hissing venomously at me to be quiet. I was somewhat puzzled. 'But Mum, I'm a true fucking Blue. Can't you hear me? I know exactly what I'm saying. The big boys told me.'

I remained gagged, sore and red-eyed for the rest of the game, which proved to be my and Mum's first and only experience of what should have been the grand atmosphere at Windsor Park. It turned out the older boys from the play park were fervent Glentoran supporters. Thanks, lads.

During the next few games, Dad felt his general play wasn't too bad, but sensed the crowd were desperate to see more goals from him; he also knew he was concentrating far too much on encouraging the younger players on the field, and in all honesty, he would have preferred it to be them scoring the goals to show that he was doing his job well as team coach. 'With all that weighty pressure crushing my shoulders, I decided to put my head down and run forward with the ball, to simply do what I knew best, and that was to bang in as many goals as possible with every scoring opportunity.'

Before arriving in Northern Ireland, he had been led to believe that the game was much slower than in the English First Division. He quickly found that to be far from the truth: 'It was relatively tougher with much keener tackling, though never really being played dirty.'

He also spotted a lot of young, raw talent that, given the opportunity, could quite easily have slotted straight into the English

League. 'What excited me most though, was the fact that I now looked forward to every single match.'

At the end of the League season Linfield finished fifth in the League and Dad had banged in a massive 55 goals. They had also won the City Cup, Gold Cup and the Antrim Shield.

Linfield were also firm favourites to win the Irish Cup after thrashing close rivals Distillery 7–1 in the semi-final. Dad cracked in four and received rave press reviews to silence a few of his critics who had written him off as just another washed-up Englishman who'd crossed the Irish Sea to play out his twilight years.

However, he then picked up a nasty injury. 'I had been out for a month but desperately wanted to play in the Irish Cup. I limped right through the game. That's not an excuse though; we were beaten by a better side on the day.' At the Oval in Belfast, Ballymena had won 3–0.

His spirits were soon lifted though, after discovering he'd been selected by a panel of sportswriters and referees as the Irish League Footballer of the Year. Everyone seemed happy, but what made Dad even happier and greatly helped spur him on was that during Linfield's matches, in his honour, the fans had penned and sung loudly their own words to Newcastle's infamous Geordie Ridley anthem 'The Blaydon Races':

> I saw a smiling face today,
> The face of Joe Mackey.
> He said the greatest thing he ever did
> Was signing on Wor Jackie.
> First Wor Jackie wasn't used
> To playing in strange places,
> 'Til Linfield bought a gramophone
> And played the Blaydon Races.

(Oh, me lads, etc. . .)

Up on the Spion Kop
The Blues supporters gathered;
Waving high the City Cup
Blended with the heather.
The Glens were leading three to two,
The Blues were none the wiser,
'Til Jackie Milburn got the ball
And scored the equaliser.

His exploits on the pitch now triggered Malcolm Brodie, the sports editor of the *Belfast Evening Telegraph*, to declare that, without a doubt, Jackie Milburn was the greatest crowd puller in the history of Irish football, reckoning that his appearance could put at least an additional 5,000 on the gate. And, not only was he an outstanding player, but he demonstrated superb sporting qualities as well, setting a great example for any parent's aspiring son to follow. Those words thrilled Dad, but not only that, they proved to be true and Linfield gradually began to recoup their outlay with soaring attendances.

At last, things seemed to be coming good and not just on the pitch. At home Mum was decorating the house the way she wanted it and we kids were enjoying life and settling nicely into the private Sullivan Upper School.

On occasion though, the very sight of that school uniform seemed to antagonise some of the kids who did not attend there. I remember taking shortcuts to school through the large estate at the back of the house, only to suffer a barrage of two-fingered gestures. Strangely though, at weekends or in the evenings when everyone tore round in their play gear, not a single nasty word was said and we all just played happily together.

I recall making my way home from school one afternoon and as I walked past one of the greens on the estate, I saw a small boy being bullied by a grinning bigger lad. Although I knew it was none of my business, the little lad looked absolutely petrified so I went across and told the bigger one to leave him be. He ran off, though to my surprise, I received no thanks from the nipper; he simply warned me what the boy's older brother would do to me when he got there. He also said I'd only made it worse for him by interfering as both brothers would probably be after him now. Nevertheless I decided to stand my ground and wait as the nipper cowered behind a tree.

Sure enough, the elder brother – who looked about my size – hurtled over the green toward me, waving his arms and screaming. I reckon I was supposed to turn heel and flee, but it was he who got the shock when I just stood still, though, in truth, I almost wet my pants. He stopped just inches from me, probably feeling a bit of a fool, and then for a few seconds neither of us knew what to do until he lunged for me and tried to grapple me to the ground. To my surprise, after a few rolls, I actually ended up pinning him down.

After he submitted, I clambered off and smugly winked towards where I thought the nipper should have been, but he was nowhere to be seen. I offered my hand to my foe, but instead of shaking it he flicked open a knife and slashed at me, shouting, 'I know who your da' is, boy!'

I turned on my heel and pelted home, not once looking back, and sighing with relief as I flew inside the house. I then ran upstairs to peek from the bedroom window, but he'd gone. The thing I found strange after that little incident was that I never clapped eyes on any of those boys again. Mind you, from then on I always took the lengthy route to and from school.

During one family Sunday dinner, Dad rose from the table and switched off the radio, which was odd because he always enjoyed listening to the BFPO programme. He sat back down and gushed, 'There'll be another mouth to feed in the Milburn household.'

We kids leapt excitedly from our seats, but I leapt higher, as no longer would I have to be the brunt of my sister's jibes at being the runt of the family. We looked at Mum but her face showed only blankness and she shrugged her shoulders, so we realised that Dad couldn't have quite meant as we'd presumed. He winked at her, and said no, there wasn't another baby on the way, but rather an African Grey parrot.

True to his word, just a few days later, a large silver cage arrived containing a grey-feathered, red-tailed parrot that Dad christened Polly. However, a few months later we discovered that 'she' was in fact a he. By then though, the talkative bird was already squawking its first string of words – 'Polly wants a chip . . . Polly wants a biscuit . . . Polly wants nuts' etc. – so, not to confuse him, he kept his effeminate name.

We soon discovered that each time he was approached he'd lunge and try to rip our fingers or any other parts he could get his beak at; not so with Dad, however. For reasons of his own, Polly would simply tilt his head and eye Dad with seemingly great affection, readily allowing himself to be picked up and stroked on the head or bounced on his knee. We four were dumbfounded.

The pair's trust and fondness for each other became notorious and anyone who ever knew Dad would know just how much the parrot meant to him. 'On occasion, Polly proved to be a pleasant distraction from the pressures of the game,' Dad remembered fondly.

Polly would be allowed out of his cage and they would sit and watch television, with us cowering in the background, yet the second Dad left the room, he'd swoop and soar over our heads, straining his neck to peck anyone in his flight path. However, as soon as Dad returned, the bird would settle in all innocence on his shoulder. I don't really think Dad ever believed our tales of his antics though. 'The poor bird must have been startled into doing that,' he said, clearly in denial.

On occasion the unshackled parrot would even follow him out to the garden and perch on the lawnmower handle as he cut the grass, although one day, as Dad was washing the car on the front drive, a passing wagon backfired and the bird shot off over the chimneys and away. Dad was distraught and searched everywhere for the rest of the day and night.

Next morning, Mum, a posse of neighbours and we kids were sent in various directions, though sadly returned empty handed. Even Mum became fraught. Next day, Dad called to ask the soldiers of the local army barracks for help and amazingly, dozens agreed as many of them recognised him and his obvious distress. But still no parrot.

Thankfully, the next morning, an excited neighbour arrived to say she'd found Polly perched on her washing line, though after approaching him he'd flown into her open coal shed; she'd then slammed the door behind him. Dad had already left for training, so it was left up to us kids and Mum to get him out of there. Armed with a tennis racket and his cage, we followed the neighbour.

We knew Polly had no fear of tennis rackets, as he'd already chewed and spat the guts from two others over the back garden, so we opened the coalhouse door. He weighed up the choice of open cage or racket, hopped cheerfully on the latter and allowed us to carry him home.

That afternoon, a happy Dad and Polly were reunited and were simply left to frolic about the floor like two long-lost brothers.

In the November of 1957, Dad had flown back to Newcastle to sign copies at the launch of his sporting autobiography *Golden Goals*. He had been approached by Stanley Paul Publishers of London to write it, so sat down and used the literary ability he'd learned while putting pen to paper for his weekly sports column in the Newcastle *Chronicle*. All the same, once edited down south it read more like something scribed by Noel Coward, using words like 'happy chappy' and 'gay little fellows', even a mind-boggling 'then nature had its biggest prank with us . . .'. Although certainly not written in Dad's native tongue, the book nevertheless sold well in both England and Northern Ireland, and he became the first ever United player to have a book published.

'While in Newcastle, I decided to part company with my little coach business. Because of the distance I could no longer have "hands-on" control, so began to search round for something else to safeguard our futures.'

Occasionally, the Linfield team stayed at the impressive 70-bedroom Pickie Hotel, located in the nearby seaside town of Bangor and Dad became friendly with the owner. After a few meetings with this man, Dad was persuaded to invest his £1,000 signing-on fee and more in the business, assured that should he ever decide to quit football he would always have the job of hotel manager to fall back on.

'Laura and I loved Northern Ireland and its open, friendly folk and the three kids had lots of new friends, so no one wanted to leave. We thought we couldn't go wrong so I agreed to part with the cash.'

Around this time, Dad brought home a cracking surprise for Mum – a little red Isetta Bubble Car and after tying a flowing white ribbon over it he proudly drove it onto the drive. She was overwhelmed.

The cute little thing also sported a canvas fold-back sunroof, so with a child or two perched on the back ledge behind the driver and front passenger, it was easy for them to poke their heads into the fresh air without feeling crushed. Mum proudly drove us everywhere in her 'modesty blowing' single-front-door-opening car, which she nicknamed 'Little Isa', albeit never at any great speed, but we always got there in the end and in what we all considered great style.

As Linda was the tallest and eldest, she always commandeered the passenger seat, so Betty and I were relegated to the rear shelf with our heads poking out. One day, after a rainstorm, we ventured out for a run, with Mum skirting around most of the puddles – if she saw them in time. Sitting higher than her and acting as lookouts, Betty and I peered warily ahead. However we were forced to screech a warning. Ahead, a huge puddle flooded the entire road.

Most sensible folk had slowed down to a snail crawl, but when it came to our turn to wade through, a smirking bus driver approached from the opposite direction and put his foot down to swamp the car with a wave of filthy brown water. It took days for her to dry out again.

Dad made regular return trips to England to watch Newcastle play – a lot of Irish League games were played on a Friday night, which left his weekends free. However, as he paid for all the trips from his own pocket, it proved too expensive for us all to go, though he and Mum felt much happier now that she had her own mode of transport to travel where she liked with us kids.

One weekend, he wanted to meet up with the Newcastle United team in Manchester, but the only available flight was a cargo one to Australia, via, of course, Manchester – only it happened to be loaded with a bunch of malodorous live pigs. Nevertheless, in sheer desperation, Dad managed to persuade the sympathetic pilot to take him on board, though he was told he'd have to sit in the rear surrounded by the pigs. As they became airborne, the jovial pilot saw the funny side, roaring with laughter as he sang, 'Seven little pigs, sitting in the back seat, kissing and a hugging with Jack . . . so why don't one of you come up and sit beside me and this is what the little pig said . . . altogether now, 1,2,3 . . .'

The 1958–59 season kicked off with a great 9–1 win for Linfield over Crusaders, in which Dad notched six goals. At 34, he felt absolutely on top of the world, filled with a brand new lease of life and determined to better his tally for the previous season. Sadly, his ambition did not make everyone in Ulster happy and he received his first ever batch of hate mail: unambiguous threats of ambush, leg and arm breakings. 'I had never received anything like that in my life, so obviously it worried me greatly,' he remembered.

He decided to discuss the situation with some of the other players, but they simply told him not to take it too much to heart. It had happened more than once before and was directly related to the religious differences in Northern Ireland. After all, Dad was playing soccer for the most prominent Protestant club in Ulster and many of the supporters of Catholic teams would never be enamoured with him banging goals past their goalkeepers.

Dad was dumbfounded and saddened: 'I was only there to play the game of football and certainly not to get involved with any religious politics I knew nothing about. I was simply a sportsman.'

However, he decided, at least for the time being anyway, to keep it all hushed from Mum. He would throw every letter on the fire, explaining them away as just junk mail, but still they continued to arrive right until the end of the season.

Success on the pitch continued nonetheless and Linfield finished at the top of the pile, ensuring the club's participation in the 1960 European Cup. They also won the City Cup and Antrim Shield, with Dad's tally of 56 goals beating his previous season's by one.

In 1958, Dad gave Northern Ireland a more than willing hand during their World Cup campaign, after Linfield paid for him to join the Irish squad in Sweden, the idea being for him to study the different techniques, tactics and training. Danny Blanchflower and Peter Doherty though, knew the value of his keen eye and so sweet-talked him into acting as their spy. He studied the future opposition carefully, attending matches of West Germany, Czechoslovakia and Argentina, and on the basis of some of his findings the Irish prepared to do battle.

Northern Ireland defeated the Czechs 1–0 in Halmstad, followed by a tough 2–2 draw with the West Germans, but then suffered a defeat at the hands of Argentina – though they had still done enough to get into the play-offs. There they once again beat the Czechs, this time 2–1 during extra time.

The Northern Irish squad and fans were ecstatic, but their luck finally ran out after they fielded a weakened and injury-blighted team against France, who kicked them into touch. Nevertheless, everyone in the squad knew they could head home with their head held high.

Being behind the scenes and watching football instead of playing it had given Dad a totally different perspective on the game, so after the Irish officials and players made a point of warmly thanking him for his positive, valuable contribution, he made a decision: 'I decided to concentrate my sights on becoming the future manager of Linfield, once I'd scraped the mud from my boots for the final time.'

Sadly though, one problem would not go away: he continued to be the recipient of sickening threat letters. Prior to the start of Linfield's next campaign, the situation worsened. 'I slumped despondently on the sitting-room sofa. I'd just torn open a particularly descriptive warning letter, signed by "one of those who took care of Jimmy Jones".'

Jimmy, a Belfast Celtic centre-forward, had been purposely injured during some particularly sickening crowd trouble back in 1951. More letters continued to arrive throughout that season, though he tried his best to push them to the back of his mind.

Before that season's end, Charlie Mitten, Newcastle United's intriguing new manager, had made several scouting trips to Windsor Park in his search for new talent. One in-form player in particular really caught his eye . . . Jackie Milburn.

'Charlie told me he desperately wanted me back at United, to play me on the right wing alongside Ivor Allchurch, Len White, George Eastham and my old pal Bobby Mitchell. Bobby was just two months my junior.'

Mitten saw Dad as the icing on the cake to re-kick United's flagging fortunes. The 'cloak and dagger' offer and the menace of the threat letters hanging over him proved just too much for Dad, so on 20 July 1959, after careful deliberation, he asked his friend, Malcolm Brodie, the sports editor of the *Belfast Telegraph*, to pen his resignation. 'I used the pretext of a new family business venture in Newcastle and Laura's ill health as my reason for wanting to be away.' Dad then handed it in to the Linfield board.

They studied it carefully, but some of them had heard rumours of a possible return to Newcastle United and asked Dad outright if they were true. 'Never a good fibber, I feebly denied it. But they gave me a knowing look and sent me home to think things over.'

Two days later, after a number of home visits from various Linfield officials, Dad withdrew his resignation. 'They told me that although the club were absolutely powerless to prevent me leaving and could not stop me taking up a coaching position elsewhere, they could and would still retain me as a player. This would prevent me playing for any team in England.' Both his and Charlie Mitten's plans for a 'reincarnation' at St James' Park were well and truly scuppered.

With both hands now firmly tied behind his back, Dad had no option other than to remain at Linfield – that is, if he wanted to continue enjoying the only thing he had ever known: playing his beloved football. He also remembered that the very same circumstances had defeated his great hero, Albert Stubbins, and also Raich Carter, who had both been left to putrefy on a club-retained list.

His remaining at Linfield now meant covering up the real reason behind it, so he duly declared to the press that he'd been persuaded to stay by the Linfield board. Later though, he admitted openly to a few press boys that he had indeed received a tentative enquiry from Newcastle, but made light of it: 'The fear of not being picked for a game might just cause me to chop off my legs.'

When Robert Howard, a reporter with the *Reynolds News*, asked Mum if she was glad to be staying in Ireland, she could only reply that at least she was happy she now knew what she was doing. Inwardly she was terribly embarrassed at her 'poor health' being used as part of Dad's excuse for leaving – or threatening to leave – as he had done when at Newcastle. She reckoned by now that most folk would expect to see him pushing her along the promenade in a bath chair, while wrapped in a nice warm woollen blanket – and her only 30. Up until then, she had reportedly suffered three mental breakdowns and umpteen severe bouts of chronic bronchitis, whereas in fact, she was really as fit as a butcher's dog.

Not long after, the *Newcastle Journal* newspaper presented Dad with a little solace when they offered him the opportunity to become a freelance sports journalist, which at least meant some form of contact with United. When Newcastle's 1959–60 season kicked off, he sent a heartfelt message from over the Irish Sea:

> How I envy you Northeast soccer fans today . . . the day of the big kick off! What I have missed more than anything since my departure from Tyneside has been the electric atmosphere created by the crowds at First Division football.

On Irish soil, Linfield were soon to create their own electric atmosphere, getting ready for the tough home leg of a two-legged tie against Swedish champions Kamraterna. And in front of 41,000 ecstatic Belfast fans, the team pulled off a tremendous 2–1 victory, with Dad hitting both of the goals.        .

For the away leg, six jubilant directors and a contingent of 75 confident supporters accompanied the team to Gothenburg. However, the Swedes had done their homework correctly and the brave Blues were hammered 6–1. 'I was marked out of the game and kicked up in the air whenever given a half chance. I was also suffering from acute fibrositis and couldn't head a ball.'

One thing that was for sure though, nothing could ever take away the sheer joy and atmosphere of the marvellous home-leg win.

Although he made fewer appearances during the rest of the season, Dad still netted a total of 34 goals and remained happy with his contribution as Linfield secured the Gold Cup, Ulster Cup and the single big one he really wanted for them, the Irish Cup. In that final, they trounced Ards 5–1.

With the long summer break upon them, he and Mum looked forward to a long, relaxing holiday. Although we kids loved everything about Ireland, we still missed seeing our Nana Nance, so Dad's mother, now widowed after Alec, at the age of 54, had died suddenly of a brain haemorrhage sustained during a fall, was invited over to stay and baby-sit us kids in Holywood, while Mum and Dad flew for a deserved three-week break in Canada.

While there, they planned to visit Mum's sister Betty and Betty's husband Roy, who by now had three young children of their own – David, Brian and Alan. Also, Mum's mother Molly and her second husband Ernest had emigrated out there too.

In the '50s, long-haul flights were something of a marathon, even with modern aircraft, so my parents braced themselves for the great trip. It proved to be worse than they had anticipated.

The pair raised their eyebrows on arrival at Nutts Corner Airport when the airline announced that, due to an unforeseen crisis in Africa, the majority of available planes had been offered to the French government to airlift their citizens to safe soil. However, a suitable replacement plane was already winging its way to Belfast.

Several hours later, as they peered wearily from the departure lounge window, a loud cheer went up from the other waiting passengers. This was hastily followed by a few gulps as their proxy craft thudded heavily onto the tarmac runway. The aircraft was ancient. Soon after, they were allowed to board and even though the smiling stewardesses assured everyone it was a 'fine old sturdy ship', some wit replied that he hoped it was and that it would float if the need arose.

Everyone buckled themselves in on the freezing aircraft and sucked nervously on the boiled sweets offered them to prevent their ears popping. 'I took that as a hopeful sign that at least the kite was expected to make the sky,' said Dad.

Suddenly, every bone in their body shook as the engines roared and the plane rattled down the runway to position itself for the big long run. 'We poked our fingers in our ears and nipped our eyes tightly shut as it began the charge.'

Mum grabbed Dad's white-knuckled hand, but to their great surprise the aircraft lifted smoothly from the ground and, through

glossy fixed grins, even the stewardesses appeared to be thankful
. . . but there was still an awful long way to go.

A few hours into the cramped flight, most passengers became
irritable due to the intense cold and rising hunger, but were
absolutely gobsmacked when offered only a boiled sweet when
someone asked for food. 'There wasn't a scrap of food on board, so
everyone ransacked their hand luggage to share what little chocolate
or nuts we had.' After what seemed an eternity, the plane skidded
down in Iceland to refuel, and all were briefly allowed off to cram
down a hasty breakfast. All too soon they were once again airborne.

Next stop was Newfoundland, where at last they were allowed
enough time for a proper feed, though found the leathery reindeer
steak wasn't quite to everyone's taste.

Before leaving Ireland, Mum and Dad had telegraphed her sister
with their expected time of arrival, which was now way behind
schedule, so knew Roy would be waiting for them at Buffalo, a long
drive from their final destination of Toronto. All they could hope for
was that he would wait there for them. Thankfully, he did.

Once in Canada, a relaxing first week was spent with Betty, Roy
and the kids, and also Molly and Ernest. The second week Mum and
Dad went to New York to see Dad's Aunt Bella and Uncle Roy, who
now both worked in service on Long Island. They had hardly seen
him since he'd arrived tearfully at Eton Mews all those years ago – a
runaway 14-year-old would-be pantry boy.

After returning to Toronto for the final week, they took in the
sights of Niagara Falls and many other beautiful places. They were
somewhat tearful when driven back to Buffalo to spend the night
before their morning flight home.

To fill in some time on the last night, they decided to go to the
cinema, but as they window-gazed the shops on their way, the
weary couple started to quarrel. Mum stormed off along the busy
sidewalk, but then quickly thought better of it and turned to face
Dad – but all she saw was a sea of strange faces and no sign of him
anywhere. Naturally she panicked. To make matters worse, she

couldn't remember the name of the hotel in which she was staying or even which direction it was in, so she frantically pushed her way through the crowds in an attempt to retrace her footsteps, but couldn't even recognise any of the towering buildings. Dad too was frantically searching for her and dashed back to the hotel to see if she had returned. No one had seen her, so he asked the receptionist to tell Mum, if she returned, that he had gone to the cinema and would be waiting inside.

Meanwhile, Mum still stumbled about the streets, but to her relief glanced up and saw '*Pollyanna*' emblazoned across the front of a cinema, knowing it was the film they'd intended seeing. She nipped inside hoping to find Dad there too. He was, but they couldn't see each other in the dark. Dad had simply presumed she must have by now stormed back to the hotel, so he sat tight just in case she did decide to come anyway, but it wasn't until the film was over that a much-relieved pair bumped into each other in the foyer.

Next morning, after checking in at the airport and stepping onto the tarmac, they spied the same old boneshaker that had brought them in the first instance. However, this time they were at least promised a meal on board.

On the flight to Canada, Dad had noticed there had been leg room in the seats nearest the doors, and as the airline policy was first come, first served as you boarded, he knew he'd have to get there first to secure one. He made a mad dash to head the queue.

The rest of the bewildered passengers nudged each other but followed at their own pace and by the time Mum boarded the plane, she found Dad sitting smugly in his chosen seat. He was soon to wish he wasn't sat there. It had been freezing during the flight out, but the pair never dreamed how cold they'd be on the return, something that was caused by the open space before them and a howling draught. All the way home they had to sit wrapped under blankets and coats, and not only that, the serving of the meals began at the other end of the plane, so they were past themselves with hunger by the time they got theirs . . . and it was cold.

Back home, we kids were having a whale of a time too, in particular on a day trip to the seaside town of Bangor with Nana Nance. While all of us strolled casually along the promenade, Betty and I got our beady eyes on some rowing boats for hire on the jetty below, but Nana, quite rightly, refused to allow us to take one out, as I was only eight and Betty ten. Eleven-year-old Linda showed no interest whatsoever and insisted instead on being taken to the nearest sweet shop to spend her pocket money. Betty and I claimed we were not hungry in the slightest and told them we'd wait outside, but the second they went inside, we pelted down to the jetty to hire a boat from a boy not much older than us.

Nana Nance paled as she came out of the shop and spied us waving from the boat below, which now bobbed precariously on the tide. Quickly we became our heroes – Betty was Captain Pugwash and I was Tom the cabin boy; however, neither of us could row the thing and soon our joy turned to tears as the crashing waves hurled us toward the harbour wall.

We swirled and spun and could see Nana crying at our plight. She left Linda on the promenade and dashed down to tackle the boy who'd hired us the boat and, though unable to speak, frantically gestured towards us.

The boy simply smiled at her, untethered another boat and calmly rowed to our rescue and towed us to safety. He did receive a severe tongue-lashing from Nana, but just stared blankly as if he'd heard it all before. And he had our money.

Shortly after Mum and Dad's arrival home, we all bade Nana a tearful farewell as she headed back to England, but before she left the four of us agreed to keep our little nautical jaunt a secret. For Dad, the 1960–61 campaign beckoned and he settled down to solid training.

It wasn't long into the season before the first intimidating letter arrived. This one was different though, as it was much more personal. It stated that if Dad was to ignore the content and score against a certain team, then Mum would be followed to where the sender knew she shopped and acid would be thrown in her face. The letter accurately described her shopping route. Dad agonized over the effect the letter could have on Mum and didn't dare reveal to her its full content. He was now so sickened to the stomach that he just knew he had to get away.

He was well aware that the handful of wicked folk who'd sent him threats, idle or otherwise, represented only a tiny fraction of the province's populace of wonderful, supportive friendly folk, but the mere fact that someone had knowledge of Mum's precise shopping habits gave him many sleepless nights.

To make matters worse, not long after a second letter arrived, this time disclosing that the sender knew specifically which school we kids attended and even described our routes to and from it. The bottom line though had nothing to do with any scoring feats and read menacingly: 'Get rid of your Catholic hedge cutter or else'.

'Not only did it send shivers down my back but the whole situation seemed unreal,' Dad said later. 'I didn't even have a clue what religion the hedge cutter was. It had never once crossed my mind to ask. Why should it? Anyway, the chap concerned only trimmed our hedge for the cuttings.'

This time, Dad drove to Windsor Park with a new determination and the club officials he spoke to this time knew he meant business. 'I was definitely leaving, regardless of any conditions imposed.'

No one seemed to know just how seriously to take the threats, though all understood just what the consequences might be if they simply ignored them. It was understood that in the interest of all parties, the whole picture would not be made public. Once again, Dad's leaving was put down to Mum's 'poor' health. It was only in later years that Dad spoke openly about what had happened.

Before leaving Northern Ireland, there was still another matter to be sorted – his hefty investment in the Pickie Hotel in Bangor. Recently it had begun to emerge that all was not running so sweetly within the walls of the business. Dad quizzed the proprietor as to why and was told that bookings were not quite as keen as usual, which he explained as purely a temporary glitch, and that things should soon return to normal. But Dad was leaving the country and he had to fight tooth and nail to get just a small portion of his much-needed cash back. He felt thoroughly duped by the whole messy state of affairs. 'I vowed there and then that it would be the last time anyone in business would ever be allowed exploit my good nature or bank balance.'

Dad boarded the ferry to England a few days before us to avoid press harassment and to find us all a place to stay. He took Polly with him. We kids were distraught at leaving behind our school and great friends, especially at such unexpected short notice. At the time though, we remained blissfully unaware of the reason why.

With everything packed and ready, it only remained for Mum to wait for the removal men and put Betty and me on a plane from Nutts Corner Airport to Newcastle. Along with Linda, she could then begin their epic journey to Ashington via ferry and hell and high water (not to mention snow blizzards) in her little red bubble car.

On a personal note, I can honestly say that, although I was only eight years of age at the time, I look back on Northern Ireland as one of the loveliest places I have ever lived.

— 7 —

# Back Home

I walked through Newcastle with him many times.
Everybody would say, 'Hello, Jackie,' and he knew half the
names. He was a very well-loved character in Newcastle.

Jack Charlton

Dad arrived back at his mother's house in the Ashington rows,
though to a quite different reception than he'd hoped for. Awaiting
him were a welcoming party of eager, hungry press boys. He was
still big news in England and speculation was running riot as to
just what his next move would be. The press demanded all the
facts.

He had offers though remained tight-lipped. 'Then a bombshell
hit me,' he recalled.

Any dreams he still harboured of a return to the Magpies, or any
other League side for that matter, were suddenly shattered the day
the Football League formally declared he was no longer eligible to
play English League football for a second time.

'It was due to the fact that I'd already drawn my entitlement of
£900 from the League Benevolent Trust,' Dad explained. 'Due to my
early release from Newcastle, I was awarded the sum with the

precondition that I couldn't return to the English Football League; however, I always kept it in the back of my mind to repay the money should future need ever arise.'

The big stumbling block was that the agreement between the League and the Inland Revenue allowed the full amount to be granted tax-free and although Dad wished to refund every single penny, they, in their stuffed-shirt wisdom, decided it might somehow jeopardise the whole scheme. 'In short, my English League career was well and truly over.'

Now it seemed that non-league Ashington FC must be certain favourites to secure his signature. When Davy Davison, the Colliers' then manager, publicly offered Dad the same £20 appearance money he could have expected from Newcastle United, and also a job as a tobacco area salesman, which might just double his wage, everyone expected Dad to jump.

Meanwhile, the relentless throng of inquisitive journalists continued to thump on Nance's door. To gain a little peace, Dad would often park his car several streets away, sneak in the house and hide in a corner of the living room just to give himself time to think. His poor mother was left to answer the pack's questions as best she could, though she soon learned one statement off by heart: 'I suppose he'll just do whatever's best for him and his family.'

Dad considered the Ashington offer. The one thing that really worried him about turning out in front of the knowledgeable 'football daft' pitmen was that he'd gone there years before himself to watch an old pal of his turn out, an ex-Sunderland player called Len Duns.

Len had been a skilful, gifted player in his prime, but with the evolution of time had lost a little of the edge, so the uncompromising crowd simply booed and jeered him throughout the game, sometimes even laughing when he mistimed a pass or couldn't sprint to the ball first. Dad unquestionably didn't relish the prospect of playing a stinker in front of his own folk; he wanted them only to remember his greyhound sprints, inimitable sliding tackles and great ability to crack the ball home with either foot from just about any angle or distance. 'After giving it much thought, I declined their generous offer.'

Almost immediately more proposals from other non-league clubs streamed to him from all over the country. 'It reached the point where I really didn't know which way to turn,' he remembered. One thing was for sure though: he knew he had to forget all about turning out again for Newcastle United.

While Dad was dealing with the press, Mum and Linda were having an eventful trip home. They had arrived at Stranraer ferry terminal in the early hours of the morning. As they chugged along the quayside they peered skyward to see a swirl of ominous pink and grey billows – snow was on its way.

They sped along at 25 mph, soon finding themselves winding along the narrow lanes surrounded by a bleak, barren landscape. They were making fairly good time until suddenly the bubble car began to cough and hic. Mum eyed the petrol gauge and was horrified to see the needle hovering in the reserve zone, quite certain she had filled up prior to boarding the ferry; it wasn't too long before the car spluttered to a halt.

Luckily Mum always carried a spare gallon of petrol. She told Linda not to worry as she flung open the door, though she soon became aware of a few icy snowflakes brushing her cheeks. With not a clue as to their precise whereabouts, or even how close the next filling station might be, she grew steadily concerned.

After turning the ignition key nothing happened. She tried several times more before remembering Dad having once told her that if she ever found herself in the situation she was now in, to gently rock the car back and forth. She didn't know why but did it anyway and it did the trick, but, just at the same time, the heavens released a steady flow of white flakes.

Mum was only too well aware that the car had no heating system, so once more headed south. Providence appeared to be on their side, as just a few miles on they spied a petrol pump by the side of the road, to the front of a small shop. Thankfully, someone peeked out.

Mum hurried Linda inside for a thaw, explaining the problem to a lady, who fetched her rather glum husband to check the engine for leaks.

He returned declaring he'd found no fault after filling the spare can and car, giving Mum the impression he thought she hadn't filled it properly, or had forgotten to.

Mum paid, thanked him and plodded on, grinning as the snow ahead cleared, but wishing she had put on her sheepskin mittens rather than the now sopping woollen ones, caused by her rubbing the fogged windscreen.

Suddenly the snow returned, though heavier than before, with Isa, the car, struggling to stay in a straight line, having only two thin wheels at the front and just a single at the rear, which acted like a rudder if it snagged. To cap it all, the fuel gauge slumped once more.

Linda could sense Mum's panic and the tears began to roll, yet there wasn't a soul to be seen, and the packing snow was becoming too heavy for the wiper motor to cope. Mum knew she couldn't abandon the car on such a narrow road for fear it may be buried or crushed and if they attempted to trek anywhere, they might easily get lost.

She managed to chug on for another mile or so when mercifully the snow ceased and the road ahead appeared much clearer. They stopped briefly before descending a steep, icy hill toward a cottage, but when almost at the bottom, Mum skidded into the cottage wall and wedged to a halt. The concerned occupants darted out, made sure they were all right, and then ushered them inside for a cuppa.

Within minutes, it began to snow again, so Mum asked to use their telephone to inform Dad of their plight; however, the couple didn't have one, so told them to bide for a while and see what the weather was about to do before moving on. The man then kindly checked the car for damage, but could not find any petrol leak.

Soon the sun peeped out and the grateful pair continued their journey after being told the next village with a garage was only ten miles on. The qualified mechanic there would no doubt be of more assistance. Thankfully the cheerful mechanic quickly identified the problem as a leaking fuel hose and rectified it with a few twists of his trusty screwdriver. At last, 14 hours after leaving Stranraer, the car gasped to a halt outside Nance's Ashington house and the freezing duo were plonked before a roaring fire to defrost.

From the viewpoint of us apprehensive kids, the short time the family spent back in the mining town was a disconcerting period to say the least. Even though it was only to be for a couple of weeks, we were despatched to Bothal Primary School just down the road, where some of the local kids viewed us as a little odd.

During our time in Northern Ireland we had picked up fairly broad, fast-flowing Belfast accents, so when we spoke, the lingo simply rebounded from many a baffled ear and cocked heads. It always tickled Nana Nance though and she chortled loudly before asking us to repeat things.

One person who undoubtedly wasn't too enamoured though, was my new form teacher – a rather stringent ma'am whose name I mercifully forget. Whether it was the accent which got her goat, or the fact that I had been privately educated thus far I do not know, but when I used 'joined writing' as I'd been previously taught, she flew off the handle and poked, slapped and screeched at me to revert to print, until such time as she approved otherwise.

'Who do you think you are, Milburn, upsetting my timetable?'

I was confused and certainly not trying to be bigheaded or show off; I was simply writing English the way I'd been shown.

I also found I could easily spell the words she asked the class to spell and even skip through the simple sums she set, but this just seemed to make her more belligerent toward me, until the day she discovered I had a weak spot. Oddly enough, up until then, I had never been taught the rudiments of pounds, shillings and pence.

She chalked a sum on the board and the class scribbled merrily away, eagerly thrusting their arms in the air when they'd solved it. I was the only one left sitting with my hands on the desk staring blankly at the paper . . . and she knew it.

'Problem, Milburn?'

I explained that I hadn't yet been taught this, so she smirked as she summoned me toward her desk at the front and ordered me to sit beside her, facing the class.

Whether it was nerves, or the confusing way she explained it to me, or the tittering of some of the other kids, I have no idea, but I just could not grasp anything she was trying to show me. Each time she went through it and I said I still didn't understand, she told me how stupid I was and even at that tender age I had the feeling she was enjoying every second of my humiliation.

I was eventually sent back to my own desk and told to stay there until I'd solved the sum, and when I'd done that, to bring her back the correct answer. However, my mind simply remained a total blank no matter how hard I tried, so each time I handed her my answer, she scoffed, reminded me how stupid I was, and sent me back to my desk. 'Do it again, boy!' This went on all afternoon until the bell rang and I pelted for freedom.

It affected me so much, that I lay awake all night trying to do the sum in my head, but the mental block simply wouldn't budge.

Next morning, after Dad went out, I point-blank refused to go to school and ran across the back lane to scale the dizzy heights of the netty roof, where I bawled my eyes out. I refused to tell my mother what the real problem was – something I never did until I left the school, for fear the teacher would have made my lot any worse than it was. Mum simply put it down to me not liking the school, or maybe just missing my Irish chums.

Around mid-morning I was coaxed down and then Mum dragged me to school, apologising to the teacher for my absence and putting it down to a tummy bug.

However, as soon as Mum disappeared, the teacher hauled me

outside, where, out of sight, she pinned me against a wall and slapped me hard, hissing that she knew exactly what my nasty little game was. I only wish she'd told me, because I didn't have a clue.

Years later, I wondered if she had been a Sunderland supporter.

The effect on me was comparable to what Dad had experienced after his father's reprimand following his school triumphs, and just as he had, I never again enjoyed the same self-confidence. Even today, oddly enough, if I write anything lengthy in longhand, I always print it.

After Alec's premature death, Nance struck up a friendship with a pleasant, mild-mannered chap named Harry Brooks. Harry lived with his sister in Slough and Nance would travel down and visit them quite often. Not long after we returned from Ireland, she announced her intention to marry Harry and would therefore soon be moving south for good.

It was Nance's decision, therefore, that finally influenced Dad as to which non-league club he would join. He plumped to head for Southern Counties League team, Yiewsley FC (now Hillingdon Borough FC), which was within easy travelling distance of Slough.

Once again, the suitcases were packed and the whole family, this time including Nance, migrated south. Some relations of Harry's, Isa and another Harry, lived close-by and kindly agreed to put some of us up, while the rest stayed with him and Nance. So began Mum and Dad's search for a permanent home of our own. Once again we kids were herded into yet another new school, albeit for the short term, but it was the third within a few weeks and the fourth attended up until now.

A director of Yiewsley FC, John Brown, who was also a director of Brocarston, a large house-building company, offered Dad the opportunity to rent a house his company had purchased on a prime piece of development land in the lovely Berkshire village of Crowthorne. He took us to see it. If Mum, Dad and we kids liked living there, he would give us the first option to purchase. There was never doubt: the very second we clapped eyes on the place, we all fell for it.

Appropriately called 'Little Orchard', the beautiful old house nestled among lush fruit and lofty pine trees. Green fields surrounded it and it was reached by a stretch of drive along the aptly named Pinewood Avenue.

John explained that although the surrounding land was indeed beautiful, it would soon be covered with a new housing development, but our house would retain its own decent-size garden with a new boundary wall. It was a case of suck it and see.

With all of us being so taken with the house, we couldn't wait to get in. Without further ado, Dad pleadingly rang and somehow successfully persuaded the furniture-storage firm to deliver the whole kit and caboodle on Christmas Eve, so the family could spend Christmas Day in their new home. Mum dashed about frantically to find a last-minute turkey, which thankfully proved worthwhile, and so the next day she proudly presented it on the hastily prepared table, itself plonked amongst a mountain of unpacked tea chests. She'd worked a miracle.

One winter's evening, not long after settling in, Dad was out on business when we heard a strange whining sound in the distance – something like an air-raid siren. Mum explained it as just a warning that someone may have escaped from nearby Broadmoor Prison. She told us all to sit quietly and switched off the lights before drawing the curtains.

Soon afterwards, someone hammered on the front door and all four of us froze. Mum whispered for us to keep silent before tiptoeing to the window to peek out, but just as her hand gripped the curtains, the glass rattled beneath somebody's pounding fist. She gasped and darted back in our direction.

At that time, many tales abounded as to just who was supposedly 'shackled' within Broadmoor and our minds raced. Bang! Another thump – this time shaking the back door. Mum snatched up the heavy brass poker and stormed to the door, demanding to know exactly who was out there, yelling that her husband was getting out of the bath and would soon sort them out.

There was a short silence until a composed voice replied, though now through the front letterbox, offering profuse apologies for having startled anyone. It turned out that two of the local constabulary, having been made aware that the family had only recently moved in, were simply calling to let us know what the siren was and why it had sounded off, and also that there was no need for us to worry anyway as the would-be escapee had been very quickly caught.

There was yet another Broadmoor incident, and once again Dad was away, this time travelling by train. Before setting off on the return journey, he rang Mum to give her the time of his expected arrival at Wokingham station so she could collect him.

With the bubble car sold, Mum had to use Dad's car to fetch him, but as she unlocked it was taken aback at the thick swirling fog. She could barely make out the houses across the road and began to think twice about venturing out, but then considered Dad stuck at the station. She decided to give it a try.

As she drove along Pinewood Avenue, she barely missed several parked cars, so decided to drive a little further away from the kerb. Suddenly, a head-on blaze of lights blinded her; this was followed by the driver's honking horn. She jerked to a halt and he drew level, wound down his window and uttered a barrage of cussing. Mum politely allowed him to finish and then explained that several cars were parked at the front of the houses along the avenue and he too should be careful.

To that, he simply clicked his tongue, muttered something about useless women drivers and sped off, only to crumple his bonnet into a stationary vehicle. Mum listened for a few seconds, but knew he needed no assistance as she heard him swear after leaping from his car to unleash his boot against metal.

She pulled slowly away, but just as she approached the crossroads heard the Broadmoor siren, so immediately locked her car door.

Although the railway station at Wokingham wasn't too far, the conditions were worsening, and now she really didn't know whether to turn back or simply press on, suddenly thinking about us kids and presuming we must have been petrified to hear the siren, but hoping we'd had the sense to switch off all the house lights. She decided it best to press on, as Dad may not even be able to get a taxi.

About halfway, the fog thickened to the point where she could barely see the tip of the bonnet, so she pulled up, knowing she would have to turn back now, praying it would not be as dense on the return trip.

Winding the window half-down, she stuck her head out to listen for any oncoming or passing traffic before turning the car, but quickly wound it up as she heard rapidly approaching footsteps and then a cough. She rammed home first gear and pressed the accelerator, but slipped the clutch, so the car spluttered. Suddenly a hand groped the passenger door handle and then thumped the window. Too frightened to look, Mum screamed, slammed the car into reverse and jerked back, but the person ran with her, still trying to get in. Her heart pounded, but she daren't look at her attacker, then suddenly there was a heavy thud on the bonnet and she opened her eyes to see who was squatting there, but saw just an ordinary suitcase. She turned toward the passenger door and saw no madman at all, only a damp Dad.

The train had arrived early so he'd rung home, but we explained Mum was already on her way, so realising how bad the fog was, and that she would probably turn round, he'd decided just to leg it instead.

Not too long after, Mum and Dad, in no doubt that we kids were well settled into our new school and making lots of new friends, decided it was just the right place to put down firm roots, so took out a mortgage to buy the house – though soon discovered it would take more than one wage to pay it.

Dad's first game for Yiewsley had been a sorry affair against Bexleyheath, ending in a 4–0 mauling, although Dad took some comfort: 'I was really just glad not to be being bayed at in front of thousands of Ashington pitmen.' It wasn't long though before he could sigh with relief and found his name etched on the score sheet, smashing the back of the net many times, just as he had for Newcastle and Linfield.

After a short time, he really believed Yiewsley were on the verge of going places and that the Football League might just be beckoning. Even though the club had been professional for only two years, they were an extremely ambitious and a prosperous little club to boot, with a 40,000-capacity ground and a 28,000 populace. They also enjoyed their own floodlight system, a huge concert room and to cap it all, had London Airport within their boundaries.

However, within a month of Dad's appointment, the Gateshead-born manager, Bill Dodgin, decided to step aside. Dad was left feeling that his own presence had forced Bill out, even though he had no part in the decision whatsoever. 'For many years after the event, I still felt terrible pangs of guilt whenever I dwelled on it,' considered Dad.

After Dodgin's departure, there were still plenty of other Northeast connections at the club, as the chairman, Alf Whittit, hailed from Sunderland and there were several other Geordie lads already on the books. As the club were part-time only, training only in the evenings, Whittit was also able to offer Dad another part-time day job, as a sales manager within his car business, which manufactured Citröens and the sporty, prestigious Monarch car.

As job number three, Dad took on the responsibility of groundsman, and if not cutting the pitch, was often found donned in old splattered overalls, pacing and chalking the boundaries. Dad's fourth job arose when Reading FC's manager, Harry Johnston, invited him to coach their players one night a week. Then came an offer of job number five – from the Jewish boys school, Carmel College.

The initial contact letter failed to mention what kind of employment the college was offering, so with his curiosity getting much the better, he drove to the college to find out for himself. After driving through the beautifully tended grounds to the entrance, Dad was shown into a huge, wood-panelled room with an amazing stained-glass window.

The blinding sun streamed through the panes and Dad saw, standing within the rays, a tall silhouetted figure moving slowly towards him. He was offered an outstretched welcoming hand and a rich, deep voice requested, 'Come in, Mr Milburn. I am very pleased to meet you.'

Dad always swore that the experience was the nearest thing he'd ever had to a spiritual encounter, likening the black-robed, bearded man almost to a vision of God.

'My name is Rabbi Kapul Rosen,' the man continued. 'May I call you Jack? I have seen and admired you playing football many times and I think you would be just the man to coach our boys. What do you say, Jack, will you help us out?'

Dad was astonished and, as ever when in awe of particular folk or surroundings, wondered just what a pit lad was doing in such a magnificent place like that. 'I stuttered my reply, agreeing to give it a try for six months or so, though only part-time. But Rabbi Rosen declared he would eventually like me to become a full-time PE housemaster. He also offered full accommodation for the family and a free education for my son if I agreed.'

The generous offer stunned Dad, but he replied that he would need a little more time to come to such a big decision. He would let the Rabbi know soon. Rabbi Rosen finished the conversation by asking Dad not to take too long to make up his mind as he himself was suffering from an incurable illness.

Incredibly, the Rabbi somehow found the strength and determination to name himself as team captain when the staff football team prepared to take on the boys' team for the forthcoming annual run out in November 1961. But he had an extra special ace card up his sleeve for the particular match – the new 'gardener'.

The boys merely sniggered when he announced his new find, denouncing him further after his mediocre first-half performance as just another slow-moving decrepit and they easily notched up a 2–0 half-time lead. Just after the whistle blew to commence the second half, however, the laughing Rabbi Rosen yelled at the unassuming 'gardener' to let one fly. From the halfway line, he cracked the ball and it soared like a guided missile into the top left-hand corner of the goal.

Fluke, thought the boys, but soon after, from a distance of some 20 yards, another flier whistled past their goalkeeper, forcing the boys to rethink their strategy. But no matter how hard they tried to contain the 'gardener', he simply danced about them. Eventually the penny dropped when one of them recognised him as Jackie Milburn.

The gleeful Rabbi cackled with merry delight at the boys' torment and at full-time, left the field with Dad and a mile-wide smile. Then he announced to the boys that they may soon have the 'gardener' as their very own permanent coach.

Sadly, providence dealt a bitter blow, and over the following weeks Rabbi Rosen's health worsened. He subsequently died the following March from leukaemia.

'The College wasn't the same without the great man,' explained Dad, 'so I never took up the full-time position of housemaster, though did carry on part-time.'

The following summer, Mum and I went to watch Betty perform in her school sports day. Betty reckoned herself to be quite a runner and had deemed the 100-yard sprint her racing certainty of the day. She waved smugly at us from the starting line, before a grim determination came over her face.

The starting pistol cracked and the line surged. Betty made a slow start, though drew alongside the others with about 40 yards to go, her flushed face beaming up the bank at us – it had 'I told you so' written all over it. With the building excitement, Mum and I sprang to our feet, as Betty stormed ahead of the tiring pack. But then catastrophe struck as the elastic waistband on her runner's 'thick navy blues' snapped, causing them to encircle her knocking kneecaps. She stumbled forward a few steps, but then somehow managed to steady herself. It was too late and her laughing rivals simply hurtled past . . . all just a mere 20 yards from the finish.

Nevertheless, she gritted her teeth and waddled over the finish line in last place. Only the bum-covering vest she'd stuffed down her knickers saved her more blushes.

At home, Polly the parrot was still causing mayhem. Not only was he continuing to peck holes in the curtains and soft furniture, he'd now begun swearing at the most inopportune times.

During the summer months, his cage always dangled from a large hook just outside the front door and perched within he focused a sceptical eye on the multitude of building-site workers going about their business around Little Orchard. It wasn't long before he picked up streams of their 'site lingo', which no doubt a few of the lads encouraged.

Dad thought it best to keep him inside after hearing the first cuss. However, our house was having a new kitchen extension built, so the back end of it was always full of workmen. Now they too must have sworn like troopers when no one else was around, because it wasn't long before Polly began to spew out even more oaths.

In general, he would reserve himself until someone like the local vicar called for a cup of tea and biscuit before letting rip with his ghastly expletives. Now bearing in mind that Polly could accurately mimic any member of the family's voice, the mind boggles just as to what any house guest must have thought as the bird yelled from a separate room.

In a desperate attempt to gag the parrot, his cage was covered with a sheet during visits, but he soon wised up and was easily able to poke his beak through the bars to drag the cover down, or tear huge holes in it, through which he peeped and swore all the louder.

Our Aunt Mary and Uncle Fred paid us a fleeting visit on their way to stay with friends on the south coast, and for reasons of his own, Polly took an immediate shine to Uncle Fred. Admittedly, he was a nice, easygoing chap, but I think it was more his lack of fear of Polly that did it for the bird. Uncle Fred felt quite comfortable with the parrot sitting on his shoulder – that is, until his earlobe must have looked like a giant sunflower seed to Polly, who lunged at it. Fortunately, Polly stopped short, but always up for the last laugh, squeezed out a trail of green and white droppings that oozed its way down the back of Uncle Fred's smart jacket. At least he didn't swear.

One morning, Mum was thrilled with some good news. Her mother Molly and stepfather Ernest, who still lived in Canada, announced by air mail their intention to return to England to search round for a suitable property to buy. Soon after they came to stay with us in Crowthorne. Straight away, they fell in love with the place and so plumped to settle there as well. They hit upon a neat little bungalow not too far from Little Orchard, and at once felt right at home in their new surroundings, enjoying the lovely village every bit as much as the rest of us.

Not long after their arrival, village tittle-tattle (so it must have been right) declared that Jan and Vlasta Gabor, the creators of the renowned Pinky and Perky duo – the high-pitched, fast-singing TV piglets – were to move into a big house on a new housing estate at the other side of Crowthorne. All us autograph-seeking school kids were thrilled at the prospect of bumping into them going about their business in the village, but alas, I have no recollection whatsoever of seeing them anywhere along the High Street (the creators, not the piglets, that is).

I'd marvelled at those porkers for years and was devastated.

In the January of 1963, as we sat in the kitchen eating breakfast, the telephone rang and Dad answered it. After his conversation he whooped with joy as he replaced the receiver.

Unbeknown to us kids, he had applied for the managerial post at

Ipswich Town FC, now vacated by Alf Ramsey on his appointment as England's new supremo. Dad had already undergone a preliminary interview that resulted in him being placed on a shortlist of just two from a long line of some sixty other hopefuls.

He had enjoyed five years as player, coach and manager with Linfield and Yiewsley and genuinely felt he now had enough experience to handle the far greater responsibility of Division One club, Ipswich. Certainly he had been successful in his previous challenges.

Without further ado, he made a few hasty phone calls and bundled us lot into the car after Mum had hurriedly packed some overnight bags. Then, during the long cross-country haul, he explained why we were headed to Ipswich. He told us not to build our hopes too high, as the majority of pressmen seemed to favour the other aspirant, Reg Flewin, a former Portsmouth centre-half and current manager of Stockport County. But he was going to give it a go. In all honesty, and though it may have been wrong, we kids simply heaved a sigh and thought, oh no, not another house move and yet another different school.

On arrival, we found ourselves gawping around the foyer of the atmospheric White Horse Hotel, situated in Ipswich town centre. After Dad checked in, Linda and Betty were shown first to their twin room and then Mum, Dad and I were led a little further down the corridor to a large bedroom the three of us were to share. Inside, it contained lots of ancient, elegant wood furniture and two hefty, curtain-draped four-poster beds. It even had its own plush en suite bathroom.

Indeed the bell boy pointed out that the wonderful nineteenth-century writer, the great Charles Dickens himself, had once stayed in the very same room to pen his famous novel, *The Pickwick Papers*; hence the room was named the 'Pickwick Room'.

We marvelled at the picture-hung walls and noticed the frames were full of what seemed to be nineteenth-century paintings and sketches that gave the room a spooky atmosphere. Well, to me they did anyway, being just ten years old. When left alone there after dark, my mind's eye was thrown into overdrive.

That evening after dinner, as we sat in the lounge to watch some TV, an incredible sight burst onto the screen, causing most other folk in the room to either fold or peer over their newspapers. Three head-shaking, mop-haired young men, dressed in shiny, identical collarless jackets, jumped manically about a stage, while strumming like the clappers on their guitars. A fourth, with lustrous, flailing hair, pounded wildly on a set of drums and tapped at cymbals, while two of the front men belted out a harmonious song. 'The Beatles' was emblazoned across the bass drum. It was their televisual birth, as the nation was soon to find out.

Mum enjoyed them, though initially Dad didn't seem too impressed – no doubt having other things more significant to his life on his mind – but for a few minutes we kids were utterly spellbound.

Before Mum and Dad went out for the evening, they made sure Linda and Betty were safely in their beds and then came back to the Pickwick Room to draw the heavy curtains around my four-poster bed – after I had crawled somewhat reluctantly onto it. I knew only too well I was to be left there alone for what might be some time.

Although they left a lamp on, the second they left the room and closed the door behind them my imagination began to run riot and I just lay there absolutely scared stiff, quickly pulling the sheets up and over my head. From beyond the curtain, an old grandfather clock ticked loudly in one of the corners and chimed faintly the quarter hours. Every single floorboard in the room seemed to creak and strain at its nails; then for a while, there was silence.

Now I know *Oliver Twist* is nothing to do with *The Pickwick Papers*, and it was almost certainly due to my childish imagination, but I lay quaking, quite sure that Fagan was lurking in the room, waiting to lure me from my 'sanctuary' into his wicked world of thievery. I was sure I heard him hissing, 'Come to me, my boy', but had no doubt I would not be taking a peek to see whether he was simply a figment of my imagination or not. Eventually I managed to drift into a nightmarish sleep, until thankfully I was woken by Mum and Dad's welcome return, just as a pair of grimy hands wedged me up a claustrophobically narrow chimneybreast to sweep.

I barely slept a further wink until Dad clambered from his bed to use the bathroom in the morning.

# 8

# A Shattered Dream

Alf [Ramsey] didn't let Jackie into team talks. Alf always had
that way of looking at you and saying 'no'.

Jack Charlton

Later that same day, 28 January 1963, at midday, Dad entered the
boardroom of Ipswich Town FC, carrying with him a firm belief in his
ability to do the necessary job in hand – and why not? He hadn't failed
in football thus far, other than to suffer the occasional bad game.

When the ordeal was over, he emerged quietly, though felt he'd
'sold all his benefits' fairly well. He then took Mum to watch a film
at the Odeon cinema in the town centre, where the football club had
their own private box at the back of the auditorium, and for a
couple of hours 'we just sat in silence, barely casting a glance at the
screen, before returning nervously to the ground'.

One of the press boys told them that Reg Flewin had emerged
after his one-hour interview looking extremely confident and
bearing a broad smile. Camera bulbs had flashed all over him and to
many of the waiting journalists the whole thing now seemed a
forgone conclusion.

Undeterred by their early assumption, Dad took Mum for a hand-in-hand stroll across the frosty Portman Road pitch to give her a player's view of the stands. 'As edginess crept in, I pondered whether the press boys may just be right.'

They paced up and down for what seemed like an age, until they noticed the club chairman, John Cobbold, running briskly in their direction from the far side. Dad whispered to Mum, 'This is it.'

Unsmiling until he got close, Mr Cobbold's face suddenly burst into a huge grin as he offered an outstretched hand. 'Congratulations, Jack. You've got it, mate!'

As the cheerful trio made their way back to the meeting room, the sceptical, scoop-hunting press queried whether Dad would even be offered a contract, to which Mr Cobbold replied quite simply, 'He can have one if he wishes.'

However, Dad made his views perfectly clear by resolutely declaring, 'I don't want a contract, it's as simple as that. I think it's up to me to prove myself first.'

We kids were waiting impatiently back in the hotel lounge, but the look of euphoria on Dad's face as he raced over to us said it all. We were, of course, thrilled for him, but the very thought of being uprooted once again put something of a dampener on the whole occasion; we had all found Crowthorne a brilliant place to live, play and be schooled in. However, an astute Dad knew that the quick route to his children's hearts was through their ever-gaping, sweet-crazed mouths and thereby decreed an instant trebling of pocket money following the move to Ipswich. It certainly helped ease the heartache of another wrenching move.

The club house on Henley Road in Ipswich was beautiful. Large and detached, it had a long back garden with a small, tadpole-filled ornamental pond and backed onto open farmland. The immediate neighbours, the Gilberts, proved to be a nice friendly bunch too. From day one, everyone settled in great. My sisters and I were then introduced to our new schools, where the staff and pupils alike could not have been more helpful or friendly.

It's such a pity that Dad, the only reason for us being there at all, was not receiving the same response from a certain quarter at the football club. All the directors, secretary and ground staff were extremely helpful to him, but the immediate problem was that it was part of the deal for Alf Ramsey to stay on in an advisory capacity until the end of the season. Initially, Dad was thrilled about being able to receive sound advice from someone of the calibre of Ramsey, but as time progressed, he was gradually forced to change his mind. Dad began to realise that Ramsey's staying was not quite in the advisory capacity he had anticipated, but more of an outright refusal on his part to let go of the reins.

Quite understandably, Dad, as the hypothetical 'new broom', felt a trifle uncomfortable and restricted in many ways by Ramsey's domineering presence and was seldom given any time alone with his inherited squad – even to the point of being excluded from any of the team talks. 'I quickly realised I was very much *not* in the hot seat,' Dad would reveal later.

Prior to his arrival, he had watched Ipswich play a couple of times and already knew he'd spotted many of the team's strengths and weaknesses. He felt their characteristic style of play – without two wingers and using two men up the middle – which, although it had previously caused opposing teams many a problem in defence, was now well sussed and that their style of play would have to change dramatically to put them back on the right track.

Maybe this was the core of the problem. Dad had hinted to the all-eared press that he would possibly need to make changes, as most new managers do, if for no other reason than to keep the squad on their toes and bring out the best in them. But their troubled ranks seemed to close against him and his plan misfired badly. Although Ipswich had just won the First Division title the previous season, the current campaign was going badly long before Dad arrived, and Ipswich languished very near the bottom. 'Most of the players were certainly past their best, for want of better words,' Dad explained.

The fans knew it, Ramsey knew it, the directors knew it, Dad knew it and worst of all, the players themselves knew it, but with little ready money in the kitty to help buy any 'quality' players, it was going to be a long hard slog to the end of the season.

Of course, with Alf Ramsey still around, if the team dropped down into the Second Division Dad would inevitably be blamed as the new manager; however, if they avoided it, then Ramsey would be given all the credit. It was a real Catch 22. 'The euphoria that had enveloped me on my appointment seemed to be rapidly melting away and I felt a little like a pawn . . . but out of the game.'

The weight of it all soon became noticeable at home too, as Dad offloaded some of his frustration on the family. Nothing at all untoward, just the odd unnecessary snap at trivial things. He wasn't like the old happy Dad of the previous month, but more like the frustrated Newcastle player he had been before he left.

We never knew until later that he had been left to make himself scarce during Ramsey's team talks, but I think the icing on the cake of frustration was when he asked him for a look at the players' reports and scouting files. Dad was uncouthly handed the name of just one solitary Scottish full-back and the address of a part-time scout in Scotland.

Truly agitated, he rang both former teammates Bob Stokoe, the current manager of Bury, and Joe Harvey, now in the red hot seat at Newcastle. Both advised the same – speak without delay with the directors. 'Take no more bloody shit!'

Dad heeded their recommendation and hastily arranged a parley with chairman John and his brother Patrick Cobbold – a couple of prank-loving, emblematic, former public schoolboys, who, at the time, owned the Tolly Cobbold Brewery in Ipswich. After airing his grievances about his treatment and his thoughts on changing the team around, Dad was 'patted somewhat patronisingly on the shoulder and reassured that Mr Ramsey's shadow would only hang over me until the end of the current season, so to please wait until then'. After all, he had given his prior agreement to the existing set-up. Then, as had happened time and time before in the past, the age-old 'self-belief' malfunction cut in and Dad simply agreed to be tolerant until the season's end – drop or no drop, Ramsey or no Ramsey.

Looking ahead, he thought it best to get on with the business of scouting for new players and drove thousands of gruelling miles all over Britain in his search for new talent. With relatively little cash to spend though, he could only buy a few youngsters for peanuts. Still, he reckoned among them, he'd bought one or two cracking ones for the future, but the pressing problem still remained and these new buys would have to develop and bide their time . . . something he did not have a lot of.

Suddenly he found himself doing something he had never done before, and that was to seek solace with a gin bottle. Too embarrassed to drink in front of Mum and us kids, he would splash out on a bottle and sit alone at the club or in a hotel room when away scouting and sip until he'd blotted the parts from his mind that he'd intended. Later, John Gibson spoke to Dad about this period:

> I talked about his drinking with him for quite a while. Jack put pressure on himself and he was so concerned that it got him down. He would sit in the office in a darkened room and have a drink. He was too nice – all the great managers have a cutting edge, a ruthless streak. He didn't have that and it became too much for him.
>
> I know lots of players who have drunk, but that was never the case with Jackie. That's why it was such a surprise when he told me. For a short period one of the answers was to sit in the dark room. It was an off period and certainly the Jackie I knew wasn't that Jackie.

Dad's drinking wasn't heavy by many people's standards. Just one or two glasses waved their magic wand for him, even though he claimed he was 'knocking it back like it was going out of fashion'.

This was perfectly understandable considering that previously he'd been a virtual non-drinker. To him it probably felt as if he'd just downed ten pints of ale at the local social club, but although the amount he swallowed may have seemed vast, especially if the room swirled, the simple truth is – mercifully – he just couldn't hold his liquor.

This was borne out years later when he and Mum attended a function at the John Jacobs Golf Centre at Gosforth Park in Newcastle. He only drank three halves of lager and lime that evening and Mum had to help him back to the car, which of course she drove. Once home, as she helped him totter up the stairs, he asked her to make him a banana sandwich and to also bring him up a glass of milk. He kept repeating to her how sorry he was for being such a nuisance, but after returning with his sandwich, she discovered him fast asleep and snoring his head off.

At the end of that season, as luck would have it, the club successfully avoided the plummet, thankfully not creating history by being the first club to win the English First Division title only to be relegated the following season. Finally, Ramsey did let go of the leash, though he was still a regular visitor to the ground as he had a house in Ipswich.

At school, we kids endured a mixture of reactions to the team staying up.

'It wasn't your Dad who kept them up, it was Alf Ramsey.'

'Your Dad has done a great job with that bunch of old crocks. I hope he buys a new team now.'

'The both of them must have worked together well.'

'They'll be playing Newcastle in the Second Division next year, then in another two years it'll be Hartlepool – they're always lurking at the bottom of the Fourth.'

Suddenly, it seemed like some days a punch-up was never far away. Not so much for Linda and Betty, but with me being a lad, I was expected to face the music and not just stand there and take the insults. I soon found some lads were prepared to rile me until I snapped and went for them first and it was pretty hard to live with. In those days, the challenge was always, 'Boxing or wrestling?'

Being only 11 years old and quick and wiry, I always preferred the latter, simply because if the grapples became too painful I could usually squirm away. Anyway, once entwined, a probing finger up the nostril or a thumb in the ear generally proved less painful than a direct line of white knuckles thudding into the bridge of your nose. Most fights were fair, but when I say that, I remember being goaded into one that certainly wasn't. The charlatan in question squared up to me and I gawped at his much bigger frame as he challenged, 'Boxing or what?' I of course plumped for wrestling, but as I assumed my stance he lunged forward and thumped me on the chin. As I reeled, all I could think was what a cheat he was, but to make matters worse, he belted me again. It was all over and all the 'sporting' beliefs handed down from my father flew straight out the window. From that day, I vowed never to put too much faith in what others told me, so I suppose it may have been a good lesson learned.

During the long school summer holidays, Dad was barely home, even though the football season was over. He never relented in his search for new players, following up almost every single report personally. What had changed was that the reports were now being forwarded to him by the new network of scouts he had organised.

Among other new scouts was his brother-in-law Les Common, a former amateur Tow Law player. Based up in Northumberland, he was married to Dad's sister Mavis, and was fast proving himself to be something of a gem as he scoured the Northeast pitches for raw, young talent. Quite a substantial number of his discoveries eventually made the professional grade, if not at Ipswich Town then at other clubs. At long last, Ipswich were beginning to secure a youth policy.

It was a real mind-churning time for Dad though. 'In one sense, I was really pleased that Ipswich had clung on in the First Division, yet with the limited cash I had to spend, I often wondered if a drop into the Second might have given me a better chance to rebuild at the lower level to give some of the youngsters more of a chance to mature and establish themselves.'

At this time Mum was feeling the boredom. We kids were forever out playing and Dad was away such a lot, so someone from the football club recommended her to take up outdoor bowling, telling her what a nice friendly bunch they were at Ipswich Ladies Bowls Club. She jumped at the chance, though worried a little – she was only 35 and wondered whether she might just be a little young for the game, which was, in general, a more mature person's game. During her first visit however, she soon felt at ease as smiling ladies of all shapes, sizes and ages made her warmly welcome.

Dad was only too pleased that she was to take up a hobby, so he went out and bought her a moped with saddlebags in which to carry her bowls and apparel – so she quite happily 'sped' her way down to the bowls club on the outskirts of the town centre. Linda would often follow her down on her bicycle, frequently giving Mum a few minutes' head start, though she would always end up at the club first. Each time she would pass her on the steep downhill run, upon which Mum would nervously seize on the brakes and slow to 15 mph, her pleated bowling skirt swirling with the G-force. It got her there though, but for us kids, watching her hare back up the bank when the game was over was an even better spectacle.


The 1963–64 soccer season got underway. Ray Crawford was sold to Wolverhampton Wanderers, so Dad could wheel and deal with the profit to buy, among others, Joe Broadfoot, Gerry Baker, Danny Hegan and Frank Brogan. Joe Broadfoot was an exciting player who really got the crowd buzzing when he would suddenly cut in from the wing to let one fly at goal. Fair enough, a lot flew over the crossbar, but it was the anticipation of what might happen when he had the ball at his feet that really sparked the crowd.

However, it wasn't enough and some disastrous results followed.

Ipswich were beaten 7–2 at home by Manchester United, 6–0 at Bolton, 6–0 at Liverpool, 9–1 at Stoke and 6–3 at Tottenham. 'My health was rapidly beginning to suffer and my personality changed almost beyond belief,' Dad explained.

We kids never really understood the tremendous pressure he was under, all we knew was that on some days, if we made any sound or squabbled then it was certainly an early night for us – no messing. If only we'd known better.

Some Sundays, in a futile attempt to take his mind off the club problems, even for just a few hours, he would bundle the three of us in the back of the car and head down to Clacton-on-Sea or some other resort on the East Anglian coast. Mum would warn us to keep quiet and be on our best behaviour, but many a time we never even made it to the chosen destination.

It might just have been my swinging foot, either accidentally or on purpose, that kicked Linda's or Betty's, or vice-versa, but whoever's it was, it would spark off a screeching mini riot in the back seat which was just enough to make Dad stop the car and spin round to head back home. His nerves were shattered . . . but we never quite knew just how shattered.

During one particular Sunday outing, after being continually tormented by both my elder sisters' nipping fingers during the hot journey, I yelled at them to stop, quickly realising the effect my screech had on Dad by the grim look on his face reflected in the driver's rear-view mirror.

At the time I was sat in the middle of the back seat, between Linda and Betty, clutching an ice-cream cornet that Mum had purchased just a few minutes before. As I looked down in shame from my father's glare, his left hand stretched back toward me and flicked the cornet out of my hand toward my face, and it landed smack on the end of my nose. Of course the other two thought it was hilarious to see me splattered, but I didn't really see the funny side and burst into tears. But the damage was done and the car completed its habitual U-turn for home. Mum turned to me from the front passenger seat, but sniggered herself, and of course the other two were helpless by now. What upset me the most though, was the fact that Dad just kept on driving for home, and all the way never lost the scary, strange look on his face. It seemed just like he'd had enough of everything.

Never again did we dare squirm or shriek on the back seat during a Sunday outing, sometimes even sitting on our hands for most of the journey.

About this time, a sixth member nosed its way into the Milburn family – a little Yorkshire terrier called Yorky, though not everyone was happy with the newcomer. The very second Polly eyed the dog he hated him, which we all put down to jealousy. He hated it when Dad patted Yorky and would hop around his perch and swear like a trooper.

The back garden of the house was surrounded by timber-slatted fencing with narrow gaps which the dog would peep between, but that didn't satisfy his curiosity and soon he chewed them so they were big enough to squeeze himself through. Once through though, he always left his mark.

After that he was tethered on a long rope, which stopped just short the fence, though he quickly gnawed through that to head for one of his gaps. This time he didn't stop just next door and chewed his way through several more fences until he halted in a garden belonging to a very green-fingered solicitor. This man took great pride in his garden and spent every spare moment there – it was his escape from the pressures of work. The dog destroyed it. I never believed a solicitor would know such swear words. We all came out on hearing the rumpus, but as soon as the dog yelped we guessed what must have happened. For a few seconds we hid behind the fence, though knew someone would eventually have to face the music. In the end Mum bravely volunteered to attempt to use her apologetic charms on the solicitor. Dad went with her just in case that failed.

The chap took some calming down and the damage had to be paid for; however, as it would never be allowed to happen again he accepted their sincere apologies. Dad was scarlet when he returned.

Following that, he sought advice from a Yorkshire terrier breeder, who insisted, 'Strap a wide stick to his collar, Jackie, and that'll do the trick.' This was meant to prevent the dog poking any more than its head through the gaps and for a short time it worked, until one afternoon Dad peeked out of the house to check on him and, needless to say, he was gone, and so were the solicitor's freshly replanted flowerbeds.

Yorky quickly found himself living on a large farm with plenty of wide-open spaces without wooden fences.


In the whole of his career, Boxing Day 1963 was without a doubt one of the worst footballing experiences that Dad ever had to endure. That day, he discovered just what a different ball game football management was. He understood that he could now only rely on the performance of 11 others on the pitch and was unable to make any physical contribution at all. This he found totally exasperating.

As the team sat on the train bound for London and Craven Cottage to play Fulham, Dad looked on po-faced as some of his players larked about like school kids with chairman John Cobbold. Later, he wondered if some of them had been having a sly nip or two of Christmas spirits when he wasn't looking.

Cobbold was always full of boyish pranks, as if he never wanted to grow up, a real-life Peter Pan. Dad really liked and respected the man in many ways, but, probably due to the stress he was under, could never understand why he seemed to take everything so lightly. Cobbold liked to be involved in rolling 'apple pie' beds for the players and squirting the sauce from plastic ketchup bottles at them in cafés and the like – not something Dad was used to. Or was it possible that Dad had forgotten how to have fun while under such extreme pressure? I always imagined that he and George Robledo, Joe Harvey and especially cheery Charlie Crowe must have had a whale of a time playing the jokers on some of their foreign trips.

After both teams trotted onto the pitch, Dad very quickly wished that Ipswich hadn't bothered. The team were pathetic and crashed 10–1 after a brilliant display from Fulham, who were led all the way by the great Johnny Haynes. The experience was unforgettable for Dad: 'It really embarrassed me. Straight after the game I was almost lost for words.'

During the grim return journey, a much-dejected Dad found a few strong words though and shared them with joker Cobbold and several of the players he understood to be making too light of the whole sorry event. 'Some of them just looked at me as if I was a spoilsport,' he later recalled.

Throughout his entire playing career, Dad had done his utmost to give 100 per cent and always took defeat badly. He never understood how someone could simply lark about after such a mammoth defeat.

When he eventually arrived home, all the Christmas cheer had been knocked out of him and he just walked glumly into the front room, closed the door behind him and sat alone in the dark for hours, replaying the whole game over and over in his head. This was to be a regular occurrence of his.

The return home match with Fulham was in just two days. This time Dad was determined Ipswich would not suffer the same humiliation.

'On the day of the match, I arrived at the ground almost too embarrassed to hold my head up,' he said. However, his previous barking at the players seemed to have done the trick . . . at least for that one day. Fulham were soundly beaten 4–2 and 'revenge tasted so sweet'.

Nevertheless, the poor results kept coming, spattered with just the odd victory: Burnley 1–3, West Ham 2–3, Birmingham 2–3, Nottingham Forest 3–4, Aston Villa 3–4, and Blackpool 3–4. Close results, undeniably, but with each, two more precious points were lost.

On one of Alf Ramsey's visits to the club, Dad asked him in his capacity as England manager if there were any particular players he could recommend to Ipswich. His question was answered with a brusque 'No', and off Ramsey walked. Nothing else, just a 'No'.

'That really puzzled me,' Dad explained, 'coming from a man who was purported to care so much about his former club.' Dad felt justified in saying that never once during his time at Ipswich, did he receive one single grain of help from Ramsey.

Ipswich visited Stoke City at the Victoria Ground in the March, only to be thrashed off the park with another humiliating thumping, this time 9–1. When Dad got home, he just didn't look the same anymore. The whole of one side of his flushed face and neck were swollen to the size of a pudding dish and a blood vessel above his temple was grotesquely enlarged, pumping furiously. He seemed to have little or no energy nor spark left and appeared in a total state of depression. The TV was switched on and Dad simply stared blankly in its direction, showing no reaction whatsoever.

His mind was made up. 'After a long conversation with Laura and plenty careful consideration, I decided to offer my resignation, but Mr Cobbold insisted he wanted me to stay at the helm, even if the club went down.'

Cobbold then went on to tell him that he was quite sure it was only a matter of time before the club's fortunes would take a turn for the better – now so more than ever, with the new youth and scouting policy firmly in place.

Ipswich did drop into the Second Division, but Dad really believed they had every chance of bouncing straight back and now, at last, he would be given the opportunity to blood some of the club's exciting young prospects at the lower level.

That summer brought a new phenomenon to the streets of Ipswich and its neighbouring lanes. The members of this movement called themselves Mods. Once or twice, a band of them on their mirrored-up scooters followed Mum on her little moped, surrounding her to poke fun, though as she wobbled between them, she certainly didn't find it quite so hilarious. The girls riding pillion howled as they thrust their transistor radios at her, blasting fuzzy music from Radio Caroline.

One particular day they teased her all the way home, but suddenly spied Dad on the driveway washing his car. The leading riders recognised him and quickly vamoosed, leaving Dad to shake his fist at them. Thankfully, they never pestered Mum again, but soon after her trusty moped went the journey.

As an occasional special treat (not that we kids deserved many), Dad allowed us to use the club's private box at the Odeon Cinema, and during one memorable visit, we were privileged to see, live on stage, a raw, relatively unknown band called The Rolling Stones. We thought they were brilliant but Dad left after ten minutes. He still preferred Nat King Cole.

Another visit saw us gawping at Gerry and the Pacemakers who were starring in the pantomime *Babes in the Wood*. We kids, among others, were lucky enough to meet them during the interval, but all of us gasped when we clocked their thick orange stage make-up and lipstick. How it 'softened' their tough Liverpool image.

In August, the 1964–65 season kicked off with great promise. Sadly Ipswich got off to a thoroughly bad start, managing to pick up only one point out of a possible eight. Dad sank very quickly to the very depths. I still wonder if the gin did too, as he claimed.

'I reflected on the 40,000 miles I'd driven over the past 18 months scouting for talent, and that did not include air or rail travel. Though it was still early days in the season, I felt completely done in and no longer able to stand the pressure. I handed in my resignation.'

To Dad's great surprise, no fewer than nine players, led by Gerry Baker and stalwart Billy Baxter, threatened to walk out, believing Dad had been sacked. Although they were wrong in their assumption, Dad was very touched by the display of loyalty, even though it was not enough to make him want to stay. 'I knew only too well the writing was on the wall and valued my health and family life too much,' he said.

Dad drove straight home from the ground and stood, ashen-faced, in the hallway. Mum was worried sick for his health and suggested that she start packing right away; she just didn't want the press boys hounding him in that state. She knew he needed to be away. She then ordered he either go straight upstairs to bed or jump on the next train to Newcastle. Without further hesitation, he grabbed a few items of clothing, stuffed them in a suitcase and asked Mum to drive him to the station. He was going home.

Mum dropped him off and returned to the house. She knew she would have to face us kids with the grim news, so she sat us down. By the look on her face, we guessed immediately there was something wrong. She explained the situation as best she could, but we were totally shattered – not only for Dad, but also for the fact that it meant yet another upheaval. I think all of us just sat and bawled our eyes out for hours.

I remember then suddenly springing from the settee and running outside, telling her I wasn't going. Selfish as it may seem, I couldn't bear facing another move and losing all my friends. Although only 12 years old, I now had a steady girlfriend called Zena and I was besotted with her. I ran from the front gates and up the Grove to my best mate Peter Ramsey's house (no relation to Alf) to break the news. 'You can hide in the cornfields and I'll bring you food whenever I can,' Peter whispered out of earshot of his mother.

We went outside to hatch our plan further when a fretting Zena and her pal Cynth came running up the Grove. They had heard the news of Dad's resignation on the radio.

With the passing of years, I think a lot of adults don't really remember the feelings of puppy love and the effect it has on kids. I was heartbroken. All four of us sat quietly in the middle of a field until reality kicked in and we grew hungry. It was then I accepted that the happy life I'd enjoyed in Ipswich was simply coming to a sad end. I went home. When I got in Mum was very sympathetic, as she'd suffered the same reaction from Linda and Betty.

That night, all we could do was take stock and think about Dad's poor health.

Next morning, we discovered Mum had been working right through the night, and all the paintings, ornaments and anything else that could be packed were wrapped and ready to be placed in tea chests when the removal men arrived in a couple of days. Even so, there was still a lot more to be done and we all set about mucking in. Later, the front doorbell rang and it was none other than the great Danny Blanchflower himself. He'd just popped in to see how Dad was faring, so Mum explained that they'd felt it best he leave Ipswich straight away.

As they sat in the kitchen chatting, we kids couldn't have wished for a better cue to escape, so tiptoed quietly out from the front door – once we'd secured Mr Blanchflower's autograph, of course. Linda and Betty headed their way and I headed mine, which was straight back up the Grove in the hope of finding Zena. Sure enough, she was there with Cynth. We spent the rest of the day in depression.

That night, an excited Dad rang Mum with some great news that had made him feel much better. He had managed to secure a home for the furniture and us, albeit temporary, just a few doors away from his sister Mavis and brother-in-law Les in Morpeth, Northumberland, where they lived with their own two kids, Dennis and Anne.

To help him relax that day, Dad had gone out to play a game of golf and by sheer chance met up with an old acquaintance on the course, a schoolteacher called Keith Swailes. Keith could see he was not looking at all well and asked him what his future plans were.

Dad, needless to say, stressed that his priority was to quickly find somewhere to live in the Northeast so he could bring the rest of the family home. He explained the house he'd lived in at Ipswich belonged not to him, but to the club he no longer managed. Keith showed immediate sympathy and told Dad to worry no more. As chance would have it, he owned a property currently standing empty on Green Lane and we could base ourselves there until such time as Dad knew what he wanted to do in the months ahead. Hence Dad was absolutely cock-a-hoop, gushing to Mum that there was now no need for the furniture to have to go into storage, or for her and the kids to be 'farmed out' with relatives. Mum told us the good news and we were really excited that Dad sounded much better in himself, though still could not help sit with faces of doom at the realisation that tomorrow we would be departing Ipswich for good and had yet to face joining another new school.

Next morning the furniture van arrived on time. Not to help matters though, all we panicking kids decided to stage a desperate last-minute revolt. Mum was just about yanking her hair out as we darted from the front door and along the road to split in different directions. One of the knowing removal men smiled compassionately at her and said, 'Don't you worry now, Mrs Milburn, they'll be back soon. We see this happen all the time.'

I had run about 20 yards when I saw Zena and Cynth half-hidden and peeping from behind a telegraph pole; she had been too shy to knock at the front door. I could barely raise a smile, though Zena said she was quite sure we'd meet up again one day and until then we'd write. We said goodbye and I dragged my feet back to the house. A sullen Linda and Betty were already there, having resigned themselves to the inevitable too, much to Mum's relief.

After ensuring Polly was securely wedged in the back of the furniture van, Mum locked the front door for the last time and piled us in the car, pulling away slowly as the neighbours waved us off. As we passed the telegraph pole Zena waved; her eyes were sad and she clasped a hand over her mouth, then she stepped onto the road and ran a few yards after the car. I was numb. Young love, eh?

One morning after we had returned to Newcastle I received a letter from Zena, but decided to wait until we moved house before replying so I could forward the new address. Once we were settled,

I decided to reply to Zena, but ended up searching everywhere for her address. It had been lost in the move. Sorry, Zena.

It was a long, cross-country haul to the A1 Great North Road and for most of the drive we just sat in stunned silence. Mum tried to cheer us up by offering to stop to buy us ice creams or sweets, or anything else that might take our fancy, but for once nothing did. Halfway up the A1, she decided she had to pull in at a rest stop for petrol and a bite to eat as she was now famished and there was still a long way to travel, but we refused to get out the car for anything, other than to nip into the toilet. I soon wished I hadn't even done that though.

To wash my hands in hot water, I turned on the wall-mounted boiler above the sink. Whoosh, scalding water covered the palm of my right hand and I ran from the toilet, screaming blue murder, to find Mum. She was busy paying the man for the petrol, but saw the agony I was in so ran me back to the toilet, quickly pushing my hand under the cold tap. The proprietor, who had heard the commotion, swiftly followed us in, gruffly pointing to the handwritten notice attached to the front of the boiler: 'Dangerous. Do not place your hands directly under the spout. To be used to fill the sink only, prior to washing your hands.' He clicked his tongue, turned on his heel and went back about his business.

Mum knew that I should have read the notice and under normal circumstances I probably would have, so she just put it down to the general stress of the day. Anyway, apart from the hurt to my pride and palm, there was no serious damage. But for the rest of the journey Mum starved, I burned and Linda and Betty froze as I dangled my hand out the window.

# 9

# Junkyard and Journalism

I always say you should never meet your heroes, but Jackie was the exception. He lived up to everything I thought of him as a schoolboy. It was a privilege to share a press box with him.

John Gibson, former sports editor of
the *Newcastle Evening Chronicle*

For the umpteenth time, everything was unpacked into yet another, albeit transitory, home. Mum and Dad could now heave a huge sigh of relief, just in time for them to put their feet up and watch the 1964 Olympic Games beamed halfway across the world by the miracle of satellite technology.

On the job front, although now just turned 40, Dad was heavily tipped by the boys on the sports pages to join his old teammate Bobby Mitchell, who was now player–manager at Third Division Gateshead FC. Bobby reckoned the pair of them still had enough spark between them to create enough pulling power to ensure bumper gates at Redheugh Park. It was now a distinct possibility too, as just two years earlier the Football League had annulled the rule governing re-entry to all players who had previously drawn their Provident Fund entitlement. (Any player who permanently intended to leave the English Football League became eligible for a tax-free lump sum from the Provident Fund.)

Dad again considered how he did not want to be remembered by the Tyneside public as just a pale shadow of his former self, his father's words swirling in his head: 'Leave them with something good to remember you by, son.' He turned the offer down flat. He also politely declined a lot of other smaller local clubs who would have relished his appearance just to attract the crowds. 'I really didn't know what I was going to do next.'

A block of shops were being constructed on the new Kirkhill housing estate in Morpeth and one of them was to be a newsagents. This pricked Dad's interest, as once the early morning papers were despatched he could leave Mum for a few hours to sell the sweets and other things, and possibly find himself a part-time job elsewhere.

He did have one hope: 'Deep down, I sorely wished above all else that the telephone might ring and Newcastle United might offer me some form of a job, maybe just with the youngsters or whatever. But they never did.'

The builder now needed a quick decision as to whether Dad would take the shop on, but there was something of a problem. There was only a small two-bedroom flat above and we were a large family of five with a noisy parrot. In the end, Dad turned down the opportunity as it would have meant farming me out permanently with relatives, while Linda and Betty would have had to bunk together in the tiny second bedroom. I secretly thanked the Lord.

Mercifully, the situation took a dramatic turn for the better when a brand-new tabloid, the *Sun*, due to hit the news stands soon, approached Dad with the offer to become their Northeast sportswriter. Dad seized the chance with both hands. 'It was a way back into football without me having to suffer the overwhelming pressures of management.'

On the strength of their offer, he decided the best thing to do would be to quickly uproot and find a new house in Newcastle – but one in which the family could stay for good this time. We all wanted finally to settle down.

The reason behind Dad's thinking was simply the logistics of travel. If he were to cover Newcastle, Sunderland and Middlesbrough then it seemed that the Toon would be the ideal place to live. It certainly had the best road links and he would always be close to the floodlights of St James' Park. So, without further ado, he and Mum began to search around for a suitable house on which to put down a deposit, which meant they'd made a solid commitment to stay.

During that interim period at Morpeth, Betty and I were installed in schools. Linda had now become of working age and so began the search for her first job. I must admit that both Betty and I found it hard to concentrate on any schoolwork as we knew we would only be there for a matter of weeks before being moved on yet again.

Eventually we set about busily unpacking boxes once more, this time into a lovely three-bedroom mock-Tudor semi-detached house in St Gabriel's Avenue, Heaton. It was certainly a nice, quiet area and we kids were warned to be on our best behaviour and zip our lips when playing outside. Of course this lasted for all of about two minutes, until we sped out on our push-bikes to explore the surrounding avenues.

The problem with the vast majority of keyed-up kids is that they cannot be quiet and we were certainly no exception, so to save any blushes in front of the new neighbours, Dad yanked us inside until our excitement quietened down. He didn't want another apple episode.

For the very first edition of the *Sun*, Dad was asked, during an interview with Frank Clough, if he was prepared to 'spill the beans' on his days at Ipswich. He replied in all honesty that he would not 'spill the beans', but simply open the can so folk could judge for themselves just what was inside. If there was one thing that Dad was not, it was a liar – he detested liars with a passion all his life. On 15 September 1964, his article read:

RAMSEY GAVE ME NO HELP

It's 12 days now since I quit Ipswich Town. Since then I've said nothing about the business. Maybe some people thought I just crept out of Portman Road, too much of a coward to face my critics. But people in the Northeast know me better than that. I never shirked an issue when I was playing with Newcastle United and I don't intend to start now.

The critics have had their say. Now I want mine. I've never been a muckraker in my life – the game has been too good to me for that – but there are some things that must be said about my disastrous 18 months with Ipswich.

I want to get one thing clear right from the start. Ipswich are a good club and the directors are gentlemen.

But I accuse Alf Ramsey! He gave me neither help nor encouragement when I took over from him. I worked with him for ten weeks and the only advice I got was that I'd have to become thick skinned to make a go of it.

I inherited from him a team that was over the top and going downhill fast. I knew it, the directors knew it, and the most disastrous thing of all, the players knew it too. Ramsey's attitude to me didn't help either. In the first few weeks I was there – Ramsey stayed on even though he had been appointed England manager – I was never invited to a team talk!

I asked him about players' reports, about their scouting files, and all I got from Ramsey was the name of one Scottish full-back and the address of a part-time scout in Scotland. Later, when Ramsey had left to take his England job, he visited us and I asked whether, during his travels looking for future England players, he could recommend any to us. Alf replied tersely: 'No'. I thought at the time: Well, that's a fine attitude from a man who is supposed to have a soft spot for his old club and the man who is asking all the League clubs for assistance.

Ramsey's attitude convinced me I was on my own in a ruthless jungle, a far cry, indeed, from the warm, human people I'd been brought up among, the folk who had gone out of their way so much to help me during my life in the Northeast.

We kept in the First Division somehow. As everyone knows, we dropped the following season, but it was a year too late for me. If we had gone down the previous season, at least I could have started rebuilding in the Second Division instead of trying to do the impossible in the First.

We dropped because we weren't good enough, and there wasn't much money to buy new players. When Ramsey left, we got rid of nine players, and only one of them was good enough to stay in the League. So I had to buy mainly young players at a small price but players I thought could do a job in the future for me if we could afford to give them grooming in the reserves. The inevitable happened. I had to push them into the first team before they were ready. But that didn't bring relief, and so we went down.

I'm convinced though, that I have given my successor the nucleus of a good team – players like Gerry Baker, Jack Bolton, Joe Broadfoot, Mick McNeil and Frank Brogan. The club says the next manager will have money to spend; that's news to me! At Ipswich I've left the basis of a good team, a scouting system and a youth policy.

This was one of the very rare occasions when Dad actually spoke out as he felt, but it was simply the truth.

With the pressure of management now off his shoulders, Dad's health gradually improved, but out of the blue he was told there was a hiccup with the *Sun* newspaper. With a mortgage around his neck, he would have to search for other work until such time as it was sorted. 'I never gave up hope that Newcastle United might yet want my services in some capacity. However, the phone remained silent.' Mum insisted that she should get out and seek work herself, but Dad would hear none of it.

Just as the bills mounted and panic set in, an old friend of his called John Jennings, who owned a large scrapyard just over the Tyne Bridge in Gateshead, heard about his plight and came rushing to the rescue with the offer of a job. Nothing fancy mind, but it meant a regular wage in his pocket every week, and with a substantial mortgage hanging over his head Dad was readily prepared to roll up his sleeves and do anything to keep the roof over the family. 'John wanted to teach me about the scrap business starting from the bottom, so I learned how to drive a crane around the scrapyard.'

We kids had never seen him really dirty and oily before, or wearing tatty overalls when he came home from work, so it came as a bit of a surprise the first time. His face was smudged too and his hands all grimy. Until that time we had only ever seen him leave or return from work in a sports jacket or a suit, except in the summer when he would wear only a shirt, generally with a smart tie.

When he returned from work on that first day, instead of just entering the house by way of the front door, as of course he always had, he crossed the threshold of the kitchen via the garage, but only after kicking off his heavy muddy boots.

Not long after that, off too went his pride and joy, the much-polished blue Austin Cambridge car, to be replaced by two little Austin Minis, one a car and the other a van, which he used daily for his work. One thing is for sure though, his appetite had returned big time and he no longer picked at his dinner plate before pushing it away as he had at Ipswich. Every meal that Mum prepared now went inside him and nowhere near the bin.

It must have been pretty wearying work though, because most

evenings, after a hot bath, he would sit quietly in his armchair and just doze in front of the television. This routine was interrupted on Wednesday and Friday nights when he and John Jennings wound their way to the local greyhound meetings at either Gosforth Stadium or Brough Park. He loved the excitement of the dogs and was really thrilled when someone named one after him: Magpie Jack. The dog won a good few races too.

In due course, the *Sun* newspaper managed to sort out its teething problems and once again approached Dad for his services. He'd missed being around the atmosphere of the football grounds so much that he simply couldn't refuse going back to them and Mr Jennings understood that all too well. He patted Dad on the back and wished him all the best, but then generously offered him a part-time job, a kind of PR role to his scrap business. He wanted him to call on local engineering companies and the like, to make sure that any scrap metal they had in their waste bins found its way to the Jennings scrapyard. Dad reckoned he now had the best of both worlds.

Linda, by now, had secured herself a job in a Newcastle department store and Betty and I were enrolled into what was to be our final schools.

Dad had taken me to Chillingham Boys School on my first day, so he could meet Mr Stephenson, the headmaster. As they stood in the playground, I distinctly remember a number of the boys whispering to each other behind cupped hands: 'Psst, that's Jackie Milburn, that lad with him must be his son'.

Long before now, I had learned to hate hearing those words, because I never quite knew what kind of a reception I would get before they got to know me for who I was and not for who my dad was. Anyway, come first break-time I soon found out.

Two or three of the big lads swaggered up to me and literally ordered me to approach certain individuals they had pointed out. My instructions were to yell at them, 'Alhayeoot!'

Now I have to admit, I had not the faintest idea what that meant, and bearing in mind that I had not lived in Geordie land since the age of five and had now inherited an East Anglian farmer's twang, the words they commanded me to say simply sounded like a Japanese idiom.

Before I dared question it, I was shoved in the direction of my first 'victim', followed by a boot up the arse. 'Go on then, Daddy's boy, get on with it!'

I reluctantly walked up to the first boy and shouted, 'Alhayeoot!'
He replied, 'No.'

I repeated it to the second and received another 'no'.

The same happened with the third and fourth until the fifth eyed me up and down and grunted, 'Aye, after school.'

I shrugged my shoulders. 'What's this alhayeoot? Those boys over there told me to say it.'

He looked at me with a different eye and his face suddenly flushed. He stomped in their direction and grabbed the one I assumed he took to be the ringleader and gave him a slap.

The others scurried off and he came back over to me smiling. 'Just as well I support the Toon, young 'un, eh? If they bother you again, come looking for me.'

I felt very much relieved, though still puzzled about the 'alhayeoot' thing, so asked him what it meant. 'It means *al* – I'll – *ha* – have – *ye* – you – *oot* – out. I'll have you out. It means I want to challenge you to a scrap.'

A nice Geordie welcome. My resentment at being dragged back 'home' was beginning to fester.

Newcastle United, still under the guiding wing of Joe Harvey, won promotion to the First Division at the end of the 1964–65 season. I'm sure Dad must have spent as much time at the ground as Joe and the players did, and not just for any newspaper gossip but for the general crack. Although he most certainly was not on United's payroll, he loved every second he spent there; after all, it was his second home.

As a journalist, he was often put in the difficult position of being given 'inside information' with regard to the various comings and goings of players. Quite often this reached him way before the players themselves knew anything. Had he been a bona fide, 'heartless bloodhound' sportswriter, then he would have sprinted to the nearest telephone box to blurt the latest 'exclusive' down the line to his story-hungry editor and probably would have received a big fat bonus for his trouble. He really couldn't do that, because if he did, then he would have lost the trust of everyone at St James' Park. What's more, because Joe was sure he could talk to Dad about everything and anything and that it would go no further, it made Dad feel as though he were a part of the whole set up. 'Which was really all I ever wanted to be.'

Anyway, Joe would always give him the nod when it was OK to go ahead and print the 'juicy stories', so Dad was more than happy, explaining that 'to go against Joe would have been to lose his faith forever, so I never did, not even once'.

As John Gibson explains, the transition from football to writing was not a difficult one for Dad:

> He was a natural footballer and so was able to be a sports journalist. His opinions carried weight because he was Jackie Milburn. Jack had contacts and his by-line on a Sunday paper meant something to the public. Joe Harvey would tell Jackie everything and Jackie printed it. I don't think he was ever going to be journalist of the year but I'm not centre-forward of the year, either! It was a great job for Jack: he played golf in the week, printed on a Sunday and spent the rest of the week smoking his Woodbines.

There was a definite spring back in Dad's step when he got up in the mornings and we all knew he found it a positive joy to face the day ahead. I only wish that I could have said the same for myself. Even though I felt very selfish about it, I just could not help but desperately miss being in Ipswich with my friends and I soon found myself falling into the trap of picking up a few bad habits from some of the 'street-wise' boys at school.

The second the bell rang at the end of the last lesson, we would rush from the school gates and pelt up the nearest back alley to light up a fag. Quite often, a large crowd of us would have to share a single Woodbine and by the time it was passed round, it was inevitably soggy and hot, so a few of us carried a pin in our lapels to prod into the stump to make it possible for us to finish it.

I wasn't alone. Often I would arrive home and see clouds of smoke pouring from the open bathroom window and knew right away that Betty was having a sly fag in there.

I think the final move back to the Northeast was, for the pair of us, the one that broke the camel's back. We were now attending our eighth school in as many years and deep down we simply weren't happy, although Linda seemed quite appeased with her lot now that she was out earning. We knew though that Mum was content and Dad was in high spirits with his lot, being back among his own folk, family and St James' Park, but that feeling of indignation was gnawing at Betty and me and many a trivial in-house argument blew out of all proportions.

A culmination of this and the arrival of our formative teenage years brought about family rifts that at the time seemed irreparable. Sometimes we just sloped around the home without speaking for days, and when we did, they were just simple terse words. Part of our home telephone number was 666 and we really did become little devils.

To make matters worse for me, I think one of the toughest days of my life was when the reality finally dawned and it was declared 'officially' that I was not going to be joining the ranks of the now well-paid professional footballers. Up until then, I had always played for my school soccer teams, mainly because I had inherited Dad's 'speed genes'. I could run like the wind and, like him, won most events on school sports days. It was different on the pitch. I had little or no ball control, even if I always carried it in the back of my mind that 'uncle' Jack Charlton had been a relatively late developer before anyone really sat up and took notice of him. So, hidden away, I practised and practised my keepy-up and dribbling skills, but about the only thing that dribbled successfully were my exasperated eyes and I couldn't even keep my socks up. The basic skill just wasn't there. I reckon Dad had probably known this from when I was a nipper and kicked my first ball, but he was just too nice to present me with the harsh fact of life. He never once forced me into practising excessively or commented harshly on my limited ability – or lack of it.

With me playing on the right wing and using my pace, I could easily outrun defenders and leave them standing, but that final cross was often just a slice to nowhere, leaving the rest of the forward line frustrated. Really, I just wasn't that hot.

The final heartbreaking crunch came when, aged 14, I travelled with Dad and my 13-year-old cousin Dennis down to Liverpool – the purpose of the trip being for the club to have a look at Dennis. He was a stocky and rugged player, a little midfield general who could read the game well and had the necessary ball skills to go with it. We stayed in a posh Liverpool hotel and were treated like royalty, but deep down I knew I was simply there as company for him. Nevertheless, I had a vivid dream that night: I was running Liverpool's front line with Ian St John and we scored a hatful between us; I woke in a delirious sweat.

The next morning, at the training ground dressing-room, strangely enough, I found myself getting changed next to none other than the great man himself. He warmly encouraged Dennis and me, and in front of the other smiling senior Liverpool players, told the pair of us to get stuck in as best we could to impress the boss man, the legendary Bill Shankly. 'Don't hold back on anything,' he said, 'this might be your one and only chance, so grab it with both hands.' I put my head down and blushed profusely, feeling far too embarrassed to admit that I was simply getting changed for a run around and that it was only Dennis they were interested in. However, within the next five minutes I felt as if a steamroller had run over me and I became as flat as a proverbial fart.

Dad led Dennis and me to a grassy area away from where the first-team players were warming up and I heaved a small sigh of relief that I was out of their view. The fact is, they probably would not have taken the slightest bit of notice anyway, but to a self-conscious adolescent like me, I was just pleased to be hidden.

Dad waved and Bill Shankly bounded across to be introduced to Dennis. Shankly then threw him a ball and asked him to run with it in and around a line of cones, which Dennis did with no problem whatsoever. He was then sent over to join in a match being played between a group of youngsters. By then I was sprinting up and down the perimeter fence, just to keep myself occupied and having the sense to do it without a football, which I probably would have tripped over anyway. I froze as Shankly shouted to me, 'What about you, young man? Aren't you going to have a go?'

I looked at Dad, who nodded and waved me over. With my tail between my legs I slowly approached them and nearly died when Shankly rolled a ball to me, telling me to repeat what Dennis had just done so successfully. Suddenly I thought, this is it – shit or bust. Reality time.

I think I hit every single cone on that short run, sending them sprawling in all directions, at the same time wishing I'd brought with me a tube of glue to stick the runaway ball onto the toe of my boot, but then that would only have put off the inevitable. I'm convinced that Dad never had the heart to bring himself to say to me the fated words, 'Sorry, son, you're not going to make it as a footballer', and this was his way of avoiding facing the issue, by letting someone else do it for him.

I glanced over my shoulder at the pair of them. Mr Shankly was shaking his head at Dad, who then looked to the ground. My heart raced as I waited for the inescapable words. Then Shankly said quite clearly, 'You're a runner, boy, not a footballer. Stick at it as you've a good turn of speed.' He then patted me on the head and ran off to join his seniors.

Even though I had fully expected what was coming, those few words cut through me like a knife. I was suddenly the lad who'd wanted a lead role in the school play only to be told he was a ham, or the wannabe racing driver who simply skids off the track at every bend. Dad asked me if I was OK, but I couldn't utter a single word, I was so choked. My eyes filled up and as I tried to focus on him through watery veils, I'm sure he was the same. Alone, the pair of us just played headers for the rest of the morning.

In the end, Dennis didn't sign for Liverpool but plumped for Aston Villa instead. I didn't have a single clue what I was going to do with the rest of my life, now that my fanciful dreams lay in tatters.

I think the culmination of this horrendous bubble-burst, the missing of Ipswich friends and the bête noir of my school, even though I'd made a few good pals like Howard McArdle, Ian Norman, Peter Crozier and Harry Ryder, now nurtured within me a profound bitterness, one much deeper than any of the family knew. I became very withdrawn, with a rebellious mind. So too did Betty.

That time was also an era of teenage exploitation by the massive recording and fashion industries.

A young American folk singer called Robert Zimmerman, employing the stage name of Bob Dylan, was busily setting Europe alight with his tour and Betty and a crowd of her pals went to see him perform at the Newcastle City Hall. So impressed was she, she breathlessly rushed out to buy any and all of his available records. The formerly relatively tranquil Milburn family home now resounded to the likes of 'The Times They Are A-Changing' and 'Blowin' In The Wind'.

The '60s 'uprising' of 'easy-to-fool' teenagers against parents with their own stolid but lifelong viewpoints had begun. No longer were there any constructive discussions on family issues, only an 'us and them' standoff from both dogmatic parties. None of us found ourselves able to back down from their specific philosophies.

Mum and Dad found this extremely hard to cope with. As with the likes of all of their generation, they had been brought up with a healthy respect for family values. Dad's shrewd words of 'You'll look back on this and laugh at yourselves', or 'You'll regret all of this in later life', for a while fell on clogged-up ears and locked minds. Of course, he was absolutely right, but it was not a healthy period in any of the family's lives and probably the least said about it the better. However, there was one incident I will never forget and that was my father really losing his temper with me.

I was 16 and had been for a run to Stamfordham with the lads on our motor scooters and while there, we popped in for a pint at the pub – and it *was* only one pint. Normally I wouldn't have bothered to have one, but this particular pub had a cellar bar with strange ceiling lighting, and it had the weird effect of making a pint of beer appear green. It was such a novelty, that we all had one, but when I arrived home and Mum sniffed the fumes on my breath, she asked outright if I'd been drinking.

From the sitting-room, Dad heard all this and completely blew his top and began to rant and rave. I then suffered the dressing down of my life, even though I was stone-cold sober. It was the stupidity of drink-driving, even in such a small quantity, that upset him.

Later, after he had calmed down, he told me that his outburst was probably only the second of his life. The first had been when Newcastle were playing an away game and his father was travelling separately to the match.

Dad had told his father to ask for him at the main entrance when he arrived at the ground so that Dad could fetch out his seat ticket, but a bureaucratic little gentleman had other ideas. Alec did just as he'd been told but was somewhat rudely told to shove off. The man flatly refused to believe Alec's story and simply would not budge. Eventually, the exchange of words led to a heated row, but the fellow still refused to check out Alec's story. Fortunately, someone just inside the doorway overheard the argument and sent a message to Dad, who rushed immediately to sort it out. Alec and the official were still at it when he reached the entrance.

As it was only minutes before the kick-off, Dad was already dressed in his black-and-white strip and he immediately saw red when he spied the distressed look on his father's face. Without hesitation, he ran at the officious chap, snatched him by the lapels, raised him from the ground and then pinned him forcefully against a wall.

It took a couple of hefty bystanders to calm down the situation, which had maybe just blown out of all proportion, but it showed what lengths Dad was prepared to go to in defence of his family. The episode only seemed to fuel Dad's passion on the pitch and he went on to score two goals that day.

In early 1967, an excited Joe Harvey had some electrifying news for Dad. The Newcastle United directors had kindly agreed to open their gates and pave the way for a Jackie Milburn testimonial match at St James' Park – after not just a little pressure from the press boys and the Newcastle United Supporters' Club.

The Supporters' Club secretary, Len Coates, wrote to the board and was given the reply from the club secretary, Dennis Barker, that they were prepared to offer Dad a suitable slot at the end of the season. Although Dad was absolutely over the moon, such was his nature that the whole affair quickly turned more into a worry and then a mad panic, and he unconfidently asked all those around him if they really thought that anyone might turn up. Dad even doubted if the Geordie public would remember or care about him: 'After all, it was ten whole years since I had last run the wings at Gallowgate.'

Most people laughed at his questions, with puzzled looks on their faces; his humbleness and lack of self-belief never ceased to amaze most folk. It took an awful lot of reassurance to convince him that they would indeed be right. Since departing for Linfield, he had dreamed about playing one final game in front of a bumper

Gallowgate crowd and dozens of former players had promised him that, should it ever happen, they would be first in the queue to turn out for him. Dad never quite believed it would all come together.

Not wanting to embarrass himself as a pale shadow of his former self, he quickly involved himself in a rigorous training schedule with a few former teammates, with circuit training and lifting weights in the St James' Park gymnasium a couple of nights a week. He had always thought highly of his good pal, chirpy Charlie Crowe, and enjoyed being in his company, so was well chuffed when Charlie agreed to join in.

Later, Charlie recalled how one night, after a fairly heavy exercise session, Dad wanted just a few more minutes' shooting practice outside in the club car park, so asked Charlie to act as a stand-in goalkeeper. They used the white sticks painted onto the surrounding wall as the goal. Charlie shrugged, agreed and walked over to ready himself in the makeshift goal, but, as the light was fading, never clearly saw the ball that Dad struck in his direction. It whistled passed his head, thudded against the brick and rebounded to Dad before he was even ready. Charlie yelled that the shot could have killed him had the ball struck him in the face and cracked his head against the wall, so quickly thought better of what he was doing and scampered off to leave Dad practising on his own.

Years later, Charlie paid him a wonderful compliment by declaring that, during the whole of his own celebrated career in football, he had never seen anyone kick a ball with such great power or precise accuracy as Jackie Milburn.

Although Dad was involved with arranging the testimonial match right from the start, a lot of hard work was going on behind the scenes. The promotion machine began to roll when a Centurion tank was brought over from Germany by the 14th/19th Lancers to be named 'Wor Jackie'. He officially christened it by smashing a bottle of Newcastle Brown Ale, as opposed to champagne, over the gun turret.

One particular chap called George Embleton proved himself a

marvellous help with regard to the sale of tickets, rolling up his sleeves and taking a whole week off work, and Stan Seymour junior also helped tremendously with the never easy task of bringing together the players. But still many a sleepless night did Mum and an anxious Dad suffer, as he lay thrashing his restless legs about the bed. Dad was still not 100 per cent confident, even after nearly all the tickets were sold, that there would be a big turn-out and began to worry himself about the weather preventing the crowd turning up.

It was Bobby Mitchell who, in the early organising stages, prevented Dad from bottling out of the whole occasion. 'He sat me down, put his arm round me and told me not to worry,' Dad explained. 'I could expect a near-50,000 crowd.'

On the morning of the testimonial, 10 May 1967 – the eve of his 43rd birthday – Mum really had to do her utmost to keep Dad calm. He relentlessly paced the floor like a cat on a hot tin roof, constantly peering out of the sitting-room window to check the current weather situation. The rest of his fretful day was spent mostly at the ground, checking that all was OK there, while periodically peeking up at the sky with his fingers crossed. But the forecast wasn't particularly good and there were intermittent sprinklings of rain.

On the night itself, most of the excited family met at the football ground long before the kick-off, each sporting new hairdos and outfits for the big occasion. I went a little later with my pal Dave Scott. As teenagers, the pair of us were a little too shy to mingle and simply headed straight to our seats. As we did, I peered around the stadium and felt a real sense of pride for Dad and so much gratitude to the 45,404 Geordies who had turned up to create the uplifting atmosphere. The really nice thing was that the overwhelming majority of them had arrived before the start of the 'big match', with only 15 latecomers missing the first game.

'I kept peeping out of the players' tunnel every few minutes to check on the size of the incoming crowd,' said Dad.

The money that was already in the pot from the excellent ticket sales would provide a financial boost to change the rest of his life, but on the night itself it was more important to Dad to be 'home', with a big crowd. He felt a need for the supporters to turn up to allow him to say a big thank you to them.

The first game was between the 'Newcastle Wembley Heroes' and the 'Guest Stars', an evocative 15-minutes-each-way affair, played purely for entertainment. The 'Wembley' team consisted of Jack Fairbrother; Bobby Cowell, Bobby Corbett; Joe Harvey; Frank Brennan, Charlie Crowe; Tommy Walker, Ernie Taylor, Jackie Milburn, Alf McMichael and Bobby Mitchell.

The 'Guests' were John Thompson; David Craig, George Hardwicke; Stan Anderson, Bob Hardisty, Ron Lewin; George Wardle, Len Shackleton, Alan Ashman, Ivor Broadis and Tom Finney.

Beaming all over his face, Dad ran past the brass band and onto the pitch, carrying a Titanic-sized lump in his throat. As he reached the centre circle and raised his arms to the crowd, the lump grew even bigger; his senses were swept over by the terrific atmosphere created by the deafening cheers of affection ringing in his ears. His eyes welled and the clock appeared to have moved back to a different era for him, and it was, beyond a shadow of a doubt, the finest birthday present he could ever have wished for. Once it was all over, he declared it had been, 'One of the proudest nights of my life.'

He welcomed both teams onto the pitch and the event became even more overwhelming as the memories flooded back. With the exception of George Robledo, who now lived halfway around the world in Chile, Dad had managed to bring together his favourite United FA Cup-winning team – the 1951 squad, the one he'd always felt most privileged to have played in.

As soon as the game kicked off, the 'Guests' allowed Dad to run straight through their ranks to slot the ball in the back of the net in just 50 seconds. The stage was set for the rest of the match. Len Shackleton performed only as Shack could and dominated some lengthy spells with his mind-boggling wizardry. Dad was thrilled at Len turning out for him, as normally his pride wouldn't allow Len to play any more. He too had wanted folk to remember him at his peak, but such was their friendship that he made a big exception for Dad, and even trained in secret for the occasion. Goalkeeper Jack Fairbrother suffered a disjointed finger after trapping it against the upright while trying to stop one of Len's infamous banana shots.

I was too young to have ever seen any of them play in their prime and I thoroughly enjoyed the wholly entertaining 30 minutes.

What followed was only taken in a slightly lighter vein, as the Jackie Milburn XI of Gordon Marshall; Cecil Irwin, Frank Clarke; Dave Elliott, George Kinnell, Jim Iley; George Herd, Wyn Davies, Jackie Milburn (substituted by Benny Craig after 25 mins), Neil Martin and Bryan ('Pop') Robson took on the International XI of Tony Waiters; Jimmy Armfield, Shay Brennan; Pat Crerand, John McGrath (in place of the injured Jack Charlton), Nobby Stiles; Alan Suddick, George Eastham, Bobby Charlton, Ferenc Puskas and George Mulhall. But sadly, after just 25 minutes of the second half, the match had to be abandoned as the steady rain developed into a relentless downpour. In spite of the rain, Dad certainly never received a single complaint from anyone who'd attended the night of '50s nostalgia.

When he got home later, so thrilled was he, that both he and Mum just lay in bed and chatted excitedly for hours about the brilliant Geordie public who had, as they had done so many times before, done him so proud. 'I always knew that they were the ones who had moulded me into what I was in the first instance,' Dad later said. 'And quite simply, without their backing, I would have been nothing. Now they had even given me financial security.'

Later in his life, quite a few of those who had attended his benefit match openly approached Dad in the streets of Newcastle to tell him that they were all too aware of the paltry sums of money to be earned playing professional football in the '50s, and that if they themselves had put in a couple of extra shifts at the pit or in the shipyards, then their own wage could quite easily have been much bigger than his. They also told him he had given them great pleasure, and were only too pleased to be able to reward a fellow Geordie with their support. Dad was moved, saying, 'Those kind words stayed with me forever.'

At an official ceremony a few days later, he was handed a cheque for the princely sum of £8,200, which enabled him to repay in full the hefty mortgage on the house and so greatly ease his financial burdens.

For the next couple of seasons, football was fairly uneventful at St James' Park, although according to Dad and many other press boys, Joe Harvey looked as if he was creating the nucleus of a good squad of players. They included the likes of Bobby Moncur, Wyn 'The Leap' Davies, Bryan ('Pop') Robson, Willie McFaul and Geoff Allen, and then with perfect timing, there came a bright cloud on the horizon when United found they had qualified to play in Europe's prestigious Inter City Fairs Cup. It may have been via the back door, under the one-city, one-club rule, but neither Joe nor anyone gave a stuff about that and the Newcastle fans began to buzz at the reality of some of Europe's finest clubs visiting Gallowgate. They buzzed even louder when in the September of 1968 Newcastle trounced Feyenoord 4–0 in the first round, in front of 46,000 at Gallowgate, with goals coming from Scott, Robson, Tommy Gibb and Davies.

Dad was thrilled to bits and even at that early stage could smell silverware, though kept firmly in the back of his mind his own first European experiences at Linfield, praying that Newcastle would not suffer a heavy second-leg defeat. 'More than anything, I really wanted them to do well to give Tyneside a boost.'

They were beaten however, but only by two goals, with tough nuts like Ollie Burton, John McNamee and goalkeeper Willie McFaul saving the day. Bobby Moncur, whom Dad always thought was a perfect captain able to lead by example, had just recovered sufficiently from a cartilage operation to play in the next round against the great Sporting Lisbon, a match which ended in a 1–1 draw in Portugal.

With their imagination now fired up, 54,000 packed into St James' for the return leg and thankfully, Pop Robson's single goal was enough to scrape the side through. Dad was absorbed by the match: 'When I got home after that game, you'd think it was me who'd been sitting in the hot seat.'

The draw for the next round was made and a few folk grimaced at the prospect of the next hurdle – Spain's Real Zaragoza, previous winners of the Fairs Cup in 1964. On New Year's Day, 1969, when Newcastle suffered a 3–2 away defeat, the Toon really had it all to do. Robson and Davies had been the scorers yet again.

This time, 56,000 squeezed in for the return match in which Pop Robson cracked one into the net from 30 yards before anyone knew anything about it, following that with a second from the head of Tommy Gibb. The fans erupted, but then quickly went silent when just before half-time Real slipped in the first opposition Fairs Cup goal to be scored at St James' Park. The aggregate score was now 4–4, setting up a nail-biting finish.

Newcastle quickly pulled their socks up and began to pile on the pressure. 'I reckon I must have chewed three pens and a full notebook before the final whistle,' Dad remarked. However, Newcastle were through on the away-goals rule.

This now meant a quarter-final match against the Portuguese side Vittoria Setubal, which took place in the usual Tyneside blizzards of March. Not being used to such extreme weather conditions, Vittoria were hammered 5–1, with the majority of their team being literally frozen out of the game. Robson grabbed two, and Davies, Foggon and Gibb got one apiece, magically spurred on by an ecstatic though crushed crowd of over 57,000. The entire city was now in a state of permanent animation waiting for the return leg and many expected a walkover. For Dad though, memories of his Swedish defeat once again kept his feet firmly on the ground and sure enough, Newcastle were defeated 3–1 after being intimidated by the restless Portuguese crowd. 'The Leap' scored the only goal. Newcastle had done enough to go through anyway.

'I now had the gut feeling that the Magpies could really go all the way,' Dad revealed. 'I was absolutely thrilled for Joe and the players, feeling even more confident after they drew the only other British club left in the competition, Glasgow Rangers.'

He was sure the team's pride would not allow them to disappoint the hungry Geordie fans, but a hard-fought 0–0 draw in front of over 75,000 fans up in Glasgow, amongst them over 10,000 travelling black and whites, left the team with it all to do at Gallowgate. Goalkeeper Willie McFaul had saved their bacon with a brilliant penalty save.

The following week, anyone who was in or around in the city of Newcastle prior to the match will clearly remember some of the horrific scenes as the Tartan invaders seized control of the streets. During the game itself, St James' Park was subjected to a hail of beer bottles flung from the predominately Scottish Gallowgate End as Rangers slipped 2–0 down. The bulk of their drunken fans were simply unable to handle the scoreline and so decided in their own wisdom to invade the pitch. With no option whatsoever, the nervous players scurried for the safety of the tunnel and it was left to the police and their snarling dogs to deal with the nasty situation as best they could.

For almost 20 minutes, sporadic battles took place, until eventually a long line of shoulder-to-shoulder policemen were able to stretch the width of the Gallowgate End and do their utmost to keep the peace for the remaining 10 minutes. 'I was really pleased that the Newcastle supporters managed to keep their cool and remained patiently on the terrace at the other end of the ground,' observed Dad. 'They neither let themselves nor their club down.' That fact was upheld at a later inquiry.

However, after the dejected Rangers supporters spewed from the ground they continued to further disgrace themselves by performing many gratuitous acts of violence on innocent bystanders, whatever their age or sex, leading to several arrests just as there had been earlier in the day.

I remember riding into town with a friend of mine, Tony Renton, on our motor scooters earlier that day, never once giving thought to any impending trouble. As we rode along Grainger Street we spotted a few Scottish blue, white and red-adorned drunks rolling about on the pavement, but really thought nothing of it and simply put it down to their being in the minority.

We turned to ride west past the Central Station on Neville Street, but to our utter horror came face to face with hundreds of staggering Rangers supporters at its front. On seeing us, they immediately saw red and threw beer cans and then as we skidded to a halt, they began a charge. We had simply no option other than to jerk about and head back against the traffic flow of the one-way street, but as we did so, we found ourselves head-on with another pack approaching from the direction of Collingwood Street. Tomorrow's newspaper headlines flashed through my mind – 'Two Youths Torn Apart By Drunken Glaswegian Mob'. Then I saw Tony suddenly wrench his bike up onto the pavement, sending fearful pedestrians scurrying, then turning sharp left only to find more honking one-way traffic on Westgate Road. I just followed as a beer can splattered on my back.

We forced our way through as the chasing pack hurled abuse, and then swung back into Grainger Street. Thirty yards up, we sped right and over the cobbles past St John's Church onto Pudding Chare, barely avoiding another group of them gathered outside the Printers Pie. After that it was down the Bigg Market, along Collingwood Street, then down Dean Street to the Quayside and home. I'll never forget that harrowing experience.

Just eight days later, United faced the first leg of the final against the mighty Hungarian side, Ujpest Dozsa. Most folk couldn't even pronounce their name properly and didn't really care to, as it was Newcastle United on the lips of the 60,000 fanatical sardines who packed themselves into the ground.

For the first hour or so it was pure deadlock, until the unexpected grand Tyneside hero of the night, Scotsman Bobby Moncur, pounced eagerly on a Wyn Davies rebound from their goalkeeper and coolly steered the ball into the back of the net with his left foot. The whole ground erupted and then Newcastle began to pile on heaps of pressure until the stadium exploded once more after a hard-hit low cracker of a shot from Moncur soared past the Hungarian keeper. To finish them off completely, Scott notched a much-deserved third.

Dad was as thrilled as anyone in the ground that night. 'Although it was a colossal team performance, I felt there was one man in particular who deserved to be singled out for special praise. Captain Bobby Moncur.' He had proved himself the Magpies' new stopper-cum-goal-scorer.

Dad could not attend the second leg, and had to be content with doing something he very rarely did at that time: tuning in his radio and listening absorbedly to every second of the game. Not since he was a youngster eagerly listening to Arsenal's FA Cup exploits on his Granny's crackling radio had he been so interested – fairly understandable after his lifetime of first-hand experience.

He felt that radio commentaries without visual action were something he could simply live without; however, this match was a little bit special and it gave Joe and the lads the opportunity to bring back to Tyneside a prime example of soccer silverware, something that had been sadly missing since way back in 1955. And there was a little something else too – the day in question was also Joe Harvey's 50th birthday.

Newcastle fielded an unchanged side in McFaul; David Craig and Frank Clark; Tommy Gibb, Ollie Burton and Bob Moncur; J.E.W. Scott, Bryan ('Pop') Robson, Wyn Davies, Ben Arentoft and J. Sinclair.

This time it was United who took a pounding and on the half hour, Ujpest, right out of the blue, took the lead as Bene drove one securely home from a difficult angle out on the right. Worse was to come as Gorocs slotted in a second just before half-time.

Joe Harvey later told Dad that he didn't tongue-lash the team during the interval, just simply reassured them that if they scored just one goal then Ujpest would fold. He told them to remember that they were still 3–2 up on aggregate.

In a better frame of mind, the players took to the field once more and this time caught their opponents on the hop. Sinclair immediately sent back in a punch-out from the Ujpest goalie and the waiting Moncur was ready, striking it venomously with his left foot straight past the perplexed keeper. He'd secured his two-legged hat-trick and became a Tyneside legend. After that, just as Joe had predicted, the Hungarians completely ran out of puff and it was now Newcastle's turn to force their opponents to back-pedal and just six minutes later, Benny Arentoft cracked in a blocked shot from 15 yards to level the score. They were white-hot now and when Alan Foggon replaced Scott, who was suffering from cramp, he seized the opportunity to add a notch to his belt by haring from just outside his own half toward their goal, firstly sweeping two of their defenders out of his way. With their goal in his sights, he belted the ball. Although their keeper got a frantic hand to it, he only managed to divert it onto the crossbar and the wily Foggon was still running on to crash the rebound into the net. It was all over and the bursting Tyneside pubs rock and rolled, celebrating the awe-inspiring victory. Beaming widely, a happy Dad switched off the radio and sipped his coffee.

During the summer football break, Dad introduced Mum to his now favourite pastime, golf. He, Joe Harvey and Len Shackleton had been happily creating divots for years, often meeting up in their spare time for practice at the John Jacobs driving range at Gosforth Park. Out of the blue, he just suggested one day that Mum should join them, so off they trotted, with her becoming one of the boys for the day.

He, Len and Joe argued the toss about her style of swing as she attempted to strike the balls to their distant target from within the narrow bay. After a while, with her ears ringing, she simply didn't know which one's 'expert' advice to listen to and eventually became so fed up of their petty bickering she told them all politely to clam up and just let her get on with it. To her great surprise they did, and from that second the pet-lipped trio just stood agog as she whacked confidently at the demon ball and proved herself quite a natural when left to do her own thing. Dad later introduced her to Morpeth Golf Club and she never looked back.

Dad's own first attempt at serious golf came about when we lived in Northern Ireland. One day he took the whole family to a quiet course near where we lived (not a lot of folk played golf in those halcyon days) after having one or two special 'junior' clubs (really, cut-down senior ones) fashioned for us small kids, probably in the hope that one of us might take up the game seriously. In reality, we were far too young to understand it, and anyway, it was only about swiping at a ridiculously small ball to get it to drop into a little hole, which we all found totally humdrum. Back at home there were bedrooms full of toys to have real fun with.

That particular day, he was frustratingly attempting to show us the correct way to swing a club and to my great surprise, patted me on the head for displaying what he called a 'canny little swing', nevertheless telling me to always remember my back-swing too. Remembering his words I did just that, though rather unfortunately, the iron tip of my club cracked the nose of the too-close-standing Betty. Here endeth the lesson.

On another day, he took me to the golf course on my own, but after just a few holes I grew increasingly bored, spending most of the time just looking around at birds and picking up twigs and the like. Dad sensed my escalating tedium and tried to make my afternoon more interesting by asking me to pick up and replace any divots he may knock out. I was much relieved, thinking anything was better than trying to hit that stupid tiny ball.

We cheerfully carried on until we were halfway to the final green, which itself was positioned quite close to the club house, and after he whacked his final shot up the fairway, Dad suggested I have one last crack at a ball with my special little club. If the truth be known, he should never have allowed me on the course at all, because the divots he removed were like peanuts compared to the whoppers I created – which, of course he always ensured were hastily replaced. In any case, he picked up my ball after my umpteenth fruitless attempt to strike it and threw it so that it landed on the green. 'There, just putt that when we get there,' he said, 'that's the easy part of the game.'

On the green, as I waited for Dad to putt his own ball first, I noticed a curious sea of faces peering out from the clubhouse window, so thought I'd try to impress them with 'my canny swing'. Dad successfully putted his ball down the hole and was busy replacing his club in his golf bag with his back to me, probably having forgotten all about my ball, and it wasn't until some frantic, screaming man came running toward the green from the clubhouse that he realised something was amiss.

I had tried to belt my ball, which lay to the edge of the green, toward the hole, but with each swing only succeeded in removing gigantic lumps of perfect, smooth green.

Dad joined a different club.


Over the next couple of seasons, Dad and Joe Harvey regularly sat in Joe's tiny Gallowgate office, sinking hot coffee and puffing worriedly on many a fag, as Newcastle tried their best to emulate the magic success of the '69 Fairs Cup. It was not to be.

In the 1969–70 season, United did well to beat Dundee United, Portuguese club Porto and Southampton, but suffered defeat at the hands of the crack Belgian side Anderlecht in the quarter-final, though only on the away-goals rule.

In 1970–71, Newcastle were unlucky to be knocked out by the relatively unknown Pesci Dozsa on penalty kicks after the two clubs tied on aggregate. Ironically, in the previous round they had tasted a sweet victory over the formidable Inter Milan, proving that football really is a funny old game.

In the September of 1970, Betty gave birth to her first child, John, causing Mum to suddenly confess to feeling a little old on becoming a grandmother. Dad simply smiled, replying, 'How do you think I feel? I'm married to one.'

Not long after their 23rd wedding anniversary on 16 February 1971, Mum felt ill and took herself off to see her doctor. The doctor immediately arranged for her to see a specialist, who in turn diagnosed her as requiring immediate surgery.

She needed a hysterectomy and very quickly found herself lying in a Hexham hospital bed. Dad tried not to let her know it, but he was absolutely beside himself, confessing this to me when he came home after paying her a visit. I was the only one living at home at that time as Linda and Betty had both married and moved out.

Thankfully, the operation itself was an absolute success, though of course Mum needed time in hospital to recuperate. Dad and I had to set about the cleaning of the house and 'cooking' for each other – otherwise we would most certainly have perished of malnourishment on a bed of dust, although I wondered later if that just might have been the easy escape as we daily dished out frazzled black chips, over-fried brittle black bacon, burst soggy fried eggs and over-boiled baked beans. Neither of us would admit to its poison though, and wedged down the lot, but there again, what type of cuisine could you expect from two ham-fisted blokes who had been thoroughly mollycoddled by Mum for years?

Mum recalls that while on the road to recovery at Hexham, the hospital suffered electrical blackouts, though she can't remember whether it was due to industrial strike action, or economics. She does remember needing the loo in the middle of the night and having to fumble her way along a long dim corridor, barely lit by what she thinks must have been low-light back-up emergency lighting. Often, she and other patients would bump into each other in the shadows and jump out of their skins, though that was not her only course of collision.

On the evening prior to her surgery, she relaxed in the rest room with some of the other patients who seemed quite amazed at her calmness, asking her if she wasn't just a little worried. Mum being Mum, always a woman who would rather face a situation than run away from it, replied that she just wanted it over and done with so she could go back home.

The other ladies gave her the impression that they believed her to be an extremely brave woman and she suddenly felt a little proud of herself. However, as she smilingly left the room to head back to the ward while cocking her ears to the others whispering about her bravado, she walked smack bang into a glass door, cracked her head and completely blew her short-lived moment of glory.

Not long after she returned home, I received one of the biggest shocks of my life.

I had spent the evening playing records in the spare front room of our house in Benton Park Road with my current girlfriend, Lorraine, and as it was getting fairly late I was about to drive her home. So, with Mum resting upstairs in bed, we went into the sitting room so Lorraine could say goodnight to Dad. To our horror we found him lying face down on the floor.

In panic, I rushed over to him and he looked up at me weakly and whispered for a glass of water. His face was ashen. I raced to the kitchen and told Lorraine to quickly ring for an ambulance, but Dad would have none of it, telling me to keep my voice down so as not to panic Mum. He just wanted the water, though was too weak to raise himself from the floor. I argued and said we must call a doctor, but as soon as he realised how serious was my intention, he hauled himself to his feet and claimed he had simply fallen when becoming dizzy after standing too quick, declaring, 'It's nothing to worry about, your mother's recovering upstairs. She's the one we have to think about.'

He managed to sit back in the chair and the colour slowly returned to his face, but then he insisted that I run Lorraine home and that he'd still be up when I got back. Though she lived a few miles away at Westerhope, I would have given Stirling Moss a good run for his money on that return journey, my mind racing as to whether I should force an issue with Dad over the ambulance.

I ran back in the house and when I entered the sitting-room he forced a smile and made me swear never to tell my mother how I'd found him and that I was only to worry about her. Then he said he was going upstairs to bed. I followed him into the hallway and stood at the bottom of the stairs to watch him go up and will never forget the way he had to drag his feet, or the sight of his left arm clutched tight to his side while his right arm pressed his chest.

That night I hardly slept a wink and early next morning, when I heard him get out of bed, followed him downstairs where he claimed to be feeling fine and I must admit his colour was fully back. When I questioned him all I got was, 'Shush, don't tell your mother', and then he went back upstairs, dressed and left in his car.

The second he pulled off the drive, I rang Dr Salkeld, his doctor, who at the time was also a Newcastle United director, to explain precisely what had happened. I was told to leave it with him. When Dad returned looking somewhat better, he winked and told me to do just what the doctor had ordered – so I knew he'd seen him. I was told never to mention what had happened to a living soul and then asked to tell Lorraine to do the same. 'End of story,' Dad said. The trouble with Dad was if he ever said no there was no arguing, full stop. I just watched him carefully over the next few weeks, but he never showed any further sign of ill health.

Around that time, Bob Stokoe, one of Dad's best-ever soccer buddies, made a triumphant return to the Northeast when he grabbed hold of the reins at Sunderland FC and set about earning his new nickname, 'The Messiah'. And it wasn't too long before he steadfastly guided Sunderland to the Twin Towers of Wembley Stadium in 1973. They were set to face Don Revie's much-feared Leeds United.

Bob became a regular visitor to our house, along with his wife

Jean. Over the years this had happened on a fairly regular basis and when younger, the pair of them and Mum and Dad had enjoyed a few holidays together. They always kept in touch. This time was different though and Bob was here to stay, so not only had Dad rekindled a dependable old friendship, he now had yet another regular golfing partner.

Bob valued Dad's opinions on up-and-coming players and not only did they sit at home or at Roker Park to discuss future prospects, they travelled a fair few miles together to run the rule over prospective new talent. As with Newcastle, Dad was never on Sunderland's payroll, it was simply an old pal's act brought about by the lifelong bond that had formed between the Newcastle United players of the early '50s.

Come Cup final day, Mum and Dad both received special invitations to be guests of the official Sunderland party at Wembley and Dad was so thrilled about that. He was, beyond the shadow of a doubt, never a one to 'freeload' or ask folk for something in return for a favour he'd maybe done them. I'm quite sure in fact that an awful lot of people played on that during his life and saw him coming, only to exploit him for their own advantage. They know who they are.

In a nutshell, he was the sort of fellow who would give you his last £5 on a Friday night after the bank had closed if he thought you needed it more than he, even if at the back of his mind he really knew you only wanted it for beer or fags and he needed it to eat. Such was his nature. Hence, Bob's kind and genuine invitation meant the world to Dad.

To the public and press, Sunderland were the firm underdogs to win the Cup and most folk just prayed they would put up a good fight, but when Ian Porterfield scored his magic goal and they hung on and fought like tigers, not to forget Jimmy Montgomery's greatest-ever Wembley final save, the whole of the Northeast felt a wonderful sense of pride that hadn't been around since the '50s. No one who has ever seen it will ever forget Bob's congratulatory sprint toward Jimmy Montgomery after the final whistle. The Cup was coming back north.

'To show my appreciation after returning home, I went straight out and bought Bob a red, black and white golf bag.'

The following year, 1974, it was at last Newcastle United's turn to reach the Twin Towers and no one in the Northeast could have been any more thrilled than Dad.

The opposition were to be the mighty Liverpool, but Joe Harvey's ace card was the man who had already scored a hat-trick against Liverpool on his debut back in 1971 – Malcolm Macdonald, or more commonly, Supermac.

From the day he'd arrived in great style at St James' Park in a limousine driven by a pal of his, complete with chauffeur's peaked cap, Malcolm had been worshipped by the Geordie fans. In fact he was a 'southern Geordie'. Dad certainly thought so anyway, and he'd taken an instant shine to him. 'I always favoured a local lad as centre-forward, feeling he would play with more passion, but inside, Malcolm really did have Geordie spirit, only without the accent. I hardly think that mattered at all.'

For Malcolm Macdonald, Dad was an important factor as he settled into the area and came to terms with the expectations on his shoulders:

> When I arrived on my first day all the press were there. I had my medical and did a press conference. Stood to one side was your dad. He came over to me and said, 'You'll need to buy a house. Have you made any plans? I'll pick you up on Friday and take you out.' He showed me all around the region and through it all he told me how to be a centre-forward for Newcastle United; it was the greatest lesson I ever had in my life. Jackie said to me, 'What you've got to remember is the lives people lead up here. They go to bed and dream of scoring the winning goal for Newcastle at St

James' Park or Wembley. You are the person who can make
their dreams come true.'

Later, Dad would speak to Malcolm after matches, giving him
advice on his game. 'He gave me priceless knowledge,' says
Malcolm, 'and I enjoyed doing it in your Dad's way.' If any one
player was going to give Newcastle a great chance of lifting the FA
Cup then it was Supermac.

Dad was interviewed several times on the radio and television
prior to the big day and always stuck to the same view: Newcastle
would win the Cup. After all, not everyone had expected the '50s
squad to beat Stanley Matthews' Blackpool in 1951 or Joe Mercer's
mighty Arsenal a year later and some even doubted they could
overcome Manchester City in 1955. However, Dad felt that if
Malcolm received the right service against Liverpool, then why not?
And Joe had built the right team to offer him just that, fielding:
Willie McFaul; Frank Clark, Alan Kennedy; Terry McDermott,
Paddy Howard, Bobby Moncur; Jimmy Smith, Tommy Cassidy,
Malcolm Macdonald, John Tudor and little Terry Hibbitt. Quite a
formidable line-up.

Dad was convinced at this time that Joe was just two or three
players away from an unstoppable side, reckoning the likes of
Keegan, Gemmill and Souness in black-and-white shirts would be
the icing on the cake.

After one particular TV interview around this time, Dad left the
studio in a hurry as he was going out that night, but as he rushed
to his car in the car park soon realised folk were pausing to gawp at
him. Puzzled, he hopped into the car and sped for home and was
almost there when he realised he had only a couple of cigarettes left,
so he pulled up outside a corner shop to buy another pack. He was
baffled as to why the lady behind the counter sniggered at him,
though she quickly stifled it, but then hastily nudged her young
assistant who reacted in the same way. The pair continued to bite
their tongues and stare as they took his cash, but said nothing.

He heard their titters after he thanked them and left the shop, but thought no more about it until he got home and looked in the mirror. To his absolute horror, he discovered his face was still plastered with thick orange studio make-up and dark lipstick. 'Needless to say, I returned to the shop the next day to assure them that I was indeed quite normal,' explained Dad.

Just before the Cup final, Dad spoke to his old pal, Liverpool manager Bill Shankly, who told him he'd heard his radio and television comments about the eventual winners. Shankly smiled, looked at Dad right in the eye and said, 'I've listened to what you've been saying, Jackie, and I admire you for it – you have to support your club. But, Jack, you *know* what's going to happen.'

The great man's words proved just what a shrewd cookie he was and Newcastle were never allowed to get into the game. Liverpool hammered them 3–0 after totally dominating the game. A lot of Geordie hearts were broken that day and so was Malcolm Macdonald's as he sat on the pitch in tears after the final whistle. Newcastle had simply been outclassed.

A thoroughly disappointed Dad did not hold back on his comments after the game, condemning the team's poor performance. Dad reckoned that the only true Geordie winner on the day had been Brendan Foster, who had stormed to victory in a warm-up, pre-match race.

After the shameful defeat, Dad really felt the team had played shoddily and that not only was he saddened, embarrassed and shocked by the performance, but also ashamed of the Magpies. His were strong words indeed. 'I felt the one saving grace that afternoon were the fabulous supporters who caused a massive lump in my throat. Even in their humiliation, they out-chanted their Liverpool counterparts with, "United, United", as Emlyn Hughes lifted the Cup.'

There was another tinge of bitterness for him too at Wembley, though a little more personal. A short while before the final, Dad discovered that Liverpool were to invite many of their 'old boys' down to Wembley and then take them on to a later banquet, so, many of the old Newcastle '50s squad were hoping the same might happen to them. However, Newcastle did not offer to wine and dine them at all, even though the former stars were prepared to fork out of their own pockets for the privilege of just being there. 'I travelled to Wembley simply in my capacity as a sports journalist,' Dad explained. Bob Stokoe was gobsmacked.

In the January of the following year, Betty gave birth to her second son, Davy, and to give Dad more excitement the following year still, Wembley Stadium once more beckoned the black-and-white hordes, though this time under the guise of the League Cup.

By that time, Bobby Moncur had left the club to grace the turf at Roker Park in a red-and-white-striped shirt, Terry Hibbitt was at Birmingham, Terry McDermott at Liverpool and both 'Jinky' Jim Smith and John Tudor were crippled with knee injuries and not only that, Joe Harvey had retired. No longer was Dad the accepted 'insider' as he had been with Joe at the helm and his nose now felt a tad out of joint.

New faces controlled St James' in the form of Blackburn Rovers' former young manager Gordon Lee and his assistant, Richard Dinnis, and Dad certainly found headline-grabbing newspaper stories a lot harder to come by as the pair kept club affairs much closer to their chest.

However, this time at Wembley the Newcastle United players most certainly did not bring shame on themselves and were very unfortunate to lose 2–1 to Manchester City in the final. They had also finished a respectable fifth in the League, but what was to follow at St James' Park was a heady time of player power and managerial chaos, resulting in the sale of every fan's favourite, Malcolm Macdonald, to Arsenal for a whopping £333,333.33.

Gordon Lee had announced on his arrival that there would be no individual 'stars' at Newcastle and so set about his task, something the Geordie public would never forgive him for. 'It brought back stark memories of Dougald Livingstone for me,' remarked Dad.

Indeed, Malcolm Macdonald *was* Newcastle United, a fact that was proven by the drop in attendances whenever it was announced, pre-match, that he was out through injury. Often, several thousand would just drift away to drown their sorrows.

Before Malcolm's transfer, Dad hinted at it in his newspaper column, prior to anything being made public. This resulted in a minor clash of words between himself and Gordon Lee. The old inferiority complex then reared its ugly head and Dad really felt he may perhaps have stirred up too big a hornet's nest, fearing it could all now backfire in his face; if it came to the worst he might just find himself barred from the ground altogether. 'That belief flattened me.'

I remember answering the telephone at home one day. It was a journalist colleague and friend of his called Joe Cummings, so I just happened to mention Dad's fears.

Joe immediately burst out laughing. 'What? Newcastle United without Jackie Milburn around would be like a car with no bloody wheels. Tell him not to be so damn ridiculous.'

I mentioned Joe's reaction to Dad but Dad still felt that he might have overstepped the mark this time. In reality, he was only doing what other case-hardened sportswriters like John Gibson, Doug Weatherall, Tony Hardisty and even Len Shackleton had been doing successfully for many a year; he'd dared enter into the world of conjecture. After a while it all blew over, but it was a long time before Dad could get to terms with it.

It was Linda's turn now to swell the ranks of the Milburn family, and in 1977 she gave birth to a boy, Darren.

At the end of that year, Gordon Lee left to go to Everton, so that left just first team coach Richard Dinnis to fill in as caretaker manager, leaving many a fan grumbling.

Dad hated that particular messy period of Newcastle's history and it seemed to have an effect on a number of fans on the terraces too – during some games it seemed more time was spent watching mass punch-ups rather than the soccer on the pitch. Once-happy crowds deserted the club.

A new season beckoned so United arranged a few friendly games, one of which was an evening match in Edinburgh against Hibernian. So that Dad could watch the match, I drove him up to Edinburgh. We had some hours free so I decided to catch up with a former girlfriend, while Dad went to call in a shop now owned by Ronnie Simpson, intending to surprise the former United skipper. Dad and I went our separate ways, arranging to meet in a café in Leith at 5 p.m. for a bite to eat before the game.

At 3.30 p.m. I drove down Leith Walk, having ended my tête-à-tête early, and was surprised to see Dad walking along the pavement, looking somewhat disconsolate. I immediately honked the horn and pulled the car over, beckoning him to hop in. I asked him if there was a problem and why he was not with Ronnie. He simply shrugged. Instead of the joyous reunion and great craic he had fully expected, Ronnie had told him he was really too busy at the moment and said he would catch up with him some other time. Dad was left to walk the streets of Edinburgh for hours.

Newcastle started the new season, 1977–78, badly and it got even worse. They lost ten games on the trot and the writing was now on the wall for Dinnis, who by that stage had been somewhat surprisingly installed as the full-time manager. Several of the players were in revolt mood. They wanted him to stay. Dad too thought Dinnis was a cracking fellow, but maybe, just as Dad had been at Ipswich, a little too yielding. Dinnis certainly had the balls to argue the toss with the directors over spending money, but their faith in him putting it to good use was the major problem. At the end of that term Newcastle dropped down into the Second Division.

The directors now felt it was time for a complete change in the style of management to bring the club back to order – and there wasn't a bigger trouble-shooter in football at that time than Wolverhampton's Bill McGarry.

McGarry's reputation as the most hated man in football management was self-acknowledged and he didn't give a damn as long as he was left to get on with the job. Dad knew him well, as he'd played alongside him for England, and McGarry had also followed in his footsteps as the next Ipswich manager after Dad had resigned. 'He'd always sung my praises for leaving the club with such a sound base for him to build on,' said Dad. 'That pleased me.' When he arrived, Dad invited him to stay short-term at his house until he found somewhere more permanent. 'Bill stayed with us for nearly a year. Must have been Laura's cooking,' Dad remarked.

One night, as the pair of them sat chatting in the sitting-room, Dad just happened to mention that all he had ever really wanted after he returned to the Northeast was a job with Newcastle United and was flabbergasted when Bill suddenly offered him one as youth development officer. Bill knew just how adept Dad was at spotting raw talent so told him to sleep on it. They would discuss it further in the morning.

'For a couple of days I was sorely tempted,' explained Dad, 'but once the story leaked to the media and I arrived home one afternoon to find a television crew setting up on the drive, that was it. I really did not want the awful pressure all over again.'

Dad simply preferred to be involved with football from behind the 'safety net' of his journalism, but just to make himself quite sure, he sat in the stands during one game and watched it from the perspective of being on the club payroll. 'Instead of enjoying the match, I sat and squirmed, wrung my hands and sweated like hell. I knew then the right answer was to say no.'

McGarry set about his trouble-shooting task with vim, weeding out the worst troublemakers but also telling the rest of the players to keep their lips sealed – at least until they understood accountability for their words. With the club now in order, which is what he was brought in for, he then attempted to build a promotion-winning side, but this proved his big failing and the closest he got to success was when United topped the table on New Year's Day by two clear points.

Alas, that proved to be their pinnacle for the season and the team slid down the table to nowhere thereafter, but what really rankled with the Geordie supporters was that Sunderland went the other way and won promotion.

Two of McGarry's big-money splash-outs had been on Scotsmen, Mark McGhee and Mike Larnach, purchased without him even having run the rule over them himself. Although some of the £250,000 was recouped when they moved on, McGarry would never live down the deal. He and the club parted company. 'I was sad to see Bill go,' said Dad, 'but he'd achieved what he set about to do and sorted out the troublemakers. Maybe he should have left then?'

Joe Harvey, now the Magpies' chief scout and with his hand firmly on the pulse, strongly recommended the next manager − Arthur Cox, though warned Arthur beforehand just how tough he may find things. The club now languished in Division Two with massive debts, but Arthur had his eyes focused on a much bigger fish.

# – 10 –

# Surprising Tributes

He never bragged. He just didn't want to talk about himself.

Sir Bobby Charlton

It was at this time Dad began to spend less of his time at the club and more of it playing golf and going caravanning. He seemed to be taking stock of his life. This certainly had nothing to do with the appointment of Arthur Cox, as the two became very firm friends. In fact Arthur rang him at home with his good news the day he was appointed.

One of the reasons for how Dad was feeling might have been that he was spending quite a lot of time on the course with his good pal, former United right-winger, George Luke. George ran his own successful carpet business and didn't really bother himself much with the comings and goings at St James' Park. Maybe that rubbed off a little on Dad, who was by now 56.

Another real possibility might have been he felt the need to change his way of life: he was suffering some fairly nasty withdrawal symptoms, both physical and mental, as he attempted to chuck the fags. Some days he would prowl around like an unfed lion – but then isn't everyone the same after suddenly kicking the habit of a lifetime?

He had been a smoker since just a youngster and in those days it was considered the 'manly' thing to do, so very few didn't. Every Hollywood hero on the big screen seemed to have a fag dangling from his lips and acted their scenes while peering slit-eyed through a fuggy haze. Anyway, he tried desperately to stick to his guns and resist temptation, but in reality, Dad felt quite lost without them and when fag-less, certainly became more of an introvert. He would last a few days and then buckle and rush out to buy a pack, finding it extremely hard to part company with a lifetime 'friend'. In reality, he had indeed lost one lifetime buddy – Polly the parrot.

After spending many years as the Milburn 'fourth child', Polly had flown to pastures new, but for no other reason than it was no longer fair to keep him now that Mum and Dad were frequently away caravanning. At first, the bird didn't seem to mind when they stayed away for the odd night, as long as he was well fed and watered, but he soon grew agitated and bored, more often than not taking it out on his wooden perch, which he regularly gnawed through, usually while still hovering on it. The poor bird would then land on the bottom with a thump. The day Mum and Dad arrived home to find him squatting and squawking on the bottom of his cage, they realised it simply wasn't fair, so looked around to find him a good home. Mum was fairly cool about him leaving, but Dad missed him terribly.

To save hauling his touring caravan about, Dad sited it permanently on a farm belonging to some friends, Edward and Joy Patterson, near Seahouses on the Northumberland coast. And of course there was the handy Seahouses Golf Club nearby.

For Dad, it was the right time of his life to begin to wind down and to spend more time with his grandchildren. Little could he expect there were still a great number of big surprises waiting just around the corner.

The first arrived in the form of a letter from the Newcastle Civic Centre. Dad was informed that he – along with several other fellow Geordies, including Cardinal Basil Hume – was to be made an

Honorary Freeman of the City of Newcastle to mark the city's 900th anniversary. His name was to be carved in stone for posterity on a wall in the Civic Centre, alongside the likes of the then president of the United States of America, Jimmy Carter. I honestly don't think that up until he opened that letter he had ever felt so honoured.

That's when the enormity of it all hit home for Dad. Once again his modest pit beginnings sprang to his mind. 'Just what am I doing etched on a wall with all those fine folk?' he queried.

Then someone quipped, 'Did you forget that Jimmy Carter was once just a peanut farmer?'

His mother Nance, now living in Stakeford, was just as thrilled as Dad. She rushed straight out to buy him a new shirt and matching tie, which he pledged to wear on the big day. At the time, she wasn't well herself and was now a widow once more after Harry, her second husband, had passed away the previous year. But she was determined to make that particular effort to get to the shops.

Sadly though, she never made it to the ceremony herself and died of lung cancer not long after making her special purchase. Dad was distraught but did his best to put on a brave face. 'Once my mother knew I was going to be made an Honorary Freeman, she died like a queen'.

The July day itself was fantastic. It was written all over Dad's face that he felt so humbled in the presence of some of the others as he stepped up to receive his scroll. But as soon as Cardinal Hume asked him for his autograph after the lunch, Dad beamed broadly and began to relax. 'We actually exchanged autographs,' he remembered warmly. Mike Neville later had these kind words to say about Dad:

> The love and respect in which Jackie was held by everybody was such that if directly elected mayors had been in vogue in his day, he would have been overwhelmingly elected and would have held the office for life!

For me, there was just one little downer on the whole wonderful occasion and that was reading someone's letter printed in the *Evening Chronicle*. The letter complained about the 'outrageous cost of the Canadian Redwood boxes in which the Freemen received their scrolls. A cost to be borne by the Newcastle rate-payers'. After a lifetime of achievement, were these men not deserving? Merry Christmas, Ebenezer.

It was not long afterwards that another unexpected honour came Dad's way when the England manager, Ron Greenwood, chose him as one of the 'Players who have made an important contribution to the history and drama of the FA Cup'.

To commemorate the Centenary Cup final, the Football Association had a dozen silver cigarette cards printed in a limited edition of 2,000, selling at £260 per set. Two other Northeasterners shared in the honour: Bobby Charlton and Raich Carter.

Dad had recently co-written *The Newcastle United Scrapbook* with his pal and journalist colleague, John Gibson, and Brian Klein, a researcher from London Weekend Television (LWT)'s *This Is Your Life* programme, read it with interest and decided Dad might just make a good subject. He telephoned the *Evening Chronicle* office to ask John if he would cooperate and John replied he'd love to, but first he'd have to contact Mum to ask her for the go-ahead.

Now, she knew only too well Dad's preference for privacy and at first was a little hesitant, but then decided to ask the family for their honest opinion. We all knew deep down that had she not agreed, Dad probably would never have found out anything about their approach, but what an honour it would be for him to miss out on without ever having known about it. Really, Mum couldn't say no.

There was one major problem though, in that LWT wanted to record the show down in London, but Mum knew there wasn't a cat-in-hell's chance of getting Dad down there without arousing his suspicions. For the first time ever, the producers of the programme agreed to a regional shoot of *This Is Your Life* at the Newcastle Tyne Tees Television studios, simply to ensure he would turn up – that in itself was a huge compliment.

Brian Klein arranged to meet Mum and some of us family at home, ensuring Dad was well out the way first on a match day, and that's where it was decided who would be saying what and who the possible guests might be. For a whole three months, which seemed like an eternity, we pulled hair, paced floors and chewed nails as the day grew closer. Mum and Dad had only ever had a single joint bank account, so to enable her to buy a new outfit for the show, Mum had to borrow the money from Dad's sister Mavis, otherwise he would have noticed the used cheque stub and questioned her as to what she'd bought and why.

The final remaining problem was how to keep him out the way on the day itself, as Mum and the rest of us had to be at the studios all day for rehearsals. That, thankfully, is where his good buddy John Gibson stepped back into the frame.

John enlisted the help of United boss Arthur Cox to keep Dad busy at St James' Park on the day and Dad had no suspicions about Mum's secret antics. She'd simply told him she would be out Christmas shopping for the day with his two sisters, Mavis and Jean. All perfectly normal stuff.

John invented a story about his wife needing his car to sort out a minor family problem, so asked Dad if he could go home with him for a bite to eat before the pair made their way to the studios, where Dad expected to be interviewed about his book for a football talk show. Naturally Dad agreed, and when the hungry pair got home, found Mum had left a couple of mince pies and an apple tart in the fridge for him to heat in the oven.

John's kitchen skills were just as sorry as Dad's and they had one heck of a job just to find the right dial to set the oven away, though in due course did accomplish their mission just before their grumbling stomachs caved in. After devouring the pies, Dad went upstairs to get washed and changed, only to find himself being followed by John, who was still petrified Dad may yet twig that something was happening and do a runner. Dad did notice John's out-of-the-ordinary behaviour: 'At the time, I found it very strange that John was following me everywhere like a lost lamb, but was too embarrassed to ask why.'

To lure Dad to the studio that evening, John and the programme producers concocted a spoof programme and named it *A Chance To Score*. 'Jackie, in his lovely innocence, never knew what was going on,' John says. Even the invited audience had no idea what was about to unfold until the huge curtains swished back and on swiftly walked Dad, followed by a wide-beaming Eamonn Andrews. Such was the audience's surprise that they erupted and as we watched his reaction on a backstage monitor, you could tell by Dad's face that he was absolutely shocked, but thrilled to bits. Mum had made the right decision, though straight after the show Dad confessed that if he had picked up on the slightest clue of what was going on, he'd have run a mile.

All the old squad from the '50s Cup-winning years appeared, as did the footballing Charlton family, some former England colleagues, including Billy Wright and Tom Finney, and the then current United squad. There was even a touching pre-recorded tribute from Cardinal Basil Hume.

The special guest, flown all the way from New York, was Dad's Aunt Bella, she who had given him his train fare home all those years ago when he was just a tearful little runaway pantry boy. However, one of his old buddies, Len Shackleton, positively refused to appear – though purely on principle and not in any way to snub dad; he just couldn't stand the show.

His old pal, and golfing partner, George Luke, was one of the very few in the audience who knew precisely what was about to happen, but when the show was over and we participants made our way to the after-programme buffet, he was sadly swept out of the exit door by the leaving audience until he found himself on the street outside the studio. Such was George's character that he simply went home, not wanting to appear as a gatecrasher by attempting to get back in the studio, but I remember Dad at the buffet looking around with a puzzled look on his face and asking, 'Where's George?'

One of the guests was a particular boyhood hero of mine, the former Manchester City goalkeeper Bert Trautmann, who I had admired since I first learned that he'd bravely kept goal throughout a whole match while suffering a broken neck. I really wanted his autograph, so after the show, somewhat excitedly took my cousin Stanley's wife, Carol, across to meet him and secure his signature. We were far from prepared for his jarring snarled response. 'Can't you see I'm busy holding a drink?' All my illusions were instantly crushed and we skulked away with our tails between our legs, both of us thinking how odd it was that everyone else we'd asked had politely obliged with a smile.

Dad was still very much on a high when he and Mum arrived home after the buffet, just as the house might have been – bungling he and John Gibson had left the scorching oven switched on high.

Just as had happened after his testimonial game, Dad and Mum chatted excitedly through the night about the programme and meeting all the old boys again, and so thrilled was he about the whole show that he rushed out the very second the shops opened to buy us kids – well, adults now – a VHS video apiece so we could record the show, which was to be broadcast that night.

The following year, Mum and Dad moved house, absolutely sickened after they were burgled for a second time, though feeling somewhat blessed that on both occasions his Cup final medals weren't filched. Some other much-cherished mementoes he had brought home from his tours of South Africa, Canada and Brazil had been during the first robbery though, and this saddened them.

They sold their Newcastle home to move into a terraced house in Bothal Terrace at the top end of Ashington, just yards from his sister Jean's, and just a few hundred yards from the Rec where, as a lad, he'd trained at every opportunity. He walked there regularly to muse over the good old days and from the pitch could even see where his Granny Thompson's house used to be, but it was long gone now, along with all the friendly corner shops to which he used to run messages for the neighbours. Now in their place stood a huge uninspired supermarket with its sprawling asphalt car park.

One day at lunchtime, he decided to pop into one of the social clubs in the Highmarket, really just to see if he could spot any of his old school or mining pals to 'catch up on the craic', but he left the empty club a tad sad.

When he entered the bar, the glum-looking club steward was propping himself on a stool at the other side of the counter and hardly bothered to look up from his morning paper, casting only a fleeting glance as he gruffly asked for payment for the half of lager. Dad sat in a corner alone and not once did the steward attempt any conversation or even look in his direction. No one else came in.

He did not expect to be recognised or anything like that, he was simply curious to see if the clubs had changed much over the past 30 years. He never again went out socially in Ashington. He should have gone to The Comrades.

Suddenly something magical appeared to be about to happen at Newcastle United. 'My interest in the club's fortunes took a dramatic upturn,' said Dad.

Rumours were flying about the possible signing from Southampton on a one-year contract of the great Kevin Keegan himself. Lo and behold, not too long after, that's precisely what happened. Arthur Cox had made the scoop of the decade and with it, the promise of great things about to unfold at St James' Park. Not since the revered Supermac had there been a bigger crowd-puller.

'Laura and I were both thrilled to be invited to Arthur Cox's home to meet Kevin,' remembered Dad fondly, 'and straight away I took an instant shine to him. We got along very well.'

Inevitably, the other press boys began to draw comparisons between the two players, something that made Dad feel quite embarrassed. They were asked to sit for photo sessions and during one in particular a blushing Kevin was asked to don a paper crown, the purpose being to signify him as the new king of St James' Park taking over the mantle from Dad.

The reason for Dad's awkwardness was that the press seemed to have forgotten all about other great goal scorers – like Len White, Wyn Davies and Malcolm Macdonald – who'd previously followed in his boots. 'Shouldn't it be Len, Malcolm or Wyn in the photograph with Kevin and not me?' questioned Dad.

In all probability it was Dad's infectious charisma the press drew their comparisons from – and Kevin Keegan certainly had an absolute shipload of that. Throughout their lives, both men were privileged (Kevin still is) to have the same rare effect that only a few people have: whenever they entered a crowded room it would hush a little, and the people therein would smile genuinely at them and just really enjoy being in their company. What it was about him that made that happen was always a mystery to Dad: 'I could never understand that of myself, but felt very blessed for it.'

There was something else: the legendary status of Newcastle's No. 9, something that, as Alan Shearer explains, continues to this day:

> I realised more than most when I was coming to United what the No. 9 shirt means, and would mean to me. There was pressure on me anyway, because I was the world's most expensive player, but the No. 9 shirt brings its own pressure because of Jackie Milburn, Malcolm Macdonald, Les Ferdinand, Andy Cole and all the great players who have scored goals wearing it.

Teetotaller Kevin proved more astute than Dad had ever been allowed to be, and signed a lucrative PR deal with Scottish and Newcastle Breweries, boosting his Tyneside income considerably during his stay. And he proved himself a total workaholic for both the club and brewery, the latter never affecting his performance on the pitch, even though it meant attending packed pub and club road shows until well after midnight.

His first match at Gallowgate was in front of a full house of 36,000 and expectations were high; Dad had not felt so excited for years and when Kevin notched the only goal of the match he leapt from his seat in the press box along with everyone else.

All of a sudden, lured by Kevin's magnetism, other fine internationals like David McCreery, Terry McDermott and Mick Channon wanted to play in a black and white shirt, though during that first season Newcastle just failed to win promotion, finishing fifth. Kevin ended up as top scorer on 21 goals. He also won the Northeast Player of the Year award.

Now though, it seemed he knew just what was required of the club to clinch promotion and refused to put pen to paper for a further season unless United promised to sign further quality players. The board agreed and Arthur Cox was duly given the money to go out and buy.

Goalkeeper Martin Thomas and full-backs John Ryan and Malcolm Brown joined the club, but to the fans' huge dismay it was announced that Imre Varadi was bound for Sheffield Wednesday. He had netted 42 goals in two seasons and was a huge crowd favourite, mainly using his incredible pace to help score goals.

Nevertheless, Arthur Cox felt he knew better and wanted a player more suited to Kevin's style of one–two play, so brought in a local lad called Peter Beardsley who had been playing over in Canada with Vancouver Whitecaps. Dad was uncertain about the signing: 'At the time, I was just a little dubious about Arthur's choice of replacement, though was quick to admit he'd been right. Peter proved to be a star.'

With Chris Waddle now firmly established on the front line, the much-feared threesome set about terrorising the opposition. Newcastle stormed to the top and with a tough new central defender, Glenn Roeder, added to the squad, they began to enjoy a string of successive victories. Then, like a bolt from the blue right in the midst of all the euphoria, Kevin announced in the February that it was his intention to retire at the end of the season. Suddenly

Tyneside fell as flat as a proverbial fart and was only slightly cheered by his pledge never to don a strip for any other League side.

With promotion already in the bag, Kevin Keegan's final game before the adoring fans ended with a 3–1 victory over Brighton, and just as he'd done in his first game for the club, he scored a fine goal, his 27th of the season. Dad and 36,000 grieving fans were sorry to see him go.

No one could forget Keegan's big finale straight after a friendly match against his old team, Liverpool, and many folk endured a walloping lump in their throat as he was whisked skyward by helicopter at the final whistle, in his own superb, inimitable showman style.

He left the club with the board of directors promising to build on the strength of what he'd left behind. A lot of pessimistic fans chuckled at that, but sadly they were proved right. In 1984 Arthur Cox left the club too, and so began the search for a successor who could continue his vision. 'On the face of it, he had lured the most "imagination-rousing" player to St James' Park in many a year,' Dad remarked. Replacing him was the problem now.

The club needed a proven manager quickly and Dad soon found himself back in the thick of things after suggesting to the board they might consider his own cousin, Jack Charlton. The ears of the board pricked and they asked Dad if he might be able to 'pull a few strings' with Big Jack. Dad was certainly keen, saying, 'I was always convinced the club could flourish under a manager with Geordie roots and Jack was available.'

Big Jack had left Middlesbrough after a successful spell, and during his time there had been voted Manager of the Year after they romped to the Second Division championship.

He'd raised a few eyebrows by first resigning to enjoy six months away from the game and then taking over as manager of Sheffield Wednesday, only to confess he felt a little unsettled there. He had grown a trifle disillusioned with football in general, and was resigned to taking another year out. He had recently made a captivating television series called *Round Britain* and another about the second great passion of his life, fishing.

'Knowing just how much Jack loved the game and would hopefully be missing it, I reckoned it was worth talking to him. I rang him at home to sound him out,' explained Dad.

At first, Dad was given an emphatic no, but refused to give up. He rang Jack again and again and then cursed when he received his phone bill. However, a short while later, Jack was officially opening a double-glazing factory in nearby Consett, Durham, so Dad pleaded with him to at least meet the United directors away from prying eyes at the club. So, finally, they agreed to meet that day at a Durham golf club, where Jack at last said yes . . . though only for a year, giving him a chance to see the lie of the land. Big Jack explains: 'Jackie insisted on me getting the Newcastle job, but I didn't want it. I thought, I'll do it for a year and keep them in the First Division.'

Jack was firmly under the impression that Newcastle were simply desperate to stay in the First Division now that Keegan and Cox had left. Resources were limited: he was given just £200,000 to spend for the whole season at that time when even an average player cost somewhere in the region of £250,000.

In order to prove his worth quickly and utilise what little cash he had, Jack spent much of his time flying up and down motorways to check out other clubs' players, and sometimes, to his fury, he'd read in the press the following day that he had casually taken time off to go fishing. None of that guff came from Dad, who knew only too well how hard Jack was grafting behind the scenes: 'Jack, Joe Harvey and I used to spend hours in his St James' office mulling over various players.' Joe was United's chief scout at this time.

Jack wasn't too displeased with his first assessment season and thought at that stage that he knew precisely what needed to be done at the club; but then Jack took an awful lot of stick when Chris Waddle suddenly announced his intention to leave.

That particular departure upset him an awful lot, as Jack had been the major cog in the wheel in persuading the then England boss, Bobby Robson, to give Waddle his first international cap in Belfast. However, from the day Waddle returned to St James', Jack was sure he'd done a deal with some club or other behind his back, though it took right until the end of the season before he found out it was Tottenham Hotspur. Waddle had flatly refused to discuss either his staying or going.

Also during that frustrating time, something else occurred that did not help the situation. Some four-star-rated moron idiotically gouged the paint from Jack's car while he was visiting his mother Cissie in their hometown of Ashington. Jack was fast becoming cheesed off, to say the least, and then during a pre-season friendly against Sheffield United, things quickly took a turn for the worse when a small organised section of the crowd aimed their embittered chants directly at him.

That morning, news had just broken about Sunderland's manager, Lawrie McMenemy, snatching the services of Ipswich's Eric Gates from right under Jack's nose. True to Big Jack's style, he simply thought, to hell with it – he had just had enough. 'I was furious after Jack told me exactly what his thoughts were,' explained Dad. 'We argued the toss in the club foyer after the match, but I had to calm him down for fear other journalists would hear us.'

What Dad found hard to come to terms with was that if a man was earning decent money at Newcastle and his prospects were fairly good, then how could he simply turn heel and walk away from the club? To make matters worse, Jack was his own flesh and blood. Jack, though, spelled it out that he simply didn't need the job or any of the hassle that went with it. It was the first time in their lives the pair had austere words, which deep down really upset Dad because he always thought the world of Big Jack.

I truly believe that Dad only ever looked at the job through black-and-white-tinted spectacles; it was *he* who could never have walked away from the manager's job at Newcastle United, while others simply could. 'I pleaded with Jack to have a rethink and he agreed to go away to his Dales home for the weekend to do just that.'

Without the pressure of the press or anyone else over the next two days, Jack was sorely tempted to return to the hot seat, but all in all, the recent events had given him the perfect excuse to leave, so when he returned to Gallowgate on the Monday morning his mind was virtually made up.

Joe Harvey was sitting waiting for him in his office and Jack asked Joe what he would do in his shoes. Not being a one to mince his words, Joe threw his cards on the table and told Jack that he himself had suffered the same abuse over the years, though unlike Jack with his other 'outside' interests, simply had nowhere else to go. 'I'd leave, Jack,' he replied.

Jack absorbed the words and packed his kit, though through time, proved to his United critics and the rest of the world just what a cracker of a manager he really was after taking over the reins of modest Eire.

# Winding Down

The name Milburn is passed on to every generation. Now, for that to happen in a football hotbed says a special thing about your dad.

Sir Bobby Robson

In 1985, now 61, Dad sat back and took careful stock of his life for a second time. The family had increased further, with Betty having given birth to two more children. Laura was born in 1982 and Katy in 1984, giving Betty a total of four kids.

Dad made the conscious decision that they should now become the focal point of his attention, though obviously he still popped into the ground on a regular basis to fish out stories for his weekly column in the *News Of The World*. Then, after carrying out his duties, he would rush home and collect Mum to be with the grandkids.

However, just when he thought he could relax for good, another totally unexpected honour was awarded to him in February 1987. 'I must have received more honours since I finished playing than I did as a player,' he marvelled. The Newcastle Sports Council, in celebration of their 20th anniversary, invited Dad to the Newcastle Civic Centre where they presented him with a fabulous Wilkinson Sword of Peace for his services to sport in the city.

Mum had to calm his nerves for days after the invitation was announced, as Dad had shied well away from any limelight over the past few years, but on the night itself, he was absolutely stunned and thrilled at the fantastic standing ovation he was given when the Duke of Edinburgh presented him with the gleaming award. The cheers he received were deafening, but when all of a sudden the entire room erupted into the hallowed Geordie anthem, 'The Blaydon Races', Dad had to fight back the tears. He really didn't know which way to turn.

I found out later, from my then boss, Peter Spark – an absolute 24-carat, black-and-white nugget, who himself was a director of sales at the Newcastle Breweries where I worked as a free-trade territory manager – that it was he himself who had set in motion the whole touching affair. 'It made me blush an awful lot, but it also made my night,' recalled Dad.

The whole pulsating scenario left the bemused-looking Duke of Edinburgh sporting a wide beam.

The honours were not over and another came his way just a few months later in the May, when he was chosen as the winner of a competition run jointly by the *Sunday Sun* and the Northeast Sportswriters Association. Together they had overwhelmingly voted him as the Northeast's greatest ever post-war player and he was absolutely flabbergasted to have come out tops above other such greats as Kevin Keegan, Peter Beardsley, Len Shackleton, Brian Clough, Wilf Mannion and Charlie Hurley.

To mark the thrilling occasion, he was presented with a beautifully inscribed silver salver. It was to be his last.

Dad had enjoyed the occasional cigar after he finally packed in the fags, but then the occasional became the habitual until he was smoking almost as many of the miniature ones each day as he had cigarettes. I had recently read a magazine article that just happened to be about that particular subject and during a visit one day mentioned it. Straight away I wished I had kept my big mouth shut as a strange look flashed over his face. It was as if I was repeating the words of that little whispering warning voice he'd dreamt about just before he chucked the fags.

At that time, I really believe he thought he had joined the ranks of the non-smoking brigade – 'After all, it's only a few cigars and not cigarettes.'

To Dad there seemed a difference, though he had admitted to Mum to feeling somewhat breathless on more than one occasion, especially on the golf course.

One day, after a particular heavy bout of coughing, Mum packed Dad off to the doctor's surgery, where he was puzzled though relieved to hear the doctor's opinion. The doctor suggested it was probably just Dad's age and that he should expect to find himself a little breathless and lacking in stamina. Dad listened intently and simply left it at that. However, just a couple of months later he was forced to go back and see the doctor again as the breathlessness seemed to be worsening.

This time, the doctor was of the opinion that Dad may need to see a psychiatrist if the problem was not going to go away and told a confused Dad that the whole thing might just all be in the mind. An appointment was made for him.

Some time later and now feeling significantly shoddier, Dad kept the appointment, but was sure his breathlessness could not simply be down to his state of mind. At home he often struggled just to climb the stairs and occasionally would spend the day in bed.

On one of those days, Mum called at the surgery on Dad's behalf to pick up a repeat prescription and spoke to the doctor in question about Dad's breathing. The doctor simply instructed Mum to tell Dad to get down to the surgery himself, even though Mum stressed how out of breath he was. The physician's attitude deeply upset her.

In early 1988, Dad stubbed out his last cigar. All he could dream about was retirement. He discussed his wishes openly with Don Evans, his long-time friend and boss at the *News Of The World*. Don understood, and even though Dad was self-employed, arranged for him to receive a small monthly pension on the day he retired, which was probably going to be at the end of the season. A couple more months passed and Dad's health simply hadn't improved at all; he was ready to pack in work immediately, but Don pleaded with him just to see the season out.

Dad could have simply walked away, but was worried it may jeopardise his pension, something he knew he would certainly need for the future. Strangely enough, as Dad was pleading with Don to retire early and Don with him to stay, it was all recorded on a telephone tape machine that Dad used when phoning in his reports. It is so sad to hear now. As ever, Dad gave in.

The 25 March 1988 was a sad day for many folk in the mining town of Ashington, a town that had been built around the pit itself. After 130 years of producing coal, the men of the final shift were about to be raised to the surface for the last time and with Dad's obvious mining links, the press, with their cameras, asked him to be on hand. 'To be honest, I hated it every time I had to go underground,' Dad revealed. 'Imagine what years of breathing that coal dust can do to your health.'

With the effort of being out and about, Dad was so physically shattered that day that as soon as he arrived home he plonked into a chair and fell asleep.

On 8 May, a mightily relieved, though quite sad Dad, wrote his last match report and sports column. His final column read:

> Today, with a million happy memories, I wave goodbye to my greatest pal: football!
>
> I've made a living out of the best game in the world – as a player, talker or writer – ever since I can remember. Lady Luck has smiled on me most of the time, but now, through minor health reasons, I'm calling it a day. And I wonder what it is going to be like now I'm not involved in a game that's been my whole life.

The final match report headline read: 'Newcastle's Gascoigne Magic Has 'Em Reeling'.

Dad had followed the fledgling Paul Gascoigne's progress with great interest. He spotted something in Gazza that made him think the young player could absolutely outshine the rest – enough to encourage Dad to go as far as declaring during a TV interview with sports presenter and former Arsenal keeper Bob Wilson, that Paul could become *the* best player in the world. Looking somewhat bemused, Bob smiled, asking 'Best in the world, Jackie?'

Dad was deadly serious and smiled back at Bob. 'If he can just keep his feet on the ground.'

Dad's eye for talented players was appreciated by the then England manager Bobby Robson, as he recently explained to me:

> I used to choose the young player of the month award, followed by the young player of the year award. Jackie was one of my scouts so he would scour the Northeast and recommend the best under-21 player that he had seen that month. I used to say, 'Jackie, come on, who's your nomination for this month?' He would nominate some real gems. We would present the awards at this big dinner at the end of each year, when Jackie would come down, and this went on for several years. I was always in touch with him and he was a good judge of a player was your dad.

Being retired, Dad really thought that was it and he could just sit back to enjoy the occasional soccer match on the telly and hope his health would improve, but he was wrong. Just the following month the award-winning local writer, Mike Kirkup, sounded him out about an idea he had with regard to writing a stage play about his life. Dad's jaw almost hit the deck. 'I didn't quite understand how a man could possibly write such a thing about someone who had only booted a bit of leather around for a living.'

Mike laughed and told him to leave that to him, if he would agree to it. He did, but the interview he gave Mike was to be his last.

In early July, after his health failed to improve, Dad revisited the doctor's surgery and was seen by a different doctor – a young locum who seemed totally amazed that he had never been sent for an X-ray and arranged for him to undergo one on 16 July. Dad and Mum were worried, but did their best to push it to the back of their minds until the results came through.

On 22 July, he was then summoned for a bronchial scope and again had to await the results. This time the hospital called him in for a discussion with a specialist, so he asked Mum to stay in the waiting room while he did just that. The specialist sat him down, looked him in the eye and told him he had lung cancer. Then he dropped the bombshell: it was too advanced for any remedial treatment. Dad froze with the horror of the words, but his next thought was how to repeat them to Mum. As soon as he re-entered the waiting room she knew by his drained face the results were not good. He immediately ushered her from the hospital and outside to the car to break the bad news. Completely stunned, the numbed pair somehow managed to drive to Cresswell on the Northumberland coast, where they just sat and stared at the waves breaking on the grey North Sea.

It was a long while before Mum and Dad could summon the strength to talk openly and felt able to discuss what might lie ahead. Mum remained resolute about one thing though: they must never give up hope.

That afternoon, one by one, we anxious kids rang Mum but all received the same numbing reply, 'It's not good news.' It was only natural that we all wanted to rush straight over, but Mum knew it was better to leave it a day or so for her and Dad to try and adjust to the full jolt. I drove immediately to Betty's house at New Hartley and will never forget the feeling of impending doom. We all cried buckets.

On 10 August, as an out-patient, Dad began a programme of radiotherapy, the sole purpose of which was to attempt to ease the pain, but it made him dreadfully sick and weak and the terrible coughing he had endured for months did not improve. Dr Evans and his empathetic nursing staff at the Newcastle General Hospital were all so kind-hearted to him that day, even finding a special place for Mum to park the car so they could come and go as discreetly as possible.

The following day, the treatment had the same terrible effect, making him feel so nauseous he couldn't even hold down a small tumbler of water; the same thing happened on the third day. After leaving the hospital that evening, Mum drove him to my house in north Newcastle, though he didn't feel strong enough to leave the car. I went outside to speak to him. Without saying it, both he and I knew it would be the last time he would be there, and that was why he had come. Yet even still he tried to make light of the whole radiotherapy thing by pointing two fingers out the car window as if they were a makeshift gun, joking he'd been well and truly 'zapped' that day.

By the middle of August, he had still kept very little food down, yet was absolutely determined to see the treatment through. It effectively finished on the 19th.

Three days later, Dr Beattie, his requested replacement doctor, paid him a visit with regard to his coughing bouts and told Dad it would probably be best for him to spend a few days in Ashington Hospital, purely as a precaution against pneumonia developing. Dad knew he had to heed the sound advice, though only agreed reluctantly as he felt much more comfortable behind the closed doors of his own home. By that time, he had lost a fair amount of weight and in all honesty, simply to avoid speculation, did not want to be seen in public. He declined the kind offer of an ambulance and Mum took him there instead.

Once at the hospital, he felt very restless to say the least, and so a few days later pleaded to be allowed home. That time I collected him and he gave a real sigh of relief as he eased himself into the passenger seat, but just a few days later he had to concede to being wrong, as he just couldn't get his appetite going at all. He went back in.

On the final day of August, he had another scan and as his cough seemed to have improved a little he once more asked to return home. The staff fully understood why and were absolutely brilliant about it, for even though he was in a small room just off the main ward, he was always aware of the other patients' visitors staring at him through the glass window and it made him feel uncomfortably embarrassed. Mum collected him two days later.

Dr Beattie began to call on a daily basis to give him his necessary injection and the pair of them got along like a house on fire. Straight after the jab, the purpose of which was to help Dad relax and sleep and should have had a 'knockout' effect after about 20 minutes, the pair would have a 50p bet to see just how long it would be before it took effect, with Dad reckoning he could last up to 60 minutes. Such a dogged fighter was he that, often enough, as Dr Beattie prepared to leave after the hour, Dad would spread out his palm and ask for the 50p, but then the second he'd secured it would drop right off. In the following days, he began to pick a bit more at his food and thankfully, what he did eat stayed down.

A week later, an unexpected visitor arrived at the house in the shape of Paul Gascoigne's mother, who'd brought with her a photograph of Dad and Paul. At that particular time, very few folk knew just how serious his illness was and the fact that she'd taken the trouble to travel the distance from Dunston to Ashington, while probably thinking he only suffered a minor health problem, pleased Dad no end.

The press boys from some of the newspapers had by now picked up on the fact his problem may be more serious than at first thought, and even though a few of his closest friends knew the real truth, such was their loyalty and respect toward him that not a single one disclosed the full facts. Get-well cards, letters, flowers and fruit flooded into the house and the telephone never stopped ringing, and I reckon it was at that time that Dad actually realised he had so many genuine friends in the world.

On occasion, Betty stayed with Mum to give her a well-earned break, as Dad was now forced to spend more and more of his time in bed and there was a huge amount of running up and down stairs to be done. Linda had a young baby girl to look after, having given birth to Alexandria the previous year, and with Darren being aged just 11 and husband Brian suffering from serious back problems, her hands were badly needed at home.

To show just how appreciative he was of all Mum's marvellous hard work over the past few weeks, Dad sat her on the edge of the bed one afternoon, looked her straight in the eye, and told her, 'You really are a one in a million and I love you.' Mum just broke down.

Apart from Dr Beattie's regular calls, Joyce Robertson, a local Ashington nurse, also popped in frequently to keep a watchful eye on him and the pair struck up a great rapport. It seemed they spent most of the time winding each other up, though both appeared to thoroughly enjoy the giggle they got from it. However, by the end of September, Dad was growing weaker and the joking became much less frequent.

One afternoon he sat up and put his arms around Mum and told her again how much he loved and cared for her, but then confessed to feeling so weary and declared that if the time he had left were to be spent feeling like that then he would rather go now. They talked for ages and he expressed a great relief at having been granted his small pension from the *News Of The World* and that it might just help to keep Mum's head above water. Later, as Mum switched off the bedroom light, he said he felt his time was almost here.

That night, he dreamed he was standing at the back of a long queue and peering up it to the front, and waiting for him were his smiling mother and father, his Uncle Tom and Granny Thompson.

By now I was calling in every day, and he told Mum he was pleased about that; I don't know what it was, maybe just to have a man-to-man or father-to-son chat, whatever it was, he wanted me there and I wanted to be there. During our entire lives, we had never had a real 'buddy–buddy' or arm-around-the-shoulder, 'Let's-go-for-a-pint-son-eh?' relationship, basically because he didn't drink, but on the other hand, apart from the scooter drink-driving incident 20 years before, we had never really had a seriously cross word.

It was during our natters together that he told me many stories about his early life, his fears of being down the pit, his school days and loads of other such things and it was a time I will never forget, often now wishing we had sat down and done it many years before. Anyhow, to allow Mum and Betty a good night's sleep I stayed overnight for a week or so in the same room with him.

Each day was different, as his health went up and down. One morning he decided he wanted to take a bath and made a great effort to do so. As he came out of the bathroom, he surprised everyone when he shouted down the stairs to tell Mum that he quite fancied a small glass of lager and lime. Mum, Betty and I trooped up with it, only to find him sitting in his pyjamas and dressing gown on a chair in the hall at the top of the stairs. He took the glass from her and took a small sip, then asked for a comb. The very second he flicked the comb through the famous quiff of his still-damp hair, he looked just like his old happy-go-lucky self and obviously sensed that we could see that. Suddenly he was making light of things and cracking jokes with us and for a while you would never know just how ill he was. That magic moment was one of the last times he ever got out of bed.

In the early hours of the morning of Sunday, 9 October 1988, as I sat with him, I suddenly became aware of a small tear rolling down his right cheek and just knew right away he was slipping away. I'm sure it was his way of telling me to go into the next room to wake and bring Mum to him.

Betty was staying in the spare room and had woken, so followed Mum in. Dad was too weak to speak, but continually turned his head toward the window with slightly opened eyes. I had closed it earlier while he slept as the room felt a little chilly though I knew he preferred it open; so I drew the curtains and opened the small top pane and just as I did so, a very faint glimmer of contentment shone over his face as he gazed out. He smiled briefly and then gave a big sigh and was gone. It was so unbelievably peaceful.

The date itself, 9 October, was so significant as it was precisely 40 years to the day since he'd scored his first England goal in his debut match, from that floating, inch-perfect Stanley Matthews cross.

# Epilogue: The After Years

He was a lovely guy who would do anything to help anyone
and that made him even more special than being Wor Jackie.

Malcolm Macdonald

Not long after the funeral, the *News Of The World* newspaper
informed a disconsolate Mum that, as a widow, she was no longer
eligible to receive Dad's small, but much-needed, pension. He himself
had received just a few payments prior to his death. After 23 years
of loyal service, I wondered just what he would have made of that.

On a much smaller scale, I myself received a boot in the teeth too
from my then employer, Scottish and Newcastle Breweries (this had
nothing to do with my former boss, Peter Spark).

After taking the necessary time off work during Dad's illness, the
purpose of which was to give my mother a much-needed break and
also to arrange and attend Dad's funeral, the kindly brewery docked
my wages, so I quickly made it known to the personnel department
that I was furious. My protest fell on deaf ears.

Throughout his career and later in life, Dad was asked to attend
many openings and functions, but he never once asked for a single
penny. I was livid to think of all the unpaid time my father had

given up to attend with me so many of the brewery's events and presentation evenings, and the only thing he was ever offered was a woollen pullover with their brewery logo emblazoned across its chest. Cheers, S and N.

Over the next few months, most of the family visited Mum on a regular, if not daily, basis and to keep herself occupied away from home she threw herself into her golf and eventually became ladies captain at Morpeth Golf Club in 1992 and not only once, but for a second spell in 1994. It became her whole life and she, as well as the rest of us, was just so grateful that Dad had introduced her to the game in the first place.

A short time after, Mum was absolutely thrilled when she received the news from the then Newcastle United director Gordon McKeag, that it was the club's intention to name the brand new west stand of St James' The Milburn Stand.

Both Mum and I were invited to attend Newcastle's League match against Ipswich Town to celebrate the occasion and we will never forget the kind, personal attention Mr McKeag showed us on that special day.

The tribute was a great acknowledgement of my father's place in the history of Newcastle United. As Sir Bobby Robson explained to me recently:

> The name Milburn means a great deal to this club. When you talk about Jackie Milburn you are talking about an icon, somebody who is identified by the people and by the supporters, even the young ones who never saw him play.

In November 1991, the first of three Jackie Milburn statues was erected in Northumberland Street, Newcastle, where a large crowd had formed for the unveiling.

Later, the proud family were treated to a fabulous reception at the

Lord Mayor's Mansion in Jesmond, and Mum felt honoured and privileged to be given a unique solo tour of the entire building.

Four years later, in October 1995, the unveiling of a second statue took place on Ashington's main street, followed by another grand reception at the local leisure centre and then, amazingly, just a year later, yet another figure appeared, though not yet cast in bronze. This time it was a local lad, Tom Maley, who sculpted it and then displayed it for a time at Ashington's Woodhorn Museum before it was re-sited on the concourse of St James' Park in the late '90s. 'We've had some great No. 9's at Newcastle,' says John Gibson, 'but there's only one statue to any footballer in the centre of Newcastle and it's to Jackie Milburn.'

At the time, because it captured his image so spectacularly, Newcastle United expressed their interest in having it cast in bronze, but then The Milburn Stand was extended, causing the existing concourse on which it stood to disappear, scuppering the plan. At the same time, the first statue in Northumberland Street was re-sited closer to the ground, so quite understandably, two statues of the same man within spitting distance of each other was not deemed a good idea.

Many Geordie folk suggested melting down the first so that Tom Maley could 'do a proper job', just as he'd done with the marvellous lifelike statue of Wilf Mannion at Middlesbrough's Riverside Stadium, but sadly, the 'preferred' statue continues to languish in the back garden of Tom's Longhirst home.

Sadly, in 1995 Mum herself began to feel unwell and after a visit to her local doctor, was quickly sent to see a specialist at the Royal Victoria Hospital in Newcastle. I drove her there myself but after driving round in circles, could find nowhere to park. With her appointment time ticking closer, she had to go inside alone and I was left to drive hopelessly around the car park with not a single space to be found. Each time I slowed to a crawl, an officious little security chap kept warning me to move on, or out.

I had told Mum I'd follow her in as soon as I was able and knew she wanted me with her, so it crossed my mind, as I became more exasperated, to simply park on the grass and suffer a fine or a yellow clamp or whatever.

In my driving mirror I could see 'Hitler' watching me like a hawk. As it was a very hot day, my temper was rising in parallel to the heat inside the car, which did not help my sticky situation in the least, so I thought it better to drive outside the hospital boundary and look for a space on Claremont Road. However, I simply found myself driving up and down with no success, so decided to pull back into the car park, where I spotted Mum already leaving the building.

Her face was ashen as she hauled herself into the passenger seat and, without any hesitation, she told me that the specialist had diagnosed her as having bowel cancer. Stunned, I just stared at her before glaring over at the bureaucratic little 'uniform'. My first reaction was to ram his head up my exhaust pipe, but fortunately, after just a split second, I realised that it would have done nothing to help Mum's dilemma and would only have succeeded in upsetting her more. However, my immediate guilt-ridden thought was that I hadn't been able to be with her when she'd received such horrible news.

As I drove her back home, she explained that her condition was operable, though without major surgery she would probably have just two years to live. If she decided to go ahead then there was a very good chance she should make a full recovery. I have never felt such a wave of relief like the one that washed over me when she said that. Back at home she broke the news to the rest of the waiting family.

Betty and I went to visit her after the operation and I must admit that seeing her lying in the hospital bed, so pale and frail and with plastic tubes sticking out everywhere, was heartbreaking. On the other hand, I had almost forgotten about her determination and positive focus of mind and when the specialist came in to check her progress the first thing she garbled at him through her oxygen mask was, 'How soon before I can play golf?'

For the next two years she did just that and gained a few more trophies into the bargain. Every six months she underwent a meticulous hospital check-up but after one particular scan, something untoward showed up on her liver and she was told the cancer had spread. She now required more major surgery.

At the age of 69 and with the thought of facing that daunting prospect once more, she actually mulled it over first. The family cajoled her by reminding her just how positive she had always been and in 1997 she was wheeled down to the operating theatre for a second time.

Thankfully, the operation was a huge success and yet again her garbled punch line to the specialist was, 'How soon before I can play golf?'

During her recuperation, the other recovering ward patients decided to hold a sweepstake to see who would draw the name of the first goal scorer in the televised Middlesbrough v. Chelsea Cup final, a game that ended in a 2–0 victory for Chelsea. As providence would have it, Mum turned up trumps when she drew Chelsea's Di Matteo, who after just 43 seconds knocked in the fastest ever Cup final goal – pipping Dad's 42-year record by two seconds. Is that irony or what?

Just before she was due to leave for home, a friendly gentleman popped into the ward and introduced himself, mentioning that he had enjoyed seeing 'Wor Jackie' play many, many times for Newcastle. They chatted for a while and before he left he said, 'Well, Mrs Milburn, it has been a great pleasure to talk about your son and to meet his dear mother.' Mum couldn't prevent herself from laughing, even though to do so painfully yanked at her stitches, replying, 'I'd be 95, not 69 if I were his mother.' The poor chap turned crimson as he realised his mistake.

That particular slip-up raised its head twice more in her life, and really, it is an easy one to make, as a lot of folk simply remember others as they appeared the last time they saw them in the flesh. More than likely the friendly chap had in his mind's eye a picture of a youthful Jackie haring down the centre of St James' Park.

Oddly enough, a similar thing happened to me at the Newcastle Racecourse during the mid-'90s, when I was in my 40s. A colleague of mine invited Kevin Keegan and Terry McDermott up into the Newcastle Breweries private box, which I was hosting. As well as being there to enjoy the racing, Kevin was also there to present the prize to the winner of the 'Jackie Milburn Apprentices' Race' and so when it was mentioned to him that 'Jackie's lad' was up in the hospitality box, he and Terry very kindly popped up to say hello. When they entered, I saw someone point them in my direction and so blushed profusely, but when Kevin stood before me and asked where 'Jackie's lad' was I felt so stupid declaring that I was he. I could see that Kevin's mind must have blanked and that he had really expected to shake hands with just a young 'un. Never mind, I was more than over the moon to shake the great man's hand.

Since the mid-'90s, Mum and I had noticed several items of memorabilia, claimed by their owners to have once been owned by Dad, were being sold at various auctions around the country. One medal in particular puzzled me. Fair enough, the face of the suggested footballer bore a slight resemblance to Dad, but he certainly never sported the 'petite' type of football shorts adorning the figure, nor the lightweight, multi-studded boots, or ever kicked a two-tone, 'patch' leather football competitively. In fact, the heavy, rounded toe-capped boots he wore when he played would have positively exploded the thing. So, other than the slight similarity of the face there was nothing else to link it with him, no inscription or anything, so I rang one of the *Journal* newspaper columnists, Tony Jones, who had expressed an interest and dismissed it as 'not one of his'. However, it still went to auction somewhere down south and reportedly fetched a four-figure sum. Not bad for a 'fake'.

Soon after, other bits and bobs were finding their way to auction houses or private sales and never once were we, the family, approached to help verify their authenticity. I agree that whilst a player, Dad sometimes simply gave stuff away at the front door if any child had the pluck to knock and ask for something, but as for the amount of 'his' former shirts being bandied about in pubs and other places, and bearing in mind the players were not simply given them after each game in those days, he must have had his own little secret black-and-white shirt production line in the back yard. I for one though, certainly don't remember the whirr of sewing machines during the dark hours.

However, it was not only this that caused Mum and I to sit down and discuss what was happening, it was also the fact that the entire family had only one England shirt between us, with not a Newcastle one to be found anywhere. Of course, all his caps and medals were still in our possession, though were now in the safekeeping of Linda, Betty and myself, with the exception of the three FA Cup winners' medals that Mum always kept. After the second burglary, Dad had suggested to Mum the collection be spread out to lessen any further risk, until such time as he requested their return, and Mum wholeheartedly agreed. But he told her to always hang onto the FA Cup winners' medals: 'They are your security should you ever fall on hard times'.

Mum looked to the future and grew worried that pieces of his collection may simply be lost or 'sold off' by future generations who could never have even met him. She asked me what I thought and in all honesty, though it seemed a shame it might happen, I had to agree that it could.

I had recently visited the Grace Darling Museum at Bamburgh and took great pleasure from seeing the various artefacts on display and wondered if any future Toon supporters might just pause at one of the statues of Jackie Milburn and question just who or what he was all about. If there was a collection of memorabilia somewhere, then at least if they wanted to, they could go somewhere to see just what he had achieved throughout his football career. We remembered Peter Grenfell's words: 'Jackie belonged to the people.'

Linda and Betty disagreed with our line of thought and therefore decided to keep hold of what was in their possession, so when

Newcastle United compassionately purchased the remainder of Dad's collection it was incomplete, minus several of his medals and caps; but fair enough, that was their decision.

These days, now in her 70s, Mum still enjoys playing and often winning at golf, though now at Burgham Golf Club, close to her new home in peaceful mid-Northumberland. It's a fair distance from the floodlights and roar of the super new St James' Park stadium and even though she was never a frequent visitor when Dad played there, and has rarely been since, it is because of his memory that it will forever hold a special place in her heart. God bless you, Dad.

# Bibliography

Gibson, John (1990) *The Jackie Milburn Story*, Sportsprint, Edinburgh

Gibson John (1989) *Newcastle United Greats*, Sportsprint, Edinburgh

Kirkup, Mike (1990) *Jackie Milburn in Black and White*, Stanley Paul & Co Ltd, London

Milburn, Jackie (1981) *Jackie Milburn's Newcastle United Scrapbook*, Souvenir Press, London

Milburn, Jackie (1957) *Golden Goals*, Stanley Paul & Co Ltd, London